The Canada-U.S. Free Trade Agreement

Final Text and Analysis

commentary prepared by

John D. Richard, Q.C.

and

Richard G. Dearden

of

GOWLING & HENDERSON
Barristers & Solicitors

CCH CANADIAN LIMITED

TAX AND BUSINESS LAW PUBLISHERS

HEAD OFFICE: 6 GARAMOND CT., DON MILLS, ONT. M3C 1Z5.
TELEPHONE (416) 441-2992. FAX NO. (416) 441-3418.

MONTREAL, PQ	OTTAWA, ON	TORONTO, ON	KITCHENER, ON	CALGARY, AB	VANCOUVER, BC
(514) 866-2771	(613) 235-8414	(416) 250-0860	(519) 741-8442	(403) 269-2169	(604) 688-7510

4242

Published by CCH Canadian Limited

USA	Commerce Clearing House Inc., Riverwoods, Illinois.
UK and EUROPE	CCH Editions Limited, Bicester, Oxfordshire.
AUSTRALIA	CCH Australia Limited, North Ryde, NSW.
NEW ZEALAND	Commerce Clearing House (NZ), Auckland.
SINGAPORE, MALAYSIA and BRUNEI	CCH Asia Limited, Singapore

Ownership of Trade Marks

The Trade Marks

COMPUTAX and **COMMERCE CLEARING HOUSE, INC.** are the

property of Commerce Clearing House Incorporated, Riverwoods, Illinois, U.S.A.

Canadian Cataloguing in Publication Data

Richard, John D.
    The Canada-U.S. free trade agreement : final
text and analysis

Includes index.
ISBN 0-88796-462-1

1. Canada - Commerce - United States.
2. United States - Commerce - Canada. 3. Canada -
Commercial treaties. 4. United States - Commercial
treaties. 5. Free trade and protection - Free
trade. 6. Reciprocity. I. Dearden, Richard G.
(Richard Georges), 1953-   II. Title.

HF1766.R53 1987   382.9'71'073   C88-093391-7

Third Printing, March, 1989
Second Printing, June, 1988

© **1988, CCH Canadian Limited**

Typeset and printed in Canada by CCH Canadian Limited.

Foreword

On December 11, 1987 the final text of The Canada–U.S. Free Trade Agreement was tabled in the House of Commons. The text of the Agreement translates the Elements of the Agreement reached on October 4, 1987 into a full legal text. Once implemented, this Agreement will create the world's largest free-trade area. The commentary in this book is a detailed analysis of the text of the Agreement which was signed January 2, 1988 and is to enter into force January 1, 1989.

During the translation period in which the Essential Elements were translated into full legal text, amendments and modifications were made. These changes are highlighted in the Summary issued by the Canadian government entitled "Elaborations and Clarifications to the Elements of the Agreement as Reflected in the Legal Text of the Free Trade Agreement Between Canada and The United States of America". This Summary as well as the full final text of the Agreement and an official Synopsis are reproduced in this book. For a detailed commentary on the Essential Elements of the Agreement readers are referred to THE CANADA–U.S. FREE TRADE AGREEMENT: COMMENTARY AND RELATED DOCUMENTS (Book No. 4246) published by CCH in October 1987.

Once the final text of the Agreement is signed and the phase-in of certain elements has begun, the full impact of the Agreement upon Canada's trading relationship with the United States will become more evident. For readers who wish to closely follow and keep up to date with this new and important aspect of Canada's trade laws, CCH Canadian Limited will be publishing, in 1988, a new loose leaf reporting service — the CANADIAN TRADE LAW REPORTER — written by John D. Richard, Q.C., and Richard G. Dearden of Gowling & Henderson, which will reproduce detailed commentary and related legislation concerning Canadian international trade and customs laws.

January, 1988

Table of Contents

PART II
Government Documents

Part I

A Look Inside:

Analysis of the Free Trade Agreement

Overview of the Agreement*

¶ 100 Introduction

The Canada–U.S. Free Trade Agreement (the Agreement) establishes the world's largest free trade area. In many respects, the Agreement will serve as a model for the *General Agreement on Tariffs and Trade* (GATT) Uruguay Round of Multilateral Trade Negotiations in that it deals with both trade in goods and services and deals with many of the issues to be addressed during the Uruguay Round.

It is an historic Agreement that will enter into force on January 1, 1989. The "essential elements" were agreed to on October 3, 1987** and were translated into a full legal text that was tabled in the House of Commons by the Prime Minister of Canada on December 11, 1987. During the translation period amendments and modifications were made to the essential elements of the Agreement. These amendments and modifications are highlighted in a summary issued by the Canadian Government entitled "Elaborations and Clarifications to the Elements of the Agreement as Reflected in the Legal Text of the Free Trade Agreement Between Canada and the United States of America".

¶ 102 Preamble and Objectives

The Preamble to the Agreement states in part that the Government of Canada and the Government of the United States of America resolved to create an expanded and secure market for the goods and services produced in their territories, to adopt clear and mutually advantageous rules governing their trade, to ensure a predictable commercial environment for business planning and investment, to reduce government-created trade distortions while preserving the Parties' flexibility to safeguard the public welfare, to build on their mutual rights and obligations under the GATT and other multilateral and bilateral instruments of cooperation, and to contribute to the harmonious development and expansion of

---

* This analysis was written by John D. Richard and Richard G. Dearden of GOWLING & HENDERSON with contributions by Alan R. O'Brien, George N. Addy, Scott Fairley, Robert Dechert, Ronald D. Lunau and David Petras, all of GOWLING & HENDERSON.

** For a commentary about the "essential elements" of the Agreement see *The Canada–U.S. Free Trade Agreement: Commentary and Related Documents* published by CCH in October, 1987.

¶ 102

world trade and to provide a catalyst to broader international cooperation.

The objectives of the Agreement are:

(1) to eliminate barriers to trade in goods and services between the territories of the Parties;

(2) to facilitate conditions of fair competition within the free trade area;

(3) to liberalize significantly conditions for investment within this free trade area;

(4) to establish effective procedures for the joint administration of this Agreement and the resolution of disputes; and

(5) to lay the foundation for further bilateral and multilateral cooperation to expand and enhance the benefits of this Agreement (Article 102).

The Preamble and the Objectives will serve as an aid to the interpretation of the provisions of the Agreement and the fulfillment of certain obligations set out therein.

¶ 104 Extent of Obligations

Canada and the U.S. have agreed to ensure that all necessary measures are taken in order to give effect to the provisions of the Agreement, including their observance, except as otherwise provided in the Agreement, by state, provincial and local governments (Article 103).

Certain provisions of the Agreement affect the provinces. The Premiers of Ontario, Manitoba and Prince Edward Island have voiced their disapproval of the Agreement. It therefore remains to be seen what the Canadian Government will do to ensure the observance by the provinces of provisions of the Agreement affecting provincial matters (e.g., wine and distilled spirits, services, procurement). It is possible that the Canadian Government will invoke its trade and commerce power as constitutional authority to enact legislation implementing the provisions affecting the provinces. In the event that this constitutional issue is litigated, the provinces which support the Agreement may find themselves supporting an argument that will widen the Canadian Government's trade and commerce power under section 91(2) of the Constitution Act, 1867.

¶ 106 Affirmation and Precedence

Canada and the U.S. have affirmed their existing rights and obligations with respect to each other, as they exist at the time of entry into force of the Agreement, under bilateral and multilateral agreements to which both are a party (Article 104(1)).

In the event of any inconsistency between the provisions of the Agreement and any other agreement entered into by Canada and the U.S., the provisions of the Agreement shall prevail to the extent of the inconsistency unless otherwise provided for in the Agreement (Article 104(2)).

¶ 108 Statistical Requirements and Publication

The Parties have agreed that all statistical requirements for the administration and enforcement of the Agreement should generally be met from data issued by Statistics Canada and the United States Department of Commerce and other United States government agencies. Data of a more detailed, specific or additional nature will be promptly exchanged upon the request of either Party (Article 2102(1)).

All laws, regulations, procedures and administrative rulings of general application respecting matters covered by the Agreement shall be published promptly. Each Party shall, to the extent possible, publish in advance and allow opportunity for comment on any law, regulation, procedure or administrative ruling of general application that it proposes to adopt respecting the matters covered by this Agreement (Article 2102(2)).

¶ 110 Amendments and Termination

Canada and the U.S. have agreed that they may modify or add to the Agreement (Article 2104). The two countries have also agreed that the Free Trade Agreement remains in force unless terminated by a Party upon six-month notice to the other Party (Article 2106).

¶ 112 Scope of the Agreement

The Canada–U.S. Free Trade Agreement is a far-reaching document and is broader in scope that any other free trade agreement negotiated under the GATT. The Agreement deals with tariffs, customs, quantitative restrictions, government procurement, technical standards, financial services, services, investment, temporary entry for business purposes, energy, automotive trade, agriculture, and wine and distilled spirits. The Agreement also creates a Canada–U.S. Trade Commission and a Binational Panel dispute settlement mechanism for antidumping and countervailing duty cases.

Implementation of the Free Trade Agreement

¶ 200 Introduction

Canada and the U.S. have recognized that the Free Trade Agreement is subject to domestic approval procedures and accordingly, have agreed to exercise their discretion in the period prior to entry into force of the Agreement so as not to jeopardize the approval process or undermine the spirit and mutual benefits of the Free Trade Agreement (Letters of Understanding between the Minister of International Trade and the United States Trade Representative dated January 2, 1988). The two countries have also agreed to ensure that all measures are taken in order to give effect to its provisions, including their observance, by state, provincial and local governments (Article 103).

¶ 202 Parliamentary Approval

The Canadian Government has the constitutional authority to bind Canada to a treaty such as the Free Trade Agreement without having to obtain the consent of Parliament or the Provinces. Notwithstanding that a treaty is binding upon Canada internationally, it has no automatic legal effect domestically. Unlike the U.S. where self-executing treaties become the law of the land, legislation and regulations will be required to implement some of the obligations assumed in the Agreement. Jurisdiction to implement the provisions of the Agreement is divided between the Parliament of Canada and the Provincial Legislatures in accordance with the division of powers set out in sections 91 and 92 of the Constitution Act, 1867. The Prime Minister of Canada tabled the text of the Canada–U.S. Free Trade Agreement in the House of Commons on December 11, 1987. The debate on the text of the Agreement commenced in the House of Commons on December 15, 1987.

On December 15, 1987, the House of Commons Standing Committee on External Affairs and International Trade presented its Report on the Elements of the Agreement. The Report reflects a division between the federal political parties — the governing party supporting the Agreement, the two opposition parties opposing it. However, the representatives of all political parties on the Committee were agreed that should changes in the U.S. fast-track procedure result in the Agreement being

¶ 202

changed by Congress in ways which impair benefits to Canada, Canada should withdraw its consent to the Agreement. The Committee also considered it important that the Agreement should be consistent with the obligations of the two countries under GATT.

The Prime Minister of Canada and the President of the United States must sign the Free Trade Agreement by January 2, 1988.

¶ 204 Congressional Approval

The Agreement had to be concluded on or before October 3, 1987 by reason of the U.S. Trade Act of 1974. Under that Act, Congress gave the President the power, during the 13-year period ending on January 3, 1988, to negotiate and enter into trade agreements with foreign countries subject to Congressional approval, the so called "fast track" process. This process provides that the President must give the Congress at least 90 days notice of his intention to enter into an agreement and after entering into the agreement, the President must submit a copy of the Agreement to the Congress together with a draft implementing bill. An executive agreement entered into pursuant to a Congressional statutory authority, such as the process described above, results in the provisions of the law overriding prior inconsistent federal laws and state laws.

The implementing bill must be introduced in both Houses of Congress (House of Representatives and the Senate) on the day it is submitted by the President. There is no statutory time limit dictating when the President must submit the implementing Bill to Congress after he has signed the Agreement. The House of Representatives has up to 60 legislative days, and the Senate has up to 90 legislative days after the Bill has been introduced, either to approve or reject the Agreement and the Bill. Under the present fast-track procedure, amendments are not in order, and a simple majority of each House is required for acceptance. Therefore, there could be a period of up to six months or longer after the Agreement is signed by the President during which time period the U.S. Congress will be considering the Canada–U.S. Free Trade Agreement.

¶ 206 Compliance With GATT

It is important to note what the Free Trade Agreement is, as well as what it is not. The Agreement is not a Customs Union such as the Treaty of Rome, that established the European Economic Community. It is a free trade area agreement within the meaning of Article XXIV of GATT. Thus, Canada and the U.S. have agreed to eliminate customs duties and other restrictive regulations of commerce on substantially all the trade in goods between the two countries. Unlike a Customs Union, which also contains this element, the Canada–U.S. Free Trade Agreement does not require Canada and the U.S. to develop a common external trade policy. Both countries continue to maintain independent trade relations with other countries.

Trade in Goods

¶ 300 Tariffs

Customs duty on goods originating in Canada and the U.S. will be eliminated in stages commencing on January 1, 1989 and ending on January 1, 1998. It is to be noted that the elimination of customs duty can be accelerated at any time. The Agreement does not affect the customs duty imposed on products originating from other countries. This will be accomplished during the GATT Uruguay Round of Multilateral Trade Negotiations which aims to reduce or eliminate customs duty.

Bilateral safeguard actions required as a result of the Agreement's reduction or elimination of customs duty are authorized by the Agreement. Specific conditions and procedures have been set out in the Agreement governing a Party's use of emergency safeguard actions against the other Party.

The Agreement also contains certain exceptions to its application such as the general exceptions set out in GATT Article XX and the measures governed by GATT's grandfather provisions. In addition, the Agreement does not apply to controls on the export of logs, beer and malt-containing beverages, softwood lumber, and controls by the Atlantic provinces on the export of unprocessed fish.

¶ 302 ELIMINATION OF CUSTOMS DUTIES

Canada and the U.S. have agreed to eliminate all customs duty on goods originating from the other country by January 1, 1998 (Article 401). The elimination of customs duty is an essential condition of GATT Article XXIV which permits the establishment of a free trade area only if duties and other restrictive regulations of commerce are eliminated on substantially all the trade between the two countries.

Customs duty will be eliminated in three stages: (1) immediately, (2) five equal steps, and (3) ten equal steps commencing January 1, 1989.

¶ 303 Immediate

Duty on certain goods will be eliminated on January 1, 1989, the day the Agreement enters into force. Examples include computers, private branch exchanges (duties on "central office, switching apparatus" will be eliminated in three equal stages commencing January 1, 1989), skis, motorcycles, some unprocessed fish, leather, yeast, unwrought aluminum, vending machines and parts, air brakes for railroad cars, skates, some paper-making machinery, some pork, fur and fur garments, whiskey, animal feeds, ferro alloys, needles, warranty repairs.

¶ 304 Five Equal Steps

Duty on certain goods will be eliminated in five equal steps commencing January 1, 1989. Examples include subway cars, printed matter, paper and paper products, paints, explosives, after-market auto parts, chemicals including resins (excluding drugs and cosmetics), furniture, hardwood plywood, most machinery.

¶ 305 Ten Equal Steps

Duty on certain goods will be eliminated in ten equal steps. For most of these goods, the elimination commences on January 1, 1989. Examples include most agricultural products, textiles and apparel, softwood plywood, rail cars, appliances, pleasure craft, tires, steel (in the case of certain specialty steel items subject to temporary emergency safeguards by the United States, tariff cuts will not begin until October 1, 1989).

¶ 306 The Harmonized System of Tariff Classification

The stages of reduction and elimination of customs duty are based upon the Harmonized System of tariff classification. The Harmonized System is to be adopted by Canada and the United States effective January 1, 1988. In Letters of Understanding signed by the Minister of International Trade and the United States Trade Representative dated January 2, 1988 it has been agreed that:

> In the event it appears that either Party is unable to complete the conversion of its Tariff Schedule to the Harmonized System prior to the entry into force of the Agreement, the Parties shall enter into consultations with a view to implementing the provisions of the Agreement, subject to domestic approval, under existing Tariff Schedules on a basis that would preserve the rights and obligations set out in the Agreement.

¶ 308 CONCESSIONARY TARIFF ITEMS

Canada has agreed to continue to exempt from customs duties certain machinery and equipment considered not available from Canadian production and certain repair and replacement parts originating in the

United States. Canada has agreed to examine this list of machinery and equipment with a view to adding to it between now and January 1, 1989.

Canada has also agreed not to increase the rate of customs duty on goods originating in the United States that will be governed by the Schedule of Statutory and Temporary Concessionary Provisions attached to the Harmonized System of tariff classification (with certain exceptions). The United States has made a similar undertaking with respect to temporary suspensions of duty on goods originating from Canada.

¶ 310 DEFINITION OF CUSTOMS DUTY

"Customs duty" is defined by the Agreement as including any customs or import duty and charge of any kind imposed in connection with the importation of goods, including any form of surtax or surcharge on imports, with the exception of: (1) antidumping or countervailing duties; (2) internal taxes imposed consistent with GATT Article III e.g., federal and retail sales taxes; (3) fees in connection with importation commensurate with the costs of services rendered (this includes the U.S. Customs user fees that are being phased out by Article 403); (4) fees applied by the U.S. Agricultural Adjustment Act.

¶ 312 EMERGENCY SAFEGUARD ACTIONS

Under certain circumstances, GATT Article XIX allows a country to take emergency action against fairly traded imported goods (i.e. goods that are not dumped or subsidized) that threaten to cause serious injury to domestic producers. Such actions are known as emergency safeguard actions, and include increases in rates of duty, imposition of quotas and surcharges. The Agreement authorizes a Party to take both bilateral safeguard actions and global safeguard actions affecting the other Party.

¶ 313 Bilateral Action

If, as a result of the Agreement's reduction or elimination of customs duty, goods originating in Canada or the U.S. are imported in such increased quantities, in absolute terms, and under such conditions that those imports alone constitute a substantial cause of serious injury to a domestic industry producing like or directly competitive goods, the importing Party may, to the extent necessary to remedy the injury: suspend the further reduction of the rate of duty on that good or increase the rate of duty on such goods.

Bilateral safeguard actions required as a result of the Agreement's reduction or elimination of duty can only be invoked during the transition period of the Agreement (i.e. 1989-1998). Such safeguard action can remain in place for only three years. Further, a safeguard action can only be taken once during the transition period against a particular good and cannot have effect beyond the expiration of the transition period unless the Parties agree otherwise (Article 1102(2)). In addition, a bilateral safeguard action cannot be instituted after the expiration of the transition period to deal with cases of serious injury to a domestic industry arising from the operation of the Agreement unless the Parties agree otherwise.

Upon the termination of the bilateral safeguard action, the rate of duty shall be the rate which would have been in effect but for the action.

¶ 314 Global Action

Canada and the U.S. have retained their respective rights and obligations under GATT Article XIX regarding emergency actions against imports on a global basis. However, each Party taking a global emergency action shall exclude the other Party from such global action unless:

(a) imports from that Party are "substantial" (imports in the range of 5% to 10% or less of total imports would normally not be considered substantial); and

(b) are contributing importantly (i.e. an important cause, but not necessarily the most important cause, of serious injury from imports) to the serious injury or threat thereof caused by the said imports (Article 1102(1)).

If a Party is initially excluded from an emergency global action taken by the other Party, the excluded Party may subsequently be included in the global action in the event of:

(a) a "surge" in imports of such goods from the excluded Party that

(b) undermines the effectiveness of such action.

"Surge" means a significant increase in imports over the trend for a reasonable recent base period for which data are available (Article 1102(2)).

If one Party intends to institute a proceeding that may result in an emergency action on a global basis the other Party must be notified without delay (regardless of whether the other Party is to be included in the global action at the outset or subsequent to the taking of the action) (Article 1102(3)). In addition, in no case shall a Party take global action:

(a) imposing restrictions on a good without prior notice and consultation with the other Party;

(b) that would have the effect of reducing imports on such goods of the other Party below the trend of imports over a reasonable recent base period with allowance for growth.

¶ 314

¶ 315 Compensation

A Party that takes bilateral emergency action or global emergency action shall provide to the other Party:

(a) mutually agreed trade liberalizing compensation in the form of concessions having substantially equivalent trade effects to the other Party;

(b) the equivalent to the value of the additional duties expected to result from the action.

If the Parties are unable to agree upon compensation, the exporting Party may take tariff action having trade effects substantially equivalent to the emergency actions taken by the importing Party.

¶ 316 Arbitration

Any dispute arising out of actual bilateral or global safeguard actions that is not resolved by consultation shall be referred to binding arbitration under Article 1806 dealt with in detail below.

¶ 320 EXCEPTIONS FOR TRADE IN GOODS

The Agreement has set out specific exceptions to its application. These exceptions include GATT Article XX (general exceptions), the grandfather provisions set out in GATT's *Protocol of Provisional Application*; controls on the export of logs of all species, beer and malt-containing beverages, softwood lumber, and controls imposed by the Atlantic provinces on the export of unprocessed fish.

¶ 321 GATT Article XX — General Exceptions

The provisions of GATT Article XX are incorporated as part of the Agreement. Article XX states in part: "subject to the requirement that such measures are not applied in a manner that would constitute a means of arbitrary or unjustifiable discrimination between countries where the same conditions prevail, or a disguised restriction on international trade, nothing in GATT shall be construed to prevent the adoption or enforcement by any Contracting Party of" certain import and export control measures. These measures include: the protection of public morals; the protection of human, animal or plant life or health (e.g., the environment, endangered species); compliance with laws or regulations which are not inconsistent with the provisions of GATT, including those relating to customs enforcement, the enforcement of monopolies operated under paragraph 4 of Article II and Article XVII, the protection of patents, trade marks and copyrights, and the prevention of deceptive practices; the protection of national treasures of artistic, historic or archaeological value; the conservation of exhaustible natural resources if such measures are made effective in conjunction with restrictions on

¶ 321

domestic production or consumption; the pursuance of obligations under any international commodity agreement (e.g., wheat, tin).

¶ 322 GATT's Protocol Of Provisional Application

The Agreement does not apply to any measure of either Party that remains exempt from the obligations of GATT by virtue of subparagraph 1(b) of the *Protocol of Provisional Application of the GATT*. This Protocol was the instrument used by the original signatories of GATT to bring GATT into force. The signatories agreed that they would fully accept certain obligations insofar as they were not inconsistent with existing legislation on January 1, 1948. An example of legislation enacted as of January 1, 1948 is the United States Jones Act that provided protection for the U.S. marine industry.

¶ 323 Export of Logs

Controls by the United States and Canada of all species of logs are not affected by the Agreement. However, the Parties have retained their rights and obligations under GATT regarding these controls.

¶ 324 Unprocessed Fish

Controls imposed by certain Atlantic provinces on the export of unprocessed fish are not affected by the Agreement. However, the Parties have retained their rights and obligations under GATT regarding these controls. Restraints on the exports of unprocessed fish caught off the coast of British Columbia are currently being discussed by Canada and the U.S. unrelated to the Agreement. It is to be noted that a recent GATT panel found that such controls contravened GATT.

¶ 325 Beer and Malt-Containing Beverages

The Agreement does not apply to beer and malt-containing beverages. However, the Parties have retained their rights and obligations under GATT regarding measures relating to the internal sale and distribution of these goods. It is to be noted that a recent GATT panel has found that such measures contravened GATT.

¶ 326 Softwood Lumber

Canada and the U.S. have agreed that the Agreement does not impair or prejudice the exercise of any rights or enforcement measures arising out of their Memorandum of Understanding on Softwood Lumber (signed December 30, 1986).

¶ 330 Customs Matters

The Free Trade Agreement sets out specific rules of origin that will dictate what goods are entitled to free trade benefits. In addition, the

Agreement deals with customs user fees, drawbacks, duty waivers, the flow of trade, and import and export restrictions.

¶ 332 RULES OF ORIGIN FOR GOODS

Specific rules of origin are critical to the operation of the Agreement to ensure that only goods originating from Canada or the U.S. receive the benefits of the Agreement.

¶ 333 General Rules

Goods originate in the territory of a Party if they are "wholly obtained or produced in the territory of either Party or both Parties" (Article 301(1)). "Goods wholly obtained or produced in the territory of either Part or both Parties" means:

(a) mineral goods extracted in the territory of either Party or both Parties;

(b) goods harvested in the territory of either Party or both Parties;

(c) live animals born and raised in the territory of either Party or both Parties;

(d) goods (fish, shellfish and other marine life) taken from the sea by vessels registered or recorded with the Party and flying its flag;

(e) goods produced on board factory ships from the goods referred to in subparagraph (d) provided that such factory ships are registered or recorded with that Party and fly its flag;

(f) goods taken by a Party or a person of a Party from the seabed or beneath the seabed outside territorial waters, provided that Party has rights to exploit that seabed;

(g) goods taken from space, provided they are obtained by a Party or a person of a Party and not processed in a third country;

(h) waste and scrap derived from manufacturing operations and used goods, provided they were collected in the territory of either Party or both Parties and are fit only for the recovery of raw materials; and

(i) goods produced in the territory of either Party or both Parties exclusively from goods referred to in subparagraphs (a) to (h) inclusive or from their derivatives, at any stage of production (Article 304).

In addition, goods originate in the territory of a Party if they have been transformed in the territory of either Party or both Parties so as to be subject to a change in tariff classification as described in Annex 301.2. The change in tariff classification is based upon the Harmonized System of tariff classification. Annex 301.2 specifically deals with the 97 chapters of the Harmonized System and sets out the rules for determining whether processing or assembly of goods in the territory of a Party results in a change of tariff classification that will constitute transformation. If such, a transformation occurs, those goods will be entitled to the benefits of the Agreement.

It is to be noted that the Harmonizd System of tariff classification is to be adopted by Canada and the United States effective January 1, 1988. In Letters of Understanding signed by the Minister of International Trade and the United States Trade Representative dated January 2, 1988 it has been agreed that:

> In the event it appears that either Party is unable to complete the conversion of its Tariff Schedule to the Harmonized System prior to the entry into force of the Agreement, the Parties shall enter into consultations with a view to implementing the provisions of the Agreement, subject to domestic approval, under existing Tariff Schedules on a basis that would preserve the rights and obligations set out in the Agreement.

A good shall not be considered to originate in the territory of a Party merely by virtue of having undergone (a) simple packaging or combining operations, (b) mere dilution with water or another substance that does not materially alter the characteristics of the good, or (c) any process or work in respect of which it is established, or in respect of which the facts as ascertained clearly justify the presumption, that the sole object was to circumvent the provisions of the rules of origin Chapter of the Agreement (Article 301(3)). Article 301(3)(c) is tantamount to an anti-avoidance provision found in income tax legislation. It is likely that Canadian and U.S. Customs authorities will invoke this provision whenever an issue arises as to the origin of goods.

Accessories, spare parts or tools delivered with any piece of equipment, machinery, apparatus or vehicle that form part of its standard equipment shall be deemed to have the same origin as that equipment, machinery, apparatus or vehicle provided the quantities and values of such accessories, spare parts or tools are customary for that equipment, machinery, apparatus or vehicle (Article 301(4)).

Annex 406 sets out the requirements for declarations of origin for imported and exported goods that are represented to qualify for the benefits of the Free Trade Agreement. The Parties have agreed to keep records that can be audited and to cooperate fully in the enforcement of their respective laws in accordance with the Agreement and other treaties, Agreements and memoranda of understanding (Annex 406(4)(5)).

¶ 334 Assembly of Goods

Annex 301.2 specifically deals with rules of origin pertaining to the "assembly" of goods. Whenever assembly of goods fails to result in a change of tariff classification because:

(a) the goods were imported into the territory of the Party in an unassembled or disassembled form and were so classified under the Harmonized System; or

(b) the tariff subheading for the goods provides for both the goods themselves and their parts,

such goods shall not be treated as goods originating in the territory of a Party (Annex 301.2(3)). However, such "assembled" goods are nonetheless considered to have been transformed in the territory of a Party and be treated as goods originating in the territory of the Party; provided that:

(a) the value of materials originating in the territory of either Party or both Parties used or consumed in the production of the goods plus direct cost of assembling the goods in the territory of either Party or both Parties constitute not less than 50% of the value of the goods when exported to the territory of the other Party; and

(b) the goods have not, subsequent to assembly, undergone processing or further assembly in a third country and have not been transshipped.

The terms "direct costs of processing or direct costs of assembling", "value of materials originating in the territory of either Party or both Parties", "value of the goods when exported to the territory of the other Party", and "materials" are defined by Article 304.

The 50% rule set out in Annex 301.2(4) is not applicable to Chapters 61 to 63 of the Harmonized System which govern "articles of apparel and clothing accessories, knitted or crotcheted" (Chapter 61), "articles of apparel and clothing accessories, not knitted or crocheted" (Chapter 62) and "other madeup textile articles"; "sets"; "worn clothing and worn textile articles"; "rags" (Chapter 63).

¶ 335 Apparel

Apparel made from fabrics woven in Canada or the United States will qualify for duty-free treatment. Apparel made from offshore fabrics will qualify for duty-free treatment up to the following levels:

	Non-Woolen Apparel	Woolen Apparel
	(in million square yard equivalent)	
Imports from Canada	50	6
Imports from U.S.	10.5	1.1

Apparel made from offshore fabrics that exceeds these levels will be considered, for tariff purposes, as products of the country from which the fabrics were obtained.

The *Synopsis* of the Agreement issued by the Canadian Government states:

> . . . goods that are further processed in a third country before being shipped to their final destination will not qualify for free trade area treatment even if they meet the rules of origin. For example, cloth woven from U.S. fibres, cut in the United States, but sewn into a shirt in Mexico, would qualify for duty-free re-entry into the United States under its outward processing program, but would not qualify for duty-free entry into Canada under the Agreement.

¶ 336 Transshipment

The rules of origin require that the goods must be shipped to the other Party without having entered the commerce of any third country and, if shipped through the territory of a third country, they do not undergo any operations other than unloading, reloading, or any operation necessary to transport them to the territory of the other Party or to preserve them in good condition. The documents related to their exportation and shipment from the territory of a Party must show the territory of the other Party as their final destination.

¶ 337 Consultation and Revision

Canada and the U.S. have agreed to consult regularly to ensure that the provisions of the rules of origin are administered effectively, uniformly and consistently within the spirit and intent of the Agreement. If either Party concludes that these provisions require revision the Agreement may be amended or modified.

¶ 338 Appeals Relating to Origin

The Parties have agreed to provide the same rights of review and appeal with respect to a decision relating to the origin of imported goods represented as meeting the rules of origin as are provided with respect to the tariff classification of imported goods. In Canada, the Tariff Board currently has the jurisdiction to hear appeals related to the tariff classification of imported goods (Annex 406(7)).

The Customs Administration in Canada and the U.S. will consult with one another concerning the uniform application of the Agreement's rules of origin and will make available to each other precedential decisions applying these principles (Annex 406(6)). Annex 406 does not indicate whether these precedential decisions will be made available to importers and exporters pursuant to the Canadian Access To Information Act and the U.S. Freedom of Information Act.

¶ 340 CUSTOMS USER FEES

Neither Canada nor the U.S. can introduce customs user fees for goods originating from the other country. The U.S. has agreed to eliminate its existing customs user fees on goods originating from Canada by

January 1, 1994 (Article 403(3)). U.S. user fees applied to goods originating in Canada will be reduced to the following levels during the next 5 years:

(1) January 1, 1990 — 80%

(2) January 1, 1991 — 60%

(3) January 1, 1992 — 40%

(4) January 1, 1993 — 20%

(5) January 1, 1994 — 0%

¶342 DRAWBACKS

Effective January 1, 1994, most duty drawbacks for bilateral trade will be eliminated by the Agreement. The rationale for the elimination of drawbacks is explained in the *Synopsis* of the Canada–U.S. Free Trade Agreement issued by the Canadian Government as follows:

> . . . both countries refund the customs duty levied on imported materials and components when these are incorporated into exported goods. This is called duty drawback. In the U.S., for example, foreign trade zones are often used as a means for U.S. exporters to avoid having to pay U.S. duties on imported components. Some of the advantages of the free trade area, however, would be eroded if a U.S. producer could source some components from a third country, manufacture a final product in a U.S. foreign trade zone without paying any duty on these components and compete in Canada with a manufacturer who has paid Canadian duties on the same components. Accordingly, the Agreement provides for duty drawbacks on third country materials and similar programs to be eliminated for bilateral trade after January 1, 1994.

There are several exceptions to the drawback contained in Articles 404(4)(5) and (8):

(1) imported citrus products;

(2) fabric not originating in the territory of either Party or both Parties and made into apparel that is subject to the Most Favoured Nation tariff when exported to the territory of the other Party (the rules of origin discussed above establish quotas for duty-free treatment of apparel made up from imported fabrics — any imported fabrics above these quotas are entitled to drawback of duties paid on fabric incorporated into apparel exported to one of the Parties);

(3) a refund of customs duties where that refund is granted by reason of the failure of the goods to conform to sample or specification or by reason of the shipment of such goods without the consent of the consignee;

(4) goods under bond for transportation and exportation to the territory of the other Party or exported to the territory of the other

Party in the same condition as when imported into the territory of the Party (testing, cleaning, repacking or inspecting the goods, preserving them in their same condition, or other like process is not a process that would change the condition of the goods);

(5) goods deemed to be exported from the territory of a Party or goods incorporated into, or directly consumed in the production of, such goods, by reason of delivery to a duty-free shop, use as stores or supplies of ships or aircraft, or use in joint undertakings of the Parties that will subsequently become the property of the other Party;

(6) dutiable goods originating in the territory of the other party that are imported into the territory of the Party and subsequently re-exported to the territory of the other Party, or are incorporated into, or directly consumed in the production of, goods subsequently exported to the territory of the other Party.

¶ 344 DUTY WAIVERS

The *Synopsis* issued by the Canadian Government describes duty waivers as follows:

Canadian customs law permits duties on imports to be refunded to specific companies if these companies meet commitments (performance requirements) related to production, exports or employment.

Article 405(1) states that neither Party shall, after the later of June 30, 1988 or the date of approval of the Agreement by the Congress of the United States, introduce:

(1) any new program;

(2) expand with respect to then existing recipients, or

(3) extend to any new recipient the application of a program existing prior to such date that waives otherwise applicable customs duties on any goods imported from any country (including the territory of the other Party) where the waiver is conditioned (explicitly or implicitly) upon the fulfillment of performance requirements.

All duty waivers must be eliminated by January 1, 1998, except for certain automotive waivers. In addition, whenever Canada or the U.S. grants a waiver with respect to goods for commercial use by a designated person, if the waiver has an adverse impact upon the commercial interests of a person of the other Party or on the other Party's economy, either make the duty waiver generally available to any importer or cease to grant the waiver (Article 405(3)).

¶ 346 FLOW OF TRADE

The Parties shall notify and consult with each other with respect to and, where possible, in advance of, major proposed changes in customs administration that would affect the flow of bilateral trade, such as the closing of a port or customs office, trade documentation required by the customs administration, customs procedures followed to implement the requirements of other agencies of a Party and the processing of travellers.

The Parties have also agreed to cooperate in customs matters in order to facilitate the flow of trade between them, particularly in matters relating to the collection of statistics with respect to the importation and exportation of goods, the harmonization of documents used in trade, and the exchange of information.

¶ 348 IMPORT AND EXPORT RESTRICTIONS

Canada and the U.S. have agreed to affirm their respective rights and obligations under GATT with respect to prohibitions or restrictions on bilateral trade in goods. The Parties understand that these GATT rights and obligations prohibit, in any circumstances in which any other form of quantitative restriction is prohibited, minimum export price requirements and, except as permitted in enforcement of countervailing and antidumping orders and undertakings, minimum import price requirements (Article 407(2)).

The *Synopsis* of the Agreement issued by the Canadian Government states:

> Nothing in the Agreement, for example, in any way prevents Canada from prohibiting the import of pornographic materials. Outside of such special circumstances, these obligations provide a guarantee that the benefits of tariff elimination will not be eroded by quotas or other restrictions. Unless specifically allowed by the Agreement, e.g., "grandfathered" or permitted under the GATT, existing quantitative restrictions will be eliminated, either immediately or according to a timetable. . . .

> Where either Canada or the United States applies restrictions on trade with other countries, it may limit or prohibit the pass-through of imports from those other countries into its own territory. It may also require that its exports to the other be consumed within the other's territory. Controls on exports to third countries for strategic reasons will thus continue to be enforced.

The Agreement also deals with restrictions on the importation from or exportation to a third country of goods. In the event that either party imposes a restriction on imports of goods from third countries, the Parties, upon the request of either Party, shall consult with a view to avoiding undue interference with or distortion of pricing, marketing and distribution arrangements in the other party (Article 407(4)).

Canada has agreed to eliminate quantitative restrictions on used or second-hand aeroplanes and aircraft of all kinds effective January 1, 1989. The United States has agreed to eliminate as of January 1, 1993 its embargo on lottery tickets, printed paper that may be used as a lottery ticket or, advertisement, for a United States lottery, printed in Canada.

Controls regarding log exports, marine transportation and unprocessed fish have been dealt with above under the heading "Exceptions For Trade In Goods".

¶ 349 Export Taxes

Neither Party shall maintain or introduce any tax, duty or charge on the export of any good to the territory of the other Party, unless such tax, duty, or charge is also maintained or introduced on such good when destined for domestic consumption (Article 408). The Canada–U.S. Memorandum of Understanding on Softwood Lumber dated December 30, 1986 is exempted from Article 408 by virtue of Article 2009 of the Agreement.

¶ 350 Other Export Measures

The Parties have agreed that under certain circumstances they may maintain or introduce a restriction justified under the provisions of: (1) GATT Article XI:2(a) — export prohibitions or restrictions temporarily applied to prevent or relieve critical shortages of foodstuffs or other products essential to the exporting contracting party, (2) GATT Article XX(g) — the conservation of exhaustible natural resources if such measures are made effective in conjunction with restrictions on domestic production or consumption, (3) GATT Article XX(i) — restrictions on exports of domestic materials necessary to ensure essential quantities of such materials to a domestic processing industry during periods when the domestic price of such materials is held below the world price as part of a governmental stabilization plan, provided that such restrictions shall not operate to increase the exports of or the protection afforded to such domestic industry, and shall not depart from the provisions of this Agreement relating to non-discrimination, (4) GATT Article XX(j) — essential to the acquisition or distribution of products in general or local supply, provided that any such measures shall be consistent with the principle that all Contracting Parties are entitled to an equitable share of the international supply of such products, in that any such measures, which are inconsistent with the other provisions of this Agreement shall be discontinued as soon as the conditions giving rise to them have ceased to exist (Article 409(1)).

The above restrictions are permitted under the Agreement only if:

(a) the restriction does not reduce the proportion of the total export shipments of the specific good made available to the other Party relative to the total supply of that good of the Party maintaining the restriction as compared to the proportion prevailing in the most recent 36-month period for which data are available prior to the imposition of the measure, or in such other representative period on which the Parties may agree;

(b) the Party does not impose a higher price for exports of a good to the other Party than the price charged for such good when consumed domestically, by means of any measure such as licenses, fees, taxation and minimum price requirements. The foregoing provision does not apply to a higher price which may result from a measure taken pursuant to subparagraph (a) that only restricts the volume of exports; and

(c) the restriction does not require the disruption of normal channels of supply to the other party or normal proportions amongst specific goods or categories of goods supplied to the other party.

The Parties have agreed to cooperate in the maintenance and development of effective controls on the export of each other's goods to third countries.

The *Synopsis* issued by the Canadian Government states:

GATT obligations recognize that circumstances may arise where export restrictions are necessary. These circumstances include situations of short supply, conservation of natural resources where domestic production or consumption is also restrained and restrictions imposed in conjunction with domestic price stabilization schemes.

Article 409 requires that export restrictions for such purposes not reduce the proportion of the good exported to the other party relative to the total supply of the good compared to the proportion exported prior to the imposition of the restriction. Any such restriction must not be designed to disrupt normal channels of supply or proportions among specific goods being restricted. It prohibits the use of licenses, fees or other measures to charge higher prices for exports than for domestic sales.

¶ 352 Government Procurement

Canada and the U.S. have reaffirmed their rights and obligations under the *GATT Code On Government Procurement* and have expanded their obligations under this Code. The Parties have agreed to actively strive to achieve, as quickly as possible, the multilateral liberalization of international government procurement policies. Any modifications that are made to the *Code On Government Procurement* will automatically be incorporated into the Free Trade Agreement. In addition, the Parties have agreed to undertake bilateral negotiations with a view to improving and expanding the procurement provisions of the Agreement.

¶ 354 ENTITIES COVERED

The entities covered by the procurement provisions of the Agreement are set out in Annex 1304.3 which reproduces verbatim the annexes for Canada and the U.S. in the *GATT Code On Government Procurement*. Twenty-two Canadian Government Departments and ten agencies are covered. The Canadian Departments of Transport, Communications and Fisheries and Oceans are not covered. Eleven out of thirteen U.S. Government Departments are covered along with forty agencies. The U.S. departments of Energy and Transport are not covered. Certain purchases reserved for small business are exempt from the Agreement.

Certain purchases (mainly non-military) by the Canadian Department of National Defence and the U.S. Department of Defence are covered by the Agreement. However, Canada's access to the U.S. defence procurement of military goods under the Defence Production Sharing Arrangements is not affected by the Free Trade Agreement. For the purposes of the Agreement, the provisions of Article VIII of the *GATT Code On Government Procurement* override the national security provisions set out in Article 2003 of the Free Trade Agreement. Article VIII of the Code states in part that a Party cannot be prevented from taking any action or not disclosing any information which it considers necessary for the protection of its essential security interests relating to the procurement of arms, ammunition or war materials, or to procurement indispensible for national security or for national defence purposes.

¶ 356 THRESHOLD — $25,000 (U.S.)

The Agreement affects federal government purchases that are above $25,000 (U.S.) (approximately $33,000 (Can.)). This is a substantial reduction of the threshold set out in the *GATT Code On Government Procurement* of $171,000 (U.S.) (approximately $238,000 (Can.)) (Article 1304).

¶ 358 PROCEDURAL OBLIGATIONS (TRANSPARENCY)

The Agreement provides for detailed procedural obligations to be accorded to "eligible goods" for procurements covered by the Agreement. "Eligible goods" is defined as "unmanufactured materials, mined or produced in the territory of either Party and manufactured materials manufactured in the territory of either Party if the cost of the goods originating outside the territories of the Parties and used in such materials is less than 50% of the cost of all the goods used in such materials" (Article 1309).

Some of the procedural obligations to be fulfilled by Canada and the U.S. for its procurements include: (1) to provide all potential suppliers equal access to pre-solicitation information and equal opportunity to compete in the pre-notification phase; (2) to provide all potential suppliers equal opportunity to be responsible to the requirements of the procuring entity in the tendering and bidding phase: (3) to use decision criteria in the qualification of potential suppliers, evaluation of bids and awarding of contracts that best meet the requirement specified in the tender documentation, are free of preferences in any form in favour of its own goods, and are clearly specified in advance; (4) to promote competition by making available information on contract awards in the post-award phase.

The Parties have agreed to equitable, timely, transparent and effective bid challenge procedures for potential suppliers of eligible goods. Each Party has agreed to provide sufficient transparency in the procurement process to ensure that the bid challenge system operates effectively. Each Party must ensure that complete documentation and records are maintained in order to allow verification that the procurement process was carried out in accordance with the obligations of the provisions of the Agreement (Article 1305).

Annex 1305.3 contains principles guiding bid challenge procedures. The Parties have agreed to a reviewing authority with no substantial interest in the outcome of the procurement having responsibility for receiving and deciding bid challenges. The reviewing authority is required to investigate the challenge expeditiously and may delay the proposed award pending resolution of the bid challenge except in cases of urgency or where the delay would be prejudicial to the public interest. The reviewing authority can determine the appropriate remedy which may include re-evaluating offers, recompeting the contract or terminating the contract. The reviewing authority is also authorized to make recommendations in writing to contracting authorities respecting all facets of the procurement process.

¶ 360 National Treatment

The Agreement requires each Party, to the extent provided in the Agreement, to accord national treatment with respect to investment and to trade in goods and services (Article 105). Canada and the U.S. have also agreed to accord national treatment to the goods of the other Party in accordance with the existing provisions of Article III of the GATT, including interpretive notes (Article 501). The Parties have agreed to apply these provisions in accordance with the existing interpretations adopted by the Contracting Parties to GATT.

GATT Article III entitled "National Treatment on Internal Taxation and Regulation" contains ten sections including notes and supplementary provisions. Section 1 of GATT Article III states: "the contracting parties recognize that internal taxes and other internal charges, and laws, regulations and requirements affecting the internal sale, offering for sale, purchase, transportation, distribution or use of products and internal quantitative regulations requiring the mixture, processing or use of products in specified amounts or proportions, should not be applied to imported or domestic products so as to afford protection to domestic production."

The Agreement states that the national treatment provisions of the Agreement regarding the treatment of like, directly competitive or substitutable goods shall mean, with respect to a province or state, treatment no less favourable than the most favourable treatment accorded by such province or state to any like, directly competitive or substitutable goods, as the case may be, of the Party of which it forms a part (Article 502). It is to be noted that "province or state" includes local governments.

The *Synopsis* of the Agreement issued by the Canadian government states:

> This Chapter incorporates the fundamental national treatment obligation of the GATT into the Free Trade Agreement. This means that once goods have been imported into either country, they will not be the object of discrimination. Such an obligation is an essential part of any agreement eliminating trade barriers since it prevents their replacement by internal measures favouring domestic goods over imports. If such a provision were not part of the Agreement, exporters in either country would have no guarantee of equal treatment.

> The practical effect of this chapter is to require that internal taxes, such as sales or excise taxes, cannot be higher on imported goods than on domestic goods and health and safety standards cannot be more rigorous for imported goods than for domestic goods. . . .

> This Chapter makes more explicit the GATT national treatment obligation to measures adopted by provinces or states. This means that a province or state cannot discriminate in respect of measures falling within its jurisdiction against imported products.

¶ 362 Technical Standards*

The provisions of Chapter Six apply to technical standards related to goods other than agricultural, food, beverage and certain related goods dealt with separately in Chapter Seven of the Agreement. The provisions of Chapter Six do not apply to measures imposed by provincial or state governments and the Parties to the Agreement are not bound to ensure the observance of the provisions by state or provincial governments. This is in stark contrast to the provisions in Chapter One of the Agreement (Objectives and Scope of the Agreement) whereby the Parties agree to "ensure that all necessary measures are taken in order to give effect to its provisions, including their observance, except as otherwise stated in the Agreement, by state, provincial and local governments". Nevertheless, recognizing that many standards are established by private organizations in both Canada and the United States (e.g., CSA and UL), the two governments have agreed to encourage greater compatibility in the standards which such organizations establish.

---

* Prepared by George N. Addy.

¶ 362

Canada and the United States have affirmed their respective rights and obligations under the GATT Tokyo Round Agreement on Technical Barriers to Trade which provide that technical regulations and standards including packaging and labelling requirements and methods for certifying conformity should not create unnecessary barriers to trade.

The essence of Chapter Six is that Canada and the United States will use their best efforts to eliminate trade barriers which present themselves as the result of standards-related measures.

Standards-related measures are permissible but, to the extent possible, the two governments will endeavour to make their respective measures more compatible to reduce obstacles to trade and costs of exporting which arise from having to meet different standards. Agricultural and fish standards are dealt with in Chapter Seven of the Agreement and specific provisions are included in Chapter Twenty for plywood. Standards-related measures are not to be used as disguised barriers to trade. Standards-related measures are permissible if their demonstrable purpose is to achieve a "legitimate domestic objective" and if they do not operate to exclude goods of the other Party that meet that legitimate domestic objective.

Legitimate domestic objective is defined to mean an objective whose purpose is to protect health, safety, essential security, the environment or consumer interests. The definition of legitimate domestic objective does not exactly track the language of the Essential Elements of the Agreement of October 4th, which referred not to "essential" security but to "national" security. The new language tracks that of the GATT technical standards agreement and is undoubtedly intended to focus on national security type issues as evidenced by the non-impairment of national security activity as set out in Article 2003.

Accreditation standards for testing facilities, inspection agencies and certification bodies of the other Party will be recognized by each Party. Accreditation will also dispense with the requirement of establishing local facilities to conduct tests, inspections or certifications. While accreditation is recognized, the Agreement contemplates the refusal by one Party of test results from bodies located in the territory of the other Party. In those circumstances, a written explanation is to be provided.

A pre-notification scheme will be implemented whereby advance notice will be given by one Party to the other Party of the implementation and text of proposed federal government standards-related measures and product approval procedures sixty days prior to their implementation. This will allow the other Party time to develop comments and discuss them with appropriate regulatory authorities. The sixty-day notice period may be dispensed with where a delay would frustrate the achievement of the legitimate domestic objective. As many standards-related measures are of state or provincial origin, the Parties have under-

¶ 362

taken to notify each other of proposed standards-related measures of state and provincial authorities which may significantly affect trade in advance, if possible, or as soon as possible after their implementation. The importance to be given to comments on proposed regulations by the trading partner will obviously be tempered by the domestic political agenda at any given point in time. Furthermore, the recognition by the Parties that they are not obligated to ensure compliance and standardization at the provincial and state levels highlights a potential roadblock to the full implementation and attainment of the objectives sought in the area of standards harmonization.

As is the case in other areas of the Agreement, the Parties have agreed to undertake additional negotiations with respect to compatibility of standards-related measures and product approval procedures, accreditation and acceptance of test data.

There are currently instances at the federal level where one Party has, on an ad hoc basis, recognized testing or specifications devised by the other Party (e.g., motor vehicles). While the accreditation and test data provisions recognize greater harmonization of standards in order to eliminate their use as barriers to entry, given the differences in climate between both countries, standards-related measures and approval procedures which pertain to products subject to climatic differences will of necessity be difficult to achieve (e.g., agri-chemical products). There are likely several areas where significant differences between the two countries mean that harmonization in real terms will not be easy. In other areas, such as motor vehicle or consumer product recall regulations, bringing Canadian reporting standards up to U.S. levels will mean higher costs to Canadian businesses.

With respect to plywood standards, a scheme has been implemented whereby if CMHC does not grant C-D grade plywood approval for use in housing financed by CMHC, the matter will be reviewed by an impartial panel of experts acceptable to both parties. If the panel of experts determines that CMHC's review was unbiased and technically accurate, tariff reduction plans for January 1, 1989 for the plywood tariff linkage category will begin. If the panel has not completed its review by January 1, 1989 or disagrees with the findings of CMHC, tariff concessions on softwood plywood may be delayed by the United States pending agreement by the Parties that the issues have been resolved satisfactorily.

The technical regulations and standards for agricultural, food, beverage and certain related goods are detailed in Chapter Seven of the Agreement. Those provisions recognize that the Parties will seek an open border policy with respect to trade in such items consistent with the legitimate need for technical regulation and standards to protect human, animal and plant life and to facilitate commerce between the Parties. The governing principles of Chapter Seven include greater harmonization of technical regulatory requirements and inspection procedures; the appli-

¶ 362

cation of import or quarantine restrictions on the basis of regional rather than national distribution of diseases or pests, where such diseases or pests are distributed regionally rather than nationally; to establish an equivalent accreditation procedure for inspection systems and inspectors; to establish reciprocal training programs and where possible utilize each other's personnel for testing and inspection of such products; and to establish common data and information requirements for submissions relating to the approval of new goods and processes. Canada and the United States will (a) endeavour to work towards the elimination of technical regulations and standards that constitute an arbitrary, unjustifiable or disguised restriction on bilateral trade, (b) exchange information related to technical regulations, standards and testing, and (c) notify and consult during the development or prior to the implementation or change in the application of any technical regulation or government standard. Working groups in various sectors of the agriculture, food, beverage and related industries will be established to further the implementation of these provisions, address other issues as they arise and report to a joint monitoring committee (to be established by the Parties to monitor the timely implementation of the provisions and report the progress of the working groups to the Minister of Agriculture for Canada and the Secretary of Agriculture for the United States and such other government representatives as may be designated) and to the Canada–U.S. Trade Commission. That Commission, established by Chapter Eighteen of the Agreement, will supervise the implementation of the Agreement, resolve disputes that may arise over its interpretation and application, oversee its further elaboration, and consider any matter that may affect its operation.

In the final analysis, the exclusion of any obligation to ensure adherence to standards-related harmonization by states or provinces (which by definition includes local governments) means that this part of the Agreement may not be as far reaching as first contemplated.

¶ 364 Agriculture

The principal elements of this part of the Agreement are to be found under the headings of subsidies, market access and technical regulations.

¶ 368 AGRICULTURAL SUBSIDIES

The Agreement recognizes that the primary goal of the parties "is to achieve, on a global basis, the elimination of all subsidies which distort agricultural trade." This is an admission that little can be done in terms of a bilateral agreement to achieve this goal and that it must be achieved through multilateral trade negotiations such as the Uruguay Round. In the meantime, Canada and the United States have agreed that neither shall introduce or maintain any export subsidy (as opposed to other subsidies) on any agricultural goods exported to the other Party and that each Party shall take into account the export interests of the other Party in the use of any export subsidy on any agricultural good exported to third countries. An export subsidy is defined in the text as a subsidy that is conditional upon the exportation of agricultural goods. Canada has also agreed to eliminate the Canadian Western Grain Transportation rail subsidies on exports to the United States shipped through Canadian West Coast ports.

There is a further provision that neither Party, i.e. the Government of Canada or the Government of the United States of America, including any *public entity* that it establishes or maintains, shall sell agricultural goods for export to the other Party "at a price below the acquisition price of the goods plus any storage, handling or other costs incurred by it with respect to those goods". What constitutes a "public entity" is not further defined but it would no doubt include marketing boards established by the Federal Government, with or without provincial participation.

¶ 370 MARKET ACCESS

The Parties have agreed to "work together to improve access to each other's markets through the elimination or reduction of import barriers".

¶ 371 Tariffs

The Agreement provides for the progressive elimination of all tariffs on agricultural goods between the two countries over a period of ten years with a snapback provision for fresh fruits and vegetables for a further ten-year period under specified conditions. A temporary duty on fresh fruits or vegetables (as defined in the text) originating in the territory of the other Party may be applied on a regional or national basis when the price of such fruit or vegetable is depressed, provided that the planted acreage for the particular fruit or vegetable is no higher than the average acreage over the preceding five years. It is further provided that any acreage increase attributed directly to a reduction in wine grape planted acreage existing on October 4, 1987, shall be excluded from the calculation of planted acreage.

¶ 372 Tariff Barriers

Meat Goods

"Meat goods" means meat of cattle (including veal), goats and sheep (except lambs), whether fresh, chilled or frozen. It is provided that neither Party shall introduce, maintain or seek any quantitative import restriction or any other measure having equivalent effect on meat goods originating in the territory of the other Party. Where one Party imposes any quantitative import restriction on meat goods from *all* third countries, or negotiates agreements limiting exports from third countries, and the other Party does not take equivalent action, then the first Party *may* impose quantitative import restrictions on meat goods originating in the

¶ 370

territory of the other Party to the extent and for such period of time only as is sufficient to prevent frustration of the action taken on imports of the meat goods from third countries. Before any such action can be taken there must be notification and consultation.

Grain and Grain Products

Canada has agreed to eliminate import licences for wheat, barley and oats and their products when U.S. grain support levels become equal to Canadian grain support levels. Wheat, oat and barley products are defined as processed or manufactured substances which contain alone or in combination more than 25% by weight of such grain or grains. The method for calculating the level of Government support is set out in detail in an annex to the Chapter. They include 13 United States Government support programs, including support provided by state governments, and 17 Canadian Government support programs including general provincial government expenditures for agriculture.

Poultry and Eggs

If Canada maintains or introduces quantitative import restrictions on chicken, turkey, eggs and their products (as defined in the text) it shall nevertheless permit the importation of such goods from the United States at a level no less than a fixed percentage of domestic production.

Sugar-Containing Products

The United States has agreed not to introduce or maintain quantitative import restrictions or import fees on any good originating in Canada containing 10% or less sugar by dry weight. Sugar means sugar derived from sugar cane or sugar beets. The original text had referred to sweeteners.

¶ 373 Saving Provisions

Supply management programs, such as marketing boards, which control imports and set domestic prices are not affected by the Agreement, but must be consistent with Canada's GATT rights and obligations.

Both countries retain the right to apply countervailing duties on imports which are unfairly subsidized.

¶ 376 TECHNICAL REGULATIONS AND STANDARDS

These provisions of the Agreement deal with the reduction of regulatory barriers and the harmonization of technical regulations. With respect to agricultural, food, beverage and certain related goods, the Parties have agreed to work toward the elimination of technical regulations and standards that constitute an arbitrary, unjustifiable or disguised restriction on bilateral trade, to exchange information and to notify and consult with each other. The Parties have agreed to establish eight working groups with equal representation who shall meet at the request of either Party but not less than once a year. A joint monitoring committee will be established with equal representation which shall meet at least annually to monitor the progress of the working groups and to report the progress of the working groups to such Minister or Cabinet-level officer as may be appropriate, and to the Commission established in Chapter 18.

¶ 378 Wine and Distilled Spirits*

The legal text of this chapter elaborates on the obligations undertaken in the October Elements of Agreement concerning reciprocal access to each Party's alcoholic beverage market. Its provisions constitute a limited exception to the principle of national treatment (Article 105, Chapter Five, Articles 501, 502) which applies to the Agreement as a whole. Nevertheless, the net result appears to be an essentially open market for wine and distilled spirits produced in and between the two countries. As such, the chapter will regulate internal sale and distribution of these commodities (Article 801, para. 1) with a view to the immediate or progressive removal of discriminatory listing, pricing and distribution policies by each Party.

This chapter does not extend to the similar regulation of beer and malt-containing beverages, an important concession to the Canadian brewing industry. However, taken together with related provisions of the Agreement (Chapters Five and Twelve, discussed below), it does freeze the status quo in terms of any derogations from the principle of national treatment for exempted commodities to "existing measures" in place as of October 4, 1987 (Article 808).

Even allowing for concessions negotiated between the Parties, these provisions demarcate a prominent concession by Canada to the United States on a long-standing trade irritant. It is also one of the few areas of the Agreement which, on the Canadian side, purports to regulate a market primarily subject to provincial regulation. Throughout all provinces of Canada, the distribution and sale of alcoholic beverages is effectively a provincial government monopoly, in part, because of federal sufferance in that, since 1928, the Importation of Intoxicating Liquors Act has made the government of each province the sole lawful importer of intoxicating liquor. The listing, pricing and distribution practices mandated by the Agreement are substantially at variance with existing practices of Liquor Control Boards in many provinces, especially those in Ontario, Quebec and British Columbia. Notwithstanding the various practices grandfathered under the Agreement discussed below, provincial practices overall are clearly incompatible with Canada's Agreement commitment to ensure freer market access for U.S. wines.

---

* Prepared by Scott Fairley, David Petras, and Alan R. O'Brien

It is well understood that the federal–provincial division of constitutional jurisdiction applicable to alcoholic beverages is, to say the least, confused and uncertain. An absence of provincial cooperation or worse, outright opposition could seriously jeopardize this chapter of the Agreement. This is one area of the Agreement where provincial government opposition to the Agreement (notably that of Ontario which controls the largest provincial market) is confident it can thwart implementation of the Agreement. While provincial powers in that regard can be overstated, the general position of the Canadian government that the subject-matter of the Agreement lies within federal jurisdiction is in this instance also open to question.

The constitutional limitations constraining Ottawa are highlighted by the fact that the practices of provincial liquor boards have already put Canada in default of its international obligations. In November, 1987, a yet-to-be released GATT panel ruling vindicated a European Community (EC) complaint that discriminatory listing practices in relation to EC wines, provincial beer-brewing requirements and grape content rules for domestic wine production were all contrary to Canada's GATT commitments. Media reports indicate that the Canadian Government is attempting to secure a negotiated settlement of this dispute in consultation with the principal provincial governments involved (e.g., Ontario, Quebec and British Columbia) in which case the GATT ruling would not be implemented. However, one possible outcome is that Canadian concessions in this chapter of the Agreement may be extended to the EC.

The immediate and phased-in requirements of the free trade regime over alcoholic beverages have been grouped under three basic headings each commanding a separate article of the Agreement.

¶ 380 Listing (Article 802)

The basic rule here is that listing practices must conform with the general principle of national treatment (Chapter Five). They must be transparent (i.e., made known to the public), not create disguised trade barriers, treat Canadian and U.S. products in the same way and be based on normal commercial considerations. Listing decisions are to be communicated promptly to applicants and, where an application is refused, accompanied by a statement of reasons. An administrative appeal process will be available to unsuccessful applicants. However, a minor exemption to national treatment entitles British Columbia estate wineries existing on October 4, 1987, producing less than 30,000 gallons annually and meeting the local content rule then in effect to an automatic listing in British Columbia, provided that British Columbia listing measures otherwise conform with the Article.

¶ 382 Pricing (Article 803)

Commencing on January 1, 1989, provincial liquor boards will be required to phase out existing mark-ups on American wine in effect as of October 4, 1987: an immediate cut of 25% on the portion of the mark-up not attributable to the cost-of-service differential for the imported product (referred to as the "base differential'); 50% by 1990; and 10% reductions thereafter until 1995 when the mark-up may be no more than the actual and audited differential in the cost-of-service between American and Canadian wine. With respect to distilled spirits, all discriminatory mark-ups are to be eliminated immediately on the coming into force of the Agreement, but cost-of-service differentials will be permitted. Similarly, all other discriminatory pricing practices are to be eliminated when the Agreement becomes effective.

¶ 384 Distribution (Article 804)

Measures relating to the distribution of wine and distilled spirits will treat American and Canadian products equally with three exceptions. First, distilleries and wineries will continue to be permitted to limit sales on their premises to wines and liquors produced on those premises. Second, private wine store outlets existing on October 4, 1987 in Ontario and British Columbia will be permitted to favour their own wine. Third, the Quebec requirement that wine sold in grocery stores be bottled in the province will be grandfathered provided that alternative Quebec outlets (i.e., SAQ stores) are provided for the sale of U.S. wine, whether or not the latter is bottled in Quebec.

¶ 386 Other Provisions

Further, with respect to distilled spirits, Canada will eliminate all mandatory blending requirements with Canadian product for bulk product imported from the United States (Article 805). Both Parties have also agreed to recognize and respect product and labelling standards for "Canadian Whiskey" and "Bourbon Whiskey" as distinctive products in accordance with the respective laws and regulations of each country and to prohibit the sale of any non-conforming product under either description (Article 806).

¶ 388 Relationship to Other Chapters

Given the potential impact of the Agreement on the Canadian wine industry, it is instructive to note that in Chapter Seven (Agriculture) there is a minor incentive to shift future land use away from grape-growing by providing that only fruit produced on land committed to wine grape production as of October 4, 1987 will be exempt from the seasonal import duties that the Parties are permitted to impose during the first 20 years of the Agreement (Article 702).

¶ 382

As noted above, beer and malt-containing beverages are not included in this chapter, which in itself is a partial derogation from the principle of national treatment (Chapter Five). Chapter Twelve of the Agreement specifically exempts beer and malt-containing beverages from Chapter Five coverage. However, this exemption applies only to existing measures (i.e., as of October 4, 1987), the continuation or prompt renewal of such existing measures, or amendments to existing measures, but only to the extent that amendments do not further extend their non-conformity with the principle of national treatment (Article 1204). It follows that the Agreement anticipates foreclosure of any new measures by one Party not conforming with the standard of national treatment for the beer and malt-containing beverage products of the other Party.

In addition, Chapter Twelve preserves the rights and obligations of the Parties under GATT for the exempted product (Article 1205). Thus, the Agreement exemption does not appear to protect the beer industries of either Party from collateral attack outside the Agreement. This may be a particular concern of the Canadian industry to the extent that current Canadian restrictions on market access for American beer producers become a serious trade irritant.

¶ 390 Energy*

"(Canada and the United States) have recognized that they have a common interest in ensuring access to each other's market and enhancing their mutual security of supply." With this introduction to Chapter 9, Canada has expressed the essential bilateral objective of access to and security of North American energy supply. No feature is more reflective of the spirit and intent of the Agreement than the provisions relating to energy.

Essentially, the Agreement removes all restrictions on trade in energy between Canada and the U.S., save decisions relating to whether and when to allow exports ("surplus tests" are retained but not so as to derogate from the non-discriminatory or proportionality principles) and the movement (pass-through) of energy from third countries.

Once energy exports are authorized, any subsequent constraints on such exports to either country are limited by a proportionate sharing arrangement which provides that any reduction in energy exports relative to total supply not result in exports being less than the proportionate amount exported in the most recent 36 months prior to the implementation of the restriction. Furthermore, no such restrictions are to disrupt access to the supply, in proportionate degree or otherwise, of other energy goods of the exporting country in normal trade supply. The price of energy in export is left primarily to market forces, with a prohibition on discriminatory taxes or charges or minimum price requirements hav-

---

* Prepared by A.R. O'Brien

ing the effect of increasing the export price beyond that prevailing in the exporting country. This same prohibition is expressed in Article 408 of the Agreement. Furthermore, energy in export from Canada is no longer to be subject to the price test of being no less than the least cost of alternative energy at the same location in the U.S. (i.e., "the least cost alternative test").

Canada has secured through the Agreement relief from U.S. restrictions on the importation of uranium for enrichment as well as potential access to Alaskan oil supplies previously denied by U.S. law. Furthermore, each country remains free to adopt and apply domestic incentives for oil and gas exploration and development directed at enhancing reserves of such energy resources.

The Agreement provides for consultation between the two countries as to any action by a regulatory agency in either country which might result in discriminatory treatment against the other country or its persons or be inconsistent with the essential principles of the Agreement.

The provisions of the Agreement relating to energy focus essentially on security of supply and price with particular attention directed to ensuring that the export price will not be artificially or discriminatorily inflated above the price of such energy when consumed domestically. Putting aside the uncertain meaning of the phrase "consumed domestically" in Article 904, it remains to ask whether the export price of natural gas might indeed be less, under essentially similar circumstances, than the domestic price. Section 1 of Annex 905.2 of the Agreement obligates Canada to delete the "least cost alternative test" from the National Energy Board Part VI Regulations, thus removing what might be described as a U.S.-based floor price. As a result of this selection the price of energy exports remains subject to the residual tests of recovery of its appropriate share of costs incurred in Canada, and the export price being not less than the price to Canadians for equivalent service in related areas. Such tests for natural gas are now monitored by the National Energy Board after the fact rather than before, and may — taken in the market-sensitive character of the Agreement — presage export energy prices for natural gas below domestic Canadian prices.

¶ 392 Automotive Trade*

The major Canadian concern in this area was to preserve the status quo under the Auto Pact (Agreement Between Canada and the United States Concerning Automotive Products, signed January 16, 1965 and in force September 16, 1966) which, in recent years, has generated a substantial trade surplus in Canada's favour. The summary of this chapter of the Agreement suggests that, although Canada has agreed not to add to those Canadian manufacturers operating under the Auto Pact, it has

---

* Prepared by David Petras and Scott Fairley

substantially achieved the objective of leaving the Auto Pact intact. Indeed, Canada and the United States have agreed to administer the Auto Pact in the best interests of employment and production in both countries (Article 1001).

This chapter ties in the benefits of progressive elimination of remaining tariffs on automotive products to a new rule of origin designed to protect the North American automotive market for genuinely domestic producers. The latter, discussed below, is set out in Chapter Three of the Agreement. Phased-in elimination of tariffs covering original equipment (over 10 years), tires (over 10 years) and aftermarket auto parts (over 5 years) are set out in detail in Chapter Four (Annex 401.2). In this chapter there is, in addition, a separate concession from Canada phasing out the long-standing Canadian embargo on the importation of used motor vehicles. Restrictions are to be removed for older automobiles (eight years or more) beginning in 1989, extending to newer vehicles over a five-year period until all restrictions are removed by 1994 (Article 1003).

A major concession on the Canadian side is in relation to the termination of certain customs duty waivers. Production-based waivers calculated on Canadian value added for certain listed non-North American automobile manufacturers will be eliminated by January 1, 1996 or by such earlier date as is specified in the individual agreements between the companies concerned and the Government of Canada (Article 1082, para 3.; Annex 1002.1, Part Three). Canada has also agreed, beginning in 1989, to exclude exports to the United States from the calculation of export-based duty waivers currently available to certain listed non-North American auto makers and to terminate such waivers completely by January 1, 1998 (Article 1002, para. 2; Annex 1002.1, Part Two). Moreover, neither Party will be permitted to grant or expand (other than in favour of certain listed North American automobile manufacturers including the Big Three) conditional duty waivers on motor vehicles or original equipment parts imported from other countries, premised on the fulfillment of performance requirements such as minimum local sourcing, import substitution, export or domestic content levels (Article 1002, para. 1). The Parties have agreed that any automotive goods waiver or waivers granted by one country (other than those permitted under the Agreement) demonstrated to have an adverse impact on the commercial interests of a person of the other country or the economy of the other country will be either terminated or made available to all importers (Article 1002, para. 4).

A chief U.S. concern in the automotive trade negotiations was that Canada was being employed as a base for increased penetration of the U.S. market by Japanese and other offshore manufacturers, primarily through the device of present and proposed assembly plants in Ontario and Quebec. The new rule of origin agreed to under the Agreement

¶ 392

(Article 1005; Chapter Three, Annex 301.2, Section XVII) is designed to confine the benefits of the Auto Pact to genuine North American automobile manufacturers. It provides that 50% of the direct cost of manufacturing vehicles and original equipment parts (on an average annual basis) must be incurred in Canada or the United States in order to be traded duty-free under the Agreement. The new Agreement rule is roughly equivalent to a 70% requirement under the present Auto Pact which, unlike the new free trade rule, permits the inclusion of overhead and other indirect costs in calculating North American content. Consequently, for the North American assembly operations of foreign automobile manufacturers (e.g., Honda and Toyota) to qualify for duty-free status, the Agreement standard is substantially tougher. The Government of Canada summary suggests that this element will give "increased opportunities" to Canadian parts manufacturers, but it may also reduce the attractiveness of additional North American assembly operations for these foreign companies.

In the result, automotive goods exported from Canada which meet the new rule of origin will have duty-free access to the United States. Manufacturers qualified under the Auto Pact which meet its safeguards can import vehicles and parts into Canada duty-free from anywhere in the world, while those not so qualifying must comply with the Agreement rule of origin to be entitled to the benefit of the declining Canada–U.S. tariffs pursuant to Chapter Four of the Agreement.

The Agreement further contemplates the creation of a bilateral Select Panel of experts to monitor the health of the North American automobile industry (Article 1004). It is envisaged that this body will propose public policy measures and private initiatives to improve the competitiveness of the North American automobile industry in domestic and foreign markets. It is further provided that the Parties will cooperate in the upcoming Uruguay Round of multilateral trade negotiations under the GATT with a view to enhancing export opportunities for North American automotive products.

In summary, the Agreement purports to enhance the integration of the North American automobile industry which began in earnest with the Auto Pact of 1966. Canada appears to have preserved its interests in this regard while accepting the fact that it cannot allow itself to be a back door to the U.S. market for offshore producers.

¶ 394 Cultural Industries*

Articles 1607 and 2005 affirm Canada's determination to insulate certain defined industries, having an influence on that country's cultural objectives, from the national treatment principles of the Agreement.

* Prepared by A.R. O'Brien

Industries engaged in film and video, music and sound recording, publishing, cable television and broadcasting activities are exempt (Article 2005) from the present or future application of the Agreement. Consequently, Canada maintains its right to review and, if necessary, deny U.S. establishment, or acquisition directly or indirectly of business enterprises falling within certain of the defined cultural industries under the Investment Canada Act, and to otherwise restrain U.S. investor involvement in others (broadcasting). However, in the case of the denial of an indirect acquisition by a U.S. investor, Canada obligates itself to purchase the enterprise from the investor at fair open market value (Article 1607). A determination by Canada to require divestiture is not subject to the dispute settlement provisions of the Agreement (Article 1608).

The exclusion of cultural industries from the operation of the Agreement is not without its latent risks for Canada. Article 2005(2) further provides that a Party to the Agreement may invoke other or similar measures of equivalent commercial effect in response to actions by the other Party as to its cultural industries otherwise inconsistent with (the principles of) the Agreement.

One particular cultural industry, cable television, is singled out in Article 2006 as the intended subject of copyright payments to U.S. owners of copyright in programs retransmitted by cable. Canada has agreed to make provision for such obligations in its Copyright Act no later than January 1, 1990. Such obligations relate to the retransmission by cable to the public of copyright programs in originating transmissions of distant U.S. signals intended for free, over-the-air reception by the general public. Such Copyright Act amendments are to further provide that the retransmission by cable of program signals not intended for free, over-the-air reception are permitted only with the permission of the holder of the copyright in the program. Certain Canadian regulatory measures relating to the deletion and substitution of substantially identical television programs as well as the deletion and substitution of commercials by cable systems carrying out such measures by condition of license as of October 4, 1987, are maintained by the Agreement.

Article 2006 also grandfathers the rights of either Party to prohibit the retransmission of a distant signal by cable where a broadcast of the program is blacked out in the local market or a network-carried program is broadcast by a local network affiliate, programming such as abusive and obscene material and prohibited advertising so long as the measures are applied in a non-discriminatory manner, certain material during an election or referendum, and authorize the pre-emption of programs for urgent matters of national importance. The article further allows either Party to introduce (new and further) measures to enable a local broadcasting licensee to fully exploit the commercial value of its copyrighted programs.

¶ 394

Upon Canada amending its Copyright Act to provide for payment by cable of copyright fees for the retransmission of programs in distant broadcast signals the Parties agree to establish a joint advisory committee, including government and private sector experts, to review retransmission rights and related issues and make recommendations within twelve months.

In the area of publications, Canada undertakes (Article 2007) to amend S.19 of the Income Tax Act so as to permit a Canadian newspaper or periodical to be published or typeset outside Canada and still retain its special status for the purposes of a Canadian advertiser intending to treat the cost of advertising in such a publication as an expense for income tax purposes.

In the area of intellectual property the Parties have agreed to cooperate in the Uruguay Round of Multilateral Trade Negotiations and in other international forums to improve protection of intellectual property (Article 2004). The *Synopsis* to the Agreement issued by the Canadian Government states: "During the course of the negotiations, the two governments worked on an overall framework covering the protection of intellectual property rights (trademarks, copyright, patents, industrial design and trade secrets). In the end, a substantial chapter was dropped . . .".

The definitive text of the Agreement appears to have assured to Canada substantial protection for its cultural infrastructure, while at the same time moving to address the long-standing cable retransmission/copyright issue. The language of Article 2006 is in some respects uncertain in matters such as the meaning of "distant signals", the intended modality of the Copyright Act amendments, or measures which might be introduced to reinforce the commercial value of a local licence. Furthermore, any future retaliatory action by the U.S. under Article 2005(2) by whatever means of like commercial value will depend on the extent to which Canada may take further protectionist action concerning its cultural industries.

Trade in Services and Investment

¶ 400 Services*

The Agreement seeks to address for the first time in a substantial way the bilateral trade in services as distinct from goods, thereby recognizing the enormous growth of the service sector in Canada–U.S. trade in the past twenty years. Although the Agreement on services is far from comprehensive, it must be viewed in the context of the present total lack of a framework of reference under GATT for the liberalization of trade and services.

The application of the Agreement to the service sector is restricted specifically to those services listed in Annex 1408 to Chapter 14. Although the services covered are specifically listed in that annex, the general headings referring to services covered include agriculture and forestry services, mining services, construction services, distributive trade services, insurance and real estate services and commercial services. In addition to the general agreement on services, three particular services are the subject of sectoral annexes to which a more comprehensive set of rules is to be applied. Those sectoral annexes are architecture, tourism and computer services and telecommunications network-based enhanced services.

The Agreement on the listed services is further restricted by paragraph 5 of Article 1402. According to that provision, the obligations and commitments of the Parties are prospective only. Thus, existing statutes regulations and administrative practices of either Party which do not conform with the agreements contained in Chapter 14 may be amended and may be continued providing that no change is made in the future which would remove from one of the listed service sectors any of the rights listed in the Agreement which are presently being enjoyed by persons of the other Party.

Paragraph 1 of Article 1401 defines the scope of the Agreement on services as applying to any measure of a Party related to the provision of a covered service by or on behalf of a person of the other Party within or

* Prepared by Robert J. Dechert.

into the territory of the first mentioned Party. Given the amorphous concept of a service, paragraph 2 of Article 1401 attempts to define the provision of a covered service as including the production, distribution and marketing of a covered service; access to any domestic distribution systems which might exist in that industry such as a telecommunication system; the establishment of a commercial presence in the jurisdiction for the purposes of distributing and marketing the covered service; and finally, the investment of a non-resident in a service business carried on in the other Party.

The operative provisions of the Agreement appear in Articles 1402 and 1403.

Paragraph 1 of Article 1402 contains a "motherhood" statement about treating the providers of a service from the other Party in a no less favourable manner than that accorded to domestic providers of that service. This is commonly referred to as "national treatment".

Paragraph 2 of Article 1402 appears to extend the concept of national treatment to the provincial and state level by requiring that providers of a service from the other Party into any state or province, are treated no less favourably than that state or province would treat providers of the service originating from other provinces or states within the same Party. This provision will continue to allow provinces and states to discriminate between the providers of services resident in their own province or state and those providers of that service originating outside of that province or state, so long as the discrimination is not based upon nationality. It is submitted that the failure to lower inter-provincial and inter-state barriers to the flow of services seriously curtails the impact of this Agreement.

The Agreement on services allows for the different treatment of Canadian and U.S. suppliers of services where the difference in treatment is no greater than that necessary for "prudential, fiduciary, health and safety, or consumer protection reasons". The different treatment of providers of the same service based upon nationality must be equivalent in effect to the treatment by the Party imposing the standard to its own persons providing the same services. Thus, providers of services trained in the other Party may be required to take extra steps to ensure to the Party in whose territory the service is being provided that the training of the non-resident provider was equal to standards required of domestic providers of the same service.

Where such discriminatory treatment is contemplated the legislating Party must provide notice in writing in advance of that measure to the other Party pursuant to the institutional requirements of Article 1803 of the Agreement.

As a caveat to the use of the unequal treatment provision of the Agreement, paragraph 4 of Article 1402 imposes on the legislating Party

¶ 400

the burden of establishing that such unequal treatment is consistent with the requirements of paragraph 3 of Article 1402.

It is worth noting that unlike other sectors referred to in the Agreement, the Parties are not required to "harmonize" their treatment of providers of services.

The burden of establishing that any legislation, regulation or administrative practice of a Party which is discriminatory to persons of the other Party is not a contravention of the terms of the Agreement, on the basis that the discriminatory treatment in question existed at the time of the making of this Agreement, rests upon the proponent of discriminatory legislation or practice.

Any measures of a Party which constitute a means of arbitrary or unjustifiable discrimination against persons of the other Party including measures requiring establishment or commercial presence within the jurisdiction, are prohibited despite the fact that those measures might be consistent with the concepts of national treatment and necessary health and safety and consumer protection standards.

Paragraph 9 of Article 1402 surprisingly excludes government procurement and subsidies from the Agreement on services. Thus, the governments of either Party may continue to unjustifiably and unfairly discriminate against the providers of services from the other Party with respect to that government's own requirements for the services in question.

For many years the most important barriers to trade in services have been the licensing and certification requirements of the Parties. Article 1403 of the Agreement attempts to construct a framework of basic rules which will govern licensing and certification requirements of both Parties with respect to the covered services. Thus, paragraph 1 of Article 1403 requires that measures governing the licensing and certification of nationals providing covered services should relate principally to competence or the ability to provide covered services. Both Parties are charged with the obligation to ensure that the purpose and effect of any proposed licensing requirement is not to discriminate, impair or restrain the access of providers of the covered service resident in the other Party to the necessary license or certification. In addition, the Parties are committed to encourage the standardization of licensing and certification requirements between the two countries.

Article 1405 contains a general agreement between the two countries to continue consultations for the purposes of extending the provisions of this service agreement to other services not presently covered by it and to more firmly secure the framework of the existing agreement by unilaterally modifying or eliminating any existing measures which may be inconsistent therewith and to negotiate further sectoral annexes. Although this provision of the Agreement has no legal force, it is sug-

¶ 400

gested that the expression of the commitment to further extend the benefits of the Agreement will become a guide in the future regulatory and administrative practices of both countries.

Article 1406 states that, subject to the general notification and consultation procedures outlined in Chapter 18 of the Agreement, the benefits of the Agreement on services may be denied to a person of the other Party where the denying Party can establish that the service in question is being indirectly provided by a person of a third country. Once again, the Party claiming the right to variation from the framework of the Agreement is charged with the burden of establishing its case.

The present practice of applying very different income tax rates as between residents and non-residents is retained with respect to providers of services, subject to the general caveat that such difference in taxation should not constitute a means of arbitrary or unjustifiable discrimination between persons of the Parties or a disguised restriction on trade and in services between the Parties. It is suggested that this provision will prohibit the heretofore popular (prior to tax reform) practice of using preferential tax rates to stimulate a particular domestic sector of the economy. Regional incentive tax measures will of course not be affected by this provision so long as providers of services from other regions of the same country and residents of the other Party are subject to similar discrimination. In addition to the general agreements referred to above with respect to the services listed in Annex 1408 (which are many and varied), the Agreement contains three specific sectoral annexes.

¶ 410 ANNEX 1404 — SECTORAL ANNEXES

¶ 412 Architecture

The first sectoral annex covers the provision of architectural services.

This particular sectoral annex arose out of much preliminary work which was conducted independently by the Royal Architectural Institute of Canada and the American Institute of Architects, prior to the negotiation of the Agreement.

Article 1 of this annex describes the scope and coverage to apply to any measure relating to the mutual recognition of professional standards and to the criteria for the licensing and conduct of architects and the provision of architectural services in either Canada or the United States.

Article 2 of the annex delegates the authority to develop the bilateral licensing and certification requirements mentioned in Article 1403 to the two professional self-regulating bodies in both countries. Those professional bodies are charged with reporting on mutually acceptable professional standards on or before December 31, 1989 and the Parties are committed to reviewing those recommendations in a timely manner and (providing that such recommendations are consistent with the general agreement on services), the Parties are committed to encouraging the adoption of those recommendations by their respective state and provincial governments. This is a situation in which the Canadian government will obviously have to seek the compliance of each of the provinces in order to fulfill its commitment under the Agreement (contrary to recent statements of the Prime Minister that no such provincial cooperation was required to give effect to the Free Trade Agreement).

Finally, Article 4 of the annex requires the establishment of a binational committee for the purposes of reviewing the compliance of the various provincial and state licensing authorities with the mutual standards devised pursuant to Article 3 of the annex.

¶ 414 Tourism*

As it applies to trade in tourism services, Chapter 14 provides for "no less favourable treatment" for all measures related to trade in tourism services. For greater certainty, these measures are defined to include:

(a) provision of tourism services in the territory of a Party, either individually or with members of a travel industry trade association;

(b) appointment, maintenance and commission of agents or representatives in the territory of a Party to provide tourism services;

(c) establishment of sales offices or designated franchises in the territory of a Party; and

(d) access to basic telecommunications transport networks.

The above instances (a) to (d) are not exhaustive of the measures included under the Agreement, since Article 2 of the Sectoral Annex on Tourism provides that the terms of Chapter 14 shall apply to "all measures" related to trade in tourism services.

Further, each Party guarantees the other Party the right to promote in the territory of the other Party travel and tourism opportunities in its own territory, provided that such promotional activities do not include the provision of tourism services for profit.

Each Party has also agreed not to impede the free flow of tourism services by imposing fees or other charges on the departure or arrival of tourists, except such fees as comply with the principle of "no less favourable treatment" under Article 1402, and as are limited in amount to the approximate cost of the services rendered.

Finally, each of the Parties has undertaken not to impose restrictions that do not conform with international agreement on the value of

---
* Prepared by Ronald D. Lunau

tourism services that its residents or visitors to its territory may purchase from persons of the other Party.

¶ 416 Computer Services and Telecommunications — Network-Based Enhanced Services*

Article 1 of Part C of Annex 1404 to Chapter Fourteen of the Agreement describes the objective of that Part as being "to maintain and support the *further development of an open and competitive market* for the provision of enhanced services and computer services within or into the territories of the Parties" (italics added).

Article 1402 of Chapter Fourteen provides that ". . . each Party shall accord to persons of the other Party treatment no less favourable than that accorded in like circumstances to its persons with respect to (Computer Services and Telecommunications Network-Based Enhanced Services)".

In effect national treatment is afforded such services to the extent of the existing access for such services in the country of the other Party. To this extent the Agreement is prospective and, pursuant to the same Article 1402, any future treatment of such services by the other Party shall be non-discriminatory and in any circumstance subject to the prior notification provision of Article 1803.

Part C then provides for the right, to the extent of existing access and as future regulation may authorize, of access for the other Party to and the use of all basic telecommunications transport services; the resale and shared use of such services; the purchase and lease of customer-premises equipment and its attachment to the basic service network, and the transborder movement of information and access to data bases within the territory of the other Party. Regulatory definitions or classifications, as between basic and enhanced services or computer services as well as standards, certification testing or approval procedures shall apply without discrimination.

The right of the establishment of a commercial presence is provided for including permanent offices, appointment of agents, installation of customers' premises equipment as well as terminal equipment for the purposes of providing enhanced or computer services.

Monopoly basic services in the country of either Party are prohibited from engaging in anticompetitive practices in any provision of enhanced services that adversely affects a person of the other Party. On the other hand, neither Party is precluded from introducing measures designed to maintain monopolistic basic telecommunications transport services or facilities within its territory, short of requiring a person of the other Party to do so.

---

* Prepared by Alan R. O'Brien

Services, as distinct from goods, have secured legitimacy in the context of trade between Canada and the U.S. The growth of computer and enhanced telecommunications-network services has made such recognition imperative and overdue. Monopoly basic services remain a probable necessity in Canada given its size and population, but enhanced services are predicated on competition with attendant commitments to research and development. The Agreement provides an opportunity, but no certainty of a Canadian presence in this continental enhanced services marketplace. The boundaries of that marketplace will be influenced by the relevant regulatory agencies in determining the meaning of "basic telecommunications transport services".

¶ 420 Temporary Entry for Business Persons*

Restrictions on the ability of foreign businessmen and employees of international corporations to temporarily enter a country for business or employment purposes are typically motivated by a desire to protect home-grown industries and the native labour market. However, these same restrictions can also pose significant barriers to trade and investment in that country. Moreover, as the Agreement notes, trade in professional and commercial services cannot take place unless people can move freely across the border.

Accordingly, to support the objective of eliminating barriers to the movement of goods, services and investments, the Agreement will lower some of these barriers by facilitating temporary entry into Canada and the United States by certain business persons based in the other country. The agreement will make no changes, however, to existing procedures for premanent entry.

"Business person" is a defined term in the Agreement meaning "a citizen of a Party who is engaged in the trade of goods or services or in investment activities . . .". Since citizenship is an element of the definition, landed immigrants or permanent residents, including entrepreneurs and investors recently admitted to Canada under the Business Immigration Program, are excluded.

The following groups of business persons are included in the Agreement:

(a) "Business Visitors";

(b) "Traders and Investors";

(c) "Professionals" engaged in one of the professions set out in Schedule 2 to Annex 1502.1 of the Agreement; and

---

* Prepared by Ronald D. Lunau

(d) "Intra-Company Transferees" employed in a capacity that is managerial, executive, or involves specialized knowledge, and employed continuously by the company for one year.

The benefits to Canadian business persons under the Agreement are significant. The most important of these may be that Canadian traders and investors meeting the requirements of Annex 1502.1(B) will be eligible to apply for treaty trader and treaty investor visas (the U.S. E-1 and E-2 visa). The E visas will be available to Canadian nationals who have, or who are employed by Canadian companies which have, substantial trade in goods or services in the United States. To be eligible, the person seeking entry must be employed in a supervisory or executive capacity, or possess essential skills, or be seeking entry to develop and direct the operations of an enterprise in which the business person has invested, or is investing, a substantial amount of capital. The advantages of this visa category are that the visa may be renewed indefinitely, and the visa may be available to those who could not qualify under the L visa category applicable to intra-company transferees.

With respect to intra-company transferees (the U.S. L-1 visa) the United States has agreed not to require labour certification tests or other procedures of similar effect for temporary entry under this category. This provision basically mirrors the existing Canadian procedure under Regulation 20(5) of the Immigration Regulations, 1978, since Canada does not impose formal employment validation requirements upon otherwise qualifying intra-company transferees, and has undertaken in the Agreement not to do so. However, it appears that the L visa category will continue to retain certain restrictions. For example, the L visa will be applicable only to Canadian citizens who have been employed continuously for one year by the firm or corporation; unlike the E visa there exists a five-year ceiling on renewals; individual labour certifications will still be required for those transferees who do not meet the rather strict requirements of employment in a capacity that is managerial, executive or involves special knowledge; there are special rules relating to the establishment of a "new office", which may impede access by Canadian companies; and there are special requirements which apply under this category when the employee to be transferred is a major shareholder of the parent Canadian company.

The changes to be implemented with respect to the U.S. B-1 visa for business visitors are generally positive. The list of eligible occupations in Schedule 1 to Annex 1502.1 will provide certainty to this category, thereby facilitating entry for these business persons at a port of entry to the United States. In addition, the United States has agreed not to apply prior approval procedures, petitions, labour certification tests or other procedures of similar effect to business visitors generally, whether or not they are listed in Schedule 1. Existing restrictions on Canadians entering the United States to install, service or repair equipment or machinery

¶ 420

sold to U.S. purchasers, or to train U.S. workers to perform such services, have also been eased. Such visits may now take place during the life of the warranty or service agreement, and are not limited to the 12-month period after the date of purchase. The Immigration and Naturalization Service of the United States had been considering lifting this restriction before the Agreement, and the change is now embodied in the Agreement.

Finally, professional business persons listed in Schedule 2 to Annex 1502.1 will be permitted to enter the United States under a new visa category, and engage in temporary employment without the need of prior filing of a visa petition or labour certification test.

The Agreement will also, of course, facilitate the temporary entry of United States business persons into Canada. The "business visitors" listed in Schedule 1 to Annex 1502.1 of the Agreement will be granted entry under section 19(1) of the Immigration Regulations, 1978. The result of this action will be to specifically remove existing requirements for these business visitors to obtain a Canadian employment authorization prior to entering Canada to engage in their temporary employment. These persons will be admitted simply upon presentation at the border of proof of citizenship and documentation demonstrating that the visitor is engaged in an occupation described in Schedule 1. Business persons other than those listed in Schedule 1 may also be granted temporary entry under section 19(1) if they can prove that they are engaged in the trade of goods or services or in investment activities. In either case, however, an employment authorization will still be required should these visitors intend to engage in secondary employment, i.e. employment which falls outside the activities described in the definition of "business person".

The other three defined groups of "business persons," namely "traders and investors", "professionals" and "intra-company transferees" will be afforded entry under section 20(5) of the Immigration Regulations. This action exempts these groups from the usual employment validation process, although these individuals will still be required to obtain an employment authorization at a port of entry.

In the case of intra-company transferees, Canada has added a new condition that the transferee must have been employed continuously for one year by the firm or corporation. This condition did not exist before the Agreement, and has apparently been added by Canada to mirror the same condition which is imposed by the United States under its domestic legislation. For the same reason, Canada has agreed to include transferees possessing "special knowledge" in this category.

On balance, the chapter of the Agreement dealing with Temporary Entry for Business Persons appears to achieve a fair and substantial quid pro quo. Such difficulties as may arise in the application of the Agreement (for example, differing interpretations of who is a "manager", "executive" or possesses "special knowledge" for the purposes of intra-company transfers) should be able to be resolved through the mandatory consultations under Article 1503 of the Agreement. For Canadians, the Agreement offers increased opportunities from the availability of the United States E visa, the new provisions for the admission of professionals, and increased certainty under the United States B visa category.

¶ 430 Investment*

The preamble to the Agreement includes a declaration that the Government of Canada and the Government of the United States of America (the Parties) are resolved to "ensure a predictable commercial environment for business planning and investment". This declaration, in conjunction with the stated objective of significantly liberalizing conditions for investment within the free trade area, set the stage for Chapter Sixteen which details the liberalization of foreign investment controls and does so within the context of the primary focus of the Agreement of granting each Party national or non-discriminatory treatment with respect to investment.

The scheme of Chapter Sixteen attempts to liberalize foreign investment controls while simultaneously preserving some flexibility to respond to national interests.

In Canada, the primary agent for foreign ownership control is Investment Canada. The agency processes review and notification filings for direct or indirect share or asset acquisitions of Canadian businesses and the establishment of new businesses in Canada by non-Canadians. Naturally, the Agreement calls for substantial amendments to the *Investment Canada Act*, which principally involve the review thresholds and the definition of what constitutes a "foreign" investment.

The current review thresholds for acquisitions of Canadian businesses are significantly altered. Canada has retained the right to review acquisitions of Canadian businesses by U.S. investors but in the case of direct acquisitions the current $5 million review threshold will be gradually raised to $150 million by January 1, 1992. In the case of indirect acquisitions, i.e. where a transaction involves the transfer of control of one foreign-controlled firm to another, the current $50 million review threshold will be phased out entirely by January 1, 1992.

Investment liberalization applies to qualifying investors, namely, the two governments or their agencies, provinces or states, their nationals or "entities" or any combination of these investors. To qualify for equal treatment "entities", which are defined as corporations, partnerships, trusts or joint ventures, must ultimately be controlled directly or

---

* Prepared by George N. Addy

indirectly through the ownership of voting interests by the listed qualifying investors or, if not controlled, qualifying investors must own a majority of voting interests. The objective here is to prevent third country investors from benefiting from investment liberalization by using domestic shell corporations. If liberalization is eventually extended to third country investors, this chapter and particularly its definitions will have to be significantly amended.

Once national treatment has been established for the investment it will be subject to the same rules as businesses owned by domestic investors. In keeping with the spirit of fair competition, domestic laws governing trade activities continue to apply; for instance, U.S. anti-trust laws will continue to govern all businesses operating in the U.S.A. and Canadian competition laws will continue to govern all businesses operating in Canada. While this may seem simple, some commentators have observed that since the delineation of the appropriate "market" is a fundamental component of any competition law analysis and since the Agreement geographically establishes a continental market for trade purposes, anti-trust policy-makers and enforcement agencies will also have to extend their perspective beyond national boundaries. The trans-border application of domestic anti-trust laws may therefore be inevitable.

Investment-related performance requirements such as domestic content and import substitution requirements, as a condition of permitting investment or in the regulation of business operations within each Party's territory, are prohibited. Such requirements may be imposed on investors of a third country except where they would have a significant impact on trade between Canada and the U.S.

The obligation to accord national treatment to investors of the other Party does not apply to measures affecting investments in the financial services, government procurement or transportation services areas. While the investment guidelines will be amended for those sectors covered by Chapter Sixteen, the existing thresholds and investment limitations appear to continue with respect to transportation sector acquisitions. This is consistent with forthcoming legislative developments such as the National Transportation Act restrictions on ownership of domestic air carrier licensees which come into force in January 1988.

Investment liberalization does not apply to ownership restrictions imposed on the acquisition or sale of existing Crown corporations. For future Crown corporations the Agreement permits ownership restrictions on the initial acquisition or sale transactions but not on subsequent resale of those interests. Another notable exception to the national treatment doctrine is the recognition that differential treatment is permitted if it is for prudential, fiduciary, health and safety, or consumer protection reasons, if the different treatment is equivalent in effect to the treatment accorded to domestic investors and if prior notification to the other

¶ 430

Party of such differential treatment has been given in accordance with the terms of the Agreement.

The provisions of Chapter Sixteen, subject to the nullification and impairment provision of the Agreement, do not apply to any subsidy which does not constitute an arbitrary or unjustifiable discrimination between investors of a Party or a disguised restriction on the benefits accorded by the Agreement.

A provision has also been included in Chapter Sixteen to prevent the indirect control of foreign investment by regulating the transfer of funds between an entity within one Party's territory to persons in the other Party's territory. In particular, apart from the equitable, non-discriminatory and good faith applications of domestic laws relating to bankruptcy and insolvency, securities, criminal or penal offences, reports of currency transfers, withholding taxes or the satisfaction of judgments in adjudicatory proceedings, each Party is prohibited from preventing an investor of the other Party from transferring profits, royalties, fees, interests or other earnings or any proceeds from the sale of all or any part of the investment.

While the agreement contemplates the free flow of revenues, dividends, and the like across the border, provisions are included which permit differential tax treatment for foreign-owned firms provided that such measures do not constitute arbitrary or unjustifiable discrimination or a disguised restriction on the benefits accorded by the Agreement.

The Parties have also agreed that they may not require an investor of the other Party, by reason of its nationality, to sell or otherwise dispose of an investment or any part thereof in its territory. The prohibition is limited to reasons of nationality. Existing domestic laws authorizing forced divestiture on a basis other than nationality continue to have full force and effect. For instance, anti-trust or competition law provisions allowing forced divestiture continue as those measures are taken not on the basis of nationality but on the basis of competitive forces within any given market and apply equally to domestic and foreign-owned entities operating within those markets. Article 2010 of the Agreement deals with the issue of monopolies. Defined to include any entity or consortium that is the sole provider of a good or covered service in the territory of a Party, monopolies, either existing or new ones, are allowed under the Agreement. Where either Party is going to establish, designate, authorize or expand the scope of a monopoly franchise to cover an additional good or covered service which may affect interests of persons of the other Party, advance notice will be given and on request, negotiations will ensue in an effort to minimize any nullification or impairment of the benefits of the Agreement. Article 2010 refers to the designation of a monopoly by a Party and does not refer to actions by a province or state which by definition includes local governments. While addressing the spirit of maintaining the legitimacy of Crown corporations, the provision leaves the question of provincial or municipal monopolies up in the air. Where monopolies are designated, the Parties have agreed to ensure non-discrimination by the monopoly in its market and to prevent the anti-competitive exercise of market power by monopolies in other markets by discrimination, cross-subsidization or through predatory conduct. The listed instances are in addition to applicable anti-trust or competition laws governing business conduct in the free trade area.

The Canadian government has agreed, in the case of a forced divestiture of a business enterprise in the cultural industry owned by an investor of the United States, to offer to purchase the business from the investor at a fair, open-market value as determined by an independent impartial assessment. Similarly, in the case of the direct or indirect nationalization for public purposes of an investment in its territory, owned by an investor of the other Party, the nationalizing Party is obligated to acquire the foreign-controlled firm in accordance with the due process of law, on a non-discriminatory basis and at fair market value.

The provisions of investment liberalization apply to future changes in law and regulations only. Existing laws, policies and practices are for the most part grandfathered (i.e., the liberalization will not apply to investments in the oil and gas and uranium mining industries). Furthermore, existing exceptions to national treatment provided in Canadian and U.S. laws, as in the case of foreign ownership in the communications and transportation industries, also continue intact.

Assuming that the provisions of the Agreement are fully implemented, the impact on the workload of Investment Canada will be significant. In effect, about 80% of the transactions currently subject to review will fall below the new thresholds. The continued existence of Investment Canada in its present form is therefore doubtful. The future role of the agency will not be the review of foreign investment, but more likely the monitoring of foreign investment in Canada. One could readily see its activities being undertaken by another department, such as the Department of External Affairs or Regional Industrial Expansion and a shift away from a responsibility to review and monitor foreign investment to an agency responsible for promoting Canada as a place for foreign interests to invest.

The next policy question that will have to be addressed by the Canadian government involving foreign investment is whether or not the liberalization of foreign investment controls contained in the Agreement should be extended to all foreign investors.

The inclusion in Chapter Sixteen of many laudable but imprecise concepts such as "significant impact", "arbitrary", "unjustifiable", "disguised" and "equitable" may allow both Parties a certain amount of room to manoeuvre. Negotiations in real terms are really only just beginning.

¶ 440 Financial Services*

The much expanded and detailed wording of the provisions of the Agreement on financial services over the description contained in the Elements of the Agreement, ironically appears to have greatly narrowed the scope of the agreement.

Article 1701 defines the scope and coverage of the financial services agreement.

Paragraph 1 of Article 1701 incorporates several other important provisions of the Agreement by reference and without further explanation.

Surprisingly, the general provisions of the Agreement on investment restrictions between the two Parties is expressly excluded from application to the financial services sector. Although there was no hint of such a circumscription in the Elements, it was indicated in the comment made by the federal minister of state for finance, Thomas Hockin that in his opinion the minister would retain his prerogative to review the entrance of U.S. financial institutions into Canada.

Paragraph 2(a) of Article 1601 allows the application of the general investment provisions of the Agreement where the financial service in question is insurance services which are otherwise not dealt with under paragraph 1 of Article 1703.

According to Article 2001 of the Agreement, the provisions of the Agreement with respect to financial services shall have no effect upon any provision of the *Canada–U.S. Income Tax Convention*. Thus interest and dividends paid by banks in either Canada or the U.S. to depositors and shareholders in the other country will continue to be subject to non-resident withholding taxes at the rates provided for in the Income Tax Convention. Specifically, Article 2001 provides that Articles XXV and XXVI of the *Canada–U.S. Income Tax Convention* will govern the interpretation of income tax legislation in both countries as it pertains to financial services. These *Canada–U.S. Income Tax Convention* articles provide for; (1) non-discrimination in income tax treatment between citizens of either Party resident in the taxing Party and the taxing party's treatment of citizens of a third state; and (2) the resolution of income tax irritants between the two Parties by the competent authorities for each of the Parties.

Article 2002, entitled "Balance of Payment" subjects the provisions of the Agreement regarding financial services to:

---

* Prepared by Robert J. Dechert

(a) Trade Restrictions in accordance with Article XII of the GATT Declaration on Trade Measures for Balance of Payments purposes dated November 28, 1979; or

(b) Restrictions on financial services by either Party on;

    (i) the making of payments and transfers for current international transactions in conformity with Article VIII of the Articles of Agreement of the International Monetary Fund, or

    (ii) International Capital Movements in accordance with Article 7, paragraphs (c) through (e), of the 1961 OECD Code of Liberalization of Capital Movements.

Each of these restrictions is subject to the general caveat that such restrictive provisions should not constitute a means of arbitrary or unjustified discrimination between persons of either Party.

The Agreement on financial services does not apply to restrictions based upon items of national security as outlined in Article 2003, discussed elsewhere herein.

Pursuant to Article 2010 of the Agreement, either Party may designate a monopoly in respect of financial services provided that:

    (i) the other Party is notified in advance of the intention to designate a monopoly; and

    (ii) prior to designation of a monopoly the designating Party must consult with the other Party if requested to do so.

Any such monopoly should be restricted such that the spirit of the Agreement is maintained. Each Party must ensure that any monopoly so designated in the area of financial services will not discriminate against citizens of the other Party in its dealings. An obvious use of this provision would be the reservation of the provision of certain financial services by the Central Banks of either Party.

The general provisions of Chapter 21 of the Agreement with respect to statistical requirements, amendments to the financial services section of the Agreement, the entry into force of the provisions of Chapter 17, and the duration and termination of the Agreement between the Parties, are specifically applied to financial services covered by Chapter 17.

The scope of the Agreement on financial services is severely restricted by paragraph 2 of Article 1701. According to that provision, no part of the Agreement on financial services shall apply to any measure of a political subdivision of either Party. Although simple in language, the effect of this restriction is quite far-reaching. As a result of paragraph 2, provincial laws governing loan companies, trust companies, mortgage companies and the securities industry will continue to be unaffected by the Agreement. Presently, foreign ownership of securities dealers is prohibited or restricted by many provincial securities law statutes.

The two main operative sections of the Agreement on financial services appear in Article 1702 and Article 1703. These articles contain the commitments of the United States and Canada respectively.

Paragraph 1 of Article 1702 contains the first of the U.S. concessions and concerns the selling and underwriting of Canadian government debt issues in the United States by Canadian and U.S. financial institutions. As a result of this provision, the dealing, underwriting and purchase of debt obligations backed by Canada (or any of its political subdivisions including provinces and municipalities) is extended to financial institutions of Canadian and U.S. origin. The wording of the Agreement may provide for the underwriting and sale of debts of Canadian Crown corporations which are guaranteed by the government of Canada or any of the provinces. This provision has been welcomed by the Canadian banking industry as a lucrative concession ensuring the banks' right of access to the entire U.S. market for the sale of these preferred securities. This represents a major policy shift in U.S. law prohibiting the sale of securities by banking institutions.

The second of the U.S. commitments contained in paragraph 2 of Article 1702, ensures that Canadian financial institutions will be treated equally to U.S. financial institutions with respect to section 5 of the International Banking Act of 1978. These provisions presently restrict foreign-controlled banks from acquiring interest in banks in more than one state. Prior to 1978, Canadian Chartered Banks had established branches in several states. These branches had been grandfathered in 1978 for 10 years, and this grandfathering protection is extended indefinitely pursuant to this provision of the Agreement.

The U.S. commitment contained in paragraph 3 of Article 1702 extends to Canadian financial institutions, identical treatment to that accorded to U.S. financial institutions with respect to amendments to the Glass-Steagall Act and associated legislation and resulting amendments to regulations and administrative practices. The Glass-Steagall Act separates the banking and securities industries in the United States. Canada (notably Ontario) has participated in recent world trends towards the obscuring of this separation of commercial and investment banking. A presently existing moratorium preventing U.S. banks from underwriting securities and selling mutual funds, insurance and mortgage-backed securities expires on March 1, 1988 well in advance of the effective date of the Agreement (January 1, 1989). If the right of the banks to participate in the securities industry in the United States is liberalized as expected, Canadian banks will be included and many will be ready to immediately participate as a result of recent acquisitions of Canadian securities dealers with U.S. operations and affiliates.

¶ 440

In addition, paragraph 4 of Article 1702 commits the United States to continue to provide Canadian-controlled financial institutions established under the laws of the United States with the rights and privileges that they now have in the United States market, as a result of existing laws, regulations, practices and stated policies of the United States. This grandfathering or "standstill provision" has been interpreted by some members of the Canadian securities industry as guaranteeing that the recent acquisition of large percentages of Canadian investment dealers with U.S. operations or subsidiaries, by Canadian banks carrying on business in the United States, may be allowed to continue despite the apparent conflict with the Glass-Steagall Act. However, it may also be argued that present cross-holdings of banks in investment dealers which also carry on both of those functions in the United States, must cease since they are presently contrary to U.S. laws. The strength of this provision for Canadian financial institutions is somewhat weakened by the final phrase of paragraph 4 which states that such rights and privileges shall be subject to "normal regulatory and prudential considerations". It is suggested that, the term "prudential considerations" could be quite widely defined.

The Canadian commitments to the Agreement on financial services are contained in Article 1703 of the Agreement. Paragraph 1 of Article 1703 states that United States persons ordinarily resident in the United States shall not be subject to restrictions that limit foreign ownership of Canadian controlled financial institutions. In accordance with this obligation such United States persons shall not be subject to; section 110(1) of the Bank Act, subsections 19(1) and 20(2) of the Canadian and British Insurance Companies Act, subsections 11(1) and 12(2) of the Investment Companies Act, subsections 45(1) and 46(2) of the Loan Companies Act (Canada) and subsections 38(1) and 39(2) of the Trust Companies Act (Canada). Each of these listed statutes presently restrict the aggregate ownership of shares of the capital stock of Schedule "A" banks, insurance companies, investment companies, and loan and trust companies by non-residents to 25%. This restriction will be removed in favour of U.S. residents as of January 1, 1989. In the case of all of the above-mentioned institutions except Schedule "A" banks, the share ownership and voting rights of any individual non-resident is presently restricted to 10%, and as a result of this provision U.S. residents will no longer be subject to this restriction. The general rule contained in section 110(3) of the Bank Act restricting the ownership by any individual of shares of the capital stock of a Schedule "A" bank to 10%, is not mentioned in the Agreement and will continue to apply to both Canadian and U.S. residents. The last sentence of paragraph 1 of Article 1703 reiterates the statement made in paragraph 2 of Article 1701 that the financial services agreement contained in the Agreement will not apply to any "provincially constituted" financial institution. The term "provincially constituted" financial institution" may apply to business corporations carrying

¶440

on the business of providing financial services as well as entities licensed under specific provincial legislation concerned with financial services such as provincial trust company legislation. This ambiguity will require some clarification.

Paragraph 2 of Article 1703 is entirely devoted to the treatment of U.S.-controlled Schedule "B" banks in Canada. Presently, section 302(7) of the Bank Act restricts the total domestic assets of all Schedule "B" banks in Canada to 16% of the total domestic assets of all banks in Canada. Pursuant to paragraph 2(a) of Article 1703 of the Agreement, Canada has committed to incorporating additional U.S.-controlled Schedule "B" banks and to increasing the authorized capital of any presently existing U.S.-controlled Schedule "B" banks without reference to the present 16% of total domestic banking assets restriction. The efficacy of this continued restriction on the aggregate value of foreign bank subsidiary assets in Canada in light of paragraph 2 of Article 1703 is seriously doubted.

Subparagraph 2(b) of Article 1703 restricts the right of the Minister of Finance to arbitrarily reduce the authorized capital of any U.S.-controlled Schedule "B" bank.

In addition, Canada is committed to allowing U.S.-controlled Schedule "B" banks to open additional branches in Canada without prior approval from the Minister of Finance.

Finally, Canada is committed to allowing for the transfer of loans from U.S.-controlled Schedule "B" banks to their U.S. resident parents subject to "prudential requirements of general application".

The changes contained in paragraph 2 of Article 1703 should satisfy what has heretofore been a major trade irritant in financial services between the two Parties.

In place of the general relaxation of investment review as set out in Chapter 16 of the Agreement, paragraph 3 of Article 1703 states that Canada shall not use review powers governing the entry of U.S.-controlled financial institutions in a manner inconsistant with the aims of Chapter 17. This provision appears to reserve the right of the Canadian government to review U.S. investment in the financial service industry for valid reasons other than the restriction of participation by U.S. residents in that sector.

In nearly identical language to that of paragraph 4 of Article 1702, paragraph 4 of Article 1703 states that Canada shall continue to provide United States-controlled financial institutions established under the laws of Canada (namely Schedule "B" banks) with the rights and privileges they now have in the Canadian market. With the exception of the general wording indicating the willingness of both Parties to continue to consult on the liberalization of trade in financial services, this paragraph has not been seen as particularly important by industry analysts.

Paragraph 1 of Article 1704 requires each Party, to the extent possible, to make public and allow opportunity for comment on, legislation and proposed regulations resulting from the agreement on financial services. This commitment to public consultation on proposed legislation is somewhat novel for Canada although it is a more common place practice in the United States. It is suggested that this specific reference to public consultation is an attempt by the negotiators to soften the impact of the lack of a dispute settlement mechanism for the financial services sector.

For unexplained reasons, the agreement on financial services is not covered by the dispute settlement procedures of the Agreement described elsewhere. Rather, paragraph 2 of Article 1704 allows either party to request consultation at any time on any matter covered by the financial services agreement and specifically states that such consultation shall be conducted between the Canadian Department of Finance and the United States Department of the Treasury. It is submitted that trade liberalization in the financial services sector will accordingly not be as secure as those parts of the Agreement which are subject to the dispute settlement mechanism. It should be pointed out that there is no mechanism provided to enforce the Agreements contained in Chapter 17 nor is there any route for the hearing of complaints voiced by the private sector with respect to same. Presumably, the only recourse of the financial service industry in either country if it believes that a law or a practice of the other Party unfairly favours or restricts the free-flow of financial services, is to complain to its own government and to request that the two governments "consult" on the issue.

Paragraph 2 of Article 1705 states generally that either Party may deny the benefits of the financial services agreement to a company of the other Party if it can establish that such company is controlled by a person of a third country. Control of a company is defined in the Agreement to mean both *de jure* or *de facto* control. It is submitted that the Agreement would allow up to 49% ownership of a financial institution in either Party by residents of a third country provided that the third country residents could not be shown to have *de facto* control of the financial institution.

The scope of the Agreement provisions on financial services are greatly dependent upon the definitions of the terms "financial service" and "financial institution" which are used throughout Chapter 17. Article 1706 defines "financial institution" as a company authorized to do business under the laws of a Party relating to financial institutions as defined by a Party, and defines "financial service" as a service of "a financial nature" offered by a financial institution. Neither of these definitions is helpful in determining what services are covered by the Agreement contained in Chapter 17. It is difficult to understand how the

Parties will enforce the provisions of the Agreements if each is left to unilaterally define what the parameters of the sector in question are. Section 190(1) of the Income Tax Act (Canada) defines a financial institution as a corporation that:

(a) is a bank,

(b) is authorized under the laws of Canada or a province to offer its services as a trustee to the public, or

(c) is authorized under the laws of Canada or a province to accept deposits from the public and carries on the business of lending money on the security of real estate or invests money in mortgages or hypothecs on real estate.

Section 254 of the Bank Act (Canada) defines a financial institution as a bank to which the Quebec Savings Bank Act applies, a corporation to which the Trust Companies Act or the Loan Companies Act applies or a financial corporation defined in section 193(1) of the Bank Act. It is clear that in Canada at least, there is presently no singular definition of "financial institution" or "financial service". It is suggested that the U.S. definition of these terms is similarly ambiguous. The Agreement obviously covers banks, securities dealers, loan and trust companies and insurance companies; however, its application to investment consultants, sales financing companies, leasing companies, and currency and commodities dealers is uncertain.

It should further be noted that by virtue of the loose definition of "ordinarily resident" contained in Article 1706, the liberalization of trade in financial services will be available to citizens of third countries who merely sojourn in either Canada or the United States for at least 183 days during a year. It is submitted that the significance of this definition may cause the extension of this Agreement to the citizens of many third countries.

Despite the more restricted scope of the agreement on financial services as set out in the Agreement, from the scope suggested by the more general wording of the Elements, it is clear that Chapter 17 has resolved several long-standing trade irritants between the Parties and has prepared a framework for future liberalization of trade in the financial services sector.

Institutional Provisions

This Part contains the institutional provisions concerning the settlement of any disputes between the Parties respecting the interpretation or application of any element of the Agreement (Chapter 18) and the provisions concerning binational dispute settlement in antidumping and countervailing duty cases (Chapter 19).

¶ 500 Canada–United States Trade Commission

¶ 502 Introduction

The Parties have established institutional provisions to deal with the operation of the Agreement and to deal with any disputes respecting the interpretation or application of any element of the Agreement. The major institution which is established for this purpose is the Canada–United States Trade Commission (the Commission). Its mandate is to supervise the implementation of the Agreement, to resolve disputes that may arise over its interpretation and application, to oversee its further elaboration, and to consider any other matter that may affect its operation. The Commission is composed of representatives of both Parties. The principal representative of each Party is the Cabinet-level officer or Minister primarily responsible for international trade or their designee. The Commission must convene at least once a year and regular sessions are to be held alternately in the two countries.

¶ 504 Procedures

The Parties have provided for the following procedures:

Notification and Information

Each Party is required to give written notice to the other of any proposed or actual measure that it considers might materially affect the operation of the agreement including a description of the reasons for the measure. This notice is to be given as far in advance as possible. Upon request, the other Party is required to promptly provide information and respond to questions pertaining to any measure whether or not notification has been given.

Consultation

Either Party may request consultations regarding any actual or proposed measure or any other matter that it considers affects the operation of the Agreement. The Parties must make an attempt to arrive at a mutually satisfactory resolution of any matter through consultation. However, if the Parties fail to resolve a matter through consultations either Party may request a meeting of the Commission stating the matter complained of and indicating what provisions of the Agreement are considered relevant. The Commission is required to convene and endeavour to resolve the dispute promptly.

Arbitration

The Agreement provides for a dispute settlement procedure should the Commission fail to arrive at a mutually satisfactory resolution. This dispute settlement procedure applies with respect to the avoidance or settlement of all disputes regarding the interpretation or application of the agreement except for disputes concerning financial services (Chapter 17) and the binational dispute settlement in antidumping and countervailing duty cases (Chapter 19). Further, any dispute arising under both the Agreement and the GATT, and agreements negotiated under the GATT, may be settled in either forum, at the discretion of the complaining Party. Once the dispute settlement provision of the Agreement or the GATT has been initiated it must be used to the exclusion of the other.

A dispute which has been referred to the Commission and has not been resolved within a period of 30 days is to be settled as follows:

(a) by compulsory arbitration, binding on both parties in the case of disputes arising from the interpretation and application of the safeguard provisions (Chapter 11);

(b) where both parties mutually agree, binding arbitration in all other disputes; or

(c) non-binding panel recommendations to the Commission which is mandated to agree on a resolution of the dispute in a manner which normally shall conform with the recommendation of the panel.

These dispute settlement procedures are in addition to the special dispute settlement mechanism established in Chapter 19 to deal with antidumping and countervailing duty issues.

The arbitration panels are composed of five members; two Canadians, two Americans and a fifth member chosen jointly from a roster developed by the Commission. It is believed that this dispute settlement mechanism along with the notification and consultation provisions will provide greater opportunity for fair and effective solutions to difficult

¶ 504

bilateral problems involving not only goods, but services (except for financial services), investment, energy, government procurement, technical standards and agriculture.

Failure on the part of the Commission to agree on the resolution of a dispute following an arbitral award entitles the complaining Party to take countermeasures.

¶ 506 Referrals

The institutional provisions in this Chapter also provide for a mechanism for consultation and agreement on the interpretation of the applicable provisions of the Agreement in the event an issue of the interpretation of the Agreement arises in any domestic judicial or administrative proceeding of either Party which either Party considers would merit its intervention or if the domestic court or administrative body solicits the views of a Party. Any agreed interpretation will be submitted to the court or administrative body in accordance with its rules. If the Parties do not reach an agreement on the interpretation of the provision it issues, then either Party may submit its own views to the court or administrative body.

What constitutes a domestic administrative proceeding is not specified in Chapter 18. However, it is a broad enough term to seem to include proceedings before boards, tribunals, government departments or agencies. It is not likely that a domestic court exercising judicial functions would seek the advice of the Parties on a matter of interpretation of the provisions of the Agreement. This procedure is limited to the interpretation of provisions of the agreement itself and not to any implementing legislation or regulations which may be enacted by either Party to give effect to the provisions of the Agreement.

¶ 508 Nullification and Impairment

Article 2011 of the Agreement provides that if a Party considers that the application of any measure, whether or not such measure conflicts with the provisions of the Agreement, causes nullification or impairment of any benefit reasonably expected to accrue to that Party, directly or indirectly under the provisions of the Agreement, that Party may, with a view to the satisfactory resolution of the matter, invoke the consultation provisions of Article 1804 and, if necessary, the dispute settlement provisions pursuant to Articles 1805, 1806 and 1807. However, this provision does not apply to Chapter 19 (Binational Panel Dispute Settlement in Antidumping and Countervailing Duty Cases) or to Article 2005 (Cultural Industries). It would appear that this provision is broad enough to include any measure taken by the Government of Canada, the provinces, or local governments. Article 103 of the Agreement provides that the Parties to the Agreement will ensure that all necessary measures are taken in order to give effect to its provisions, including their observance, by state, provincial and local governments.

¶ 510 Binational Dispute Settlement in Antidumping and Countervailing Duty Cases

¶ 512 Goods of a Party

It is provided that the provisions of Chapter 19 apply only to goods which the competent authority of the importing Party when applying its antidumping or countervailing duty law determines are goods of the other Party. Article 201 of the Agreement defines "goods of a Party" to mean domestic products as they are understood in the GATT. GATT Article 1 provides for MFN treatment "to any product originating in or destined for any country". Section 15 of the Special Import Measures Act (SIMA), which refers to the normal value of goods, refers to goods from the country of export. Revenue Canada, in recent years, has adopted the practice of identifying dumped or subsidized goods by reference to the place where they originated or are exported from. Chapter 3 of the Agreement which contains the rules of origin for goods is more limitative but does not limit the scope of the general provisions of Chapter 19. The goods with which Chapter 19 is concerned are of a broader description than the goods which are defined in Chapter 3 for other purposes. It is clear that the provisions of Chapter 19 do not apply to goods exported from a third country.

¶ 514 Provisions Concerning Present and Future Antidumping and Countervailing Duty Laws

The main features of Chapter 19 are:

(1) the retention of domestic antidumping and countervailing duty laws,

(2) the right of each party to change or modify its antidumping or countervailing duty laws,

(3) in the case of an amendment to a Party's antidumping or countervailing duty statute, effective January 1, 1989, such amendment applies to goods from the other Party only if specifically mentioned in the amending statute,

(4) the other Party must be notified in writing of the proposed amendment as far in advance as possible and the other party is entitled to request consultation prior to the enactment of the amending statute,

(5) any such amending statute must not be inconsistent with the GATT Antidumping Code or Subsidies Code or with the object and purpose of the Agreement,

(6) the other Party may request that the amending statute be referred to a binational panel for a declaratory opinion as to whether it does not conform with the GATT and the Agreement or has the effect of overturning a prior decision of a binational panel and does not conform to those provisions,

(7) the panel can recommend modifications to the amending statute to remedy a non-conformity and this triggers the requirement of further consultation between the Parties to achieve a mutually satisfactory solution to the matter,

(8) such solution may include seeking remedial legislation which if not enacted within nine months from the end of the consultation period and no other agreement has been reached, the Party that requested the panel may retaliate by taking comparable legislative or equivalent executive action or terminate the Agreement upon sixty days' written notice.

A serious drawback of the Agreement is that the Parties have reserved the right to apply existing antidumping and countervailing duty laws to goods exported by the other Party. Further, these laws can be amended and grandfathered up to January 1, 1989, without recourse to the consultation and review process provided for in the case of amendments occurring after January 1, 1989. Therefore, the current features of U.S. antidumping and countervailing duty laws which Canadian exporters have objected to remain unchanged. However, on the positive side, any amendments made after January 1, 1989, must be made specifically applicable to Canada and if they do not conform with the provisions of the Agreement, can be referred to an independent binational panel, and if found not to be in conformity with the Agreement must be reviewed. Also, account must be taken of the other provisions in Chapter 19 which require both Parties to establish a working group to develop a substitute system of rules in both countries for antidumping and countervailing duties as applied to their bilateral trade.

¶ 516 Provisions Concerning the Review of Final Antidumping and Countervailing Duty Determinations

The text of the Agreement states that "the Parties shall replace judicial review of final antidumping and countervailing duty determinations with binational panel review". Either Party may request that a panel review, based on the administrative record, a final antidumping or countervailing duty determination of a competent investigating authority of either Party to determine whether such determination was in accordance with the antidumping or countervailing duty law of the importing Party. However, the agreement does not eliminate judicial review in all circumstances. If the recourse to review a final determination by a binational panel is not sought by those who are entitled to trigger such a review then recourse may be had to judicial review or appeal as otherwise provided in each country's domestic legislation. Further, the binational panel review process applies only to a final determination of a competent investigating authority as this expression is defined in Chapter 19. It does not apply to other types of determinations and, in particular, it does not apply to a preliminary determination concerning dumping or subsidizing. A competent investigating authority means in the case of Canada the Canadian Import Tribunal (CIT) or the Deputy Minister of National Revenue for Customs and Excise and in the case of the United States the International Trade Commission or the International Trade Administration of the United States Department of Commerce or their successor. The binational panel review process is a significant departure from current practice and a unique mechanism. It would oust the jurisdiction of the Federal Court of Canada to review decisions of the Canadian Import Tribunal and of the Tariff Board to consider certain appeals from the Deputy Minister of National Revenue. It would oust the jurisdiction of the U.S. Court of International Trade and the Court of Appeals for the Federal Circuit over final determinations.

The final agreement has sought to achieve symmetry in the application of panel reviews. A final determination in the case of the Canadian Import Tribunal includes an affirmative or negative finding of injury under subsection 43(1) of the Special Import Measures Act (SIMA), a decision to initiate a review pursuant to subsection 76(3) of SIMA, an order under subsection 76(4) of SIMA continuing a finding made under subsection 43(1) and a reconsideration pursuant to subsection 91(3) of SIMA. Not included are the reports made under subsection 45(1), and under section 48 of SIMA or advice given to the Deputy Minister as a result of any referral to the Tribunal under sections 33, 34, 35 and 90 of SIMA. A final determination in the case of the Deputy Minister includes a determination pursuant to section 41 of SIMA, a redetermination pursuant to section 59 of SIMA and a review of an undertaking pursuant to subsection 53(1) of SIMA. It is to be noted that SIMA does not presently provide for an appeal from a final determination of dumping or subsidizing made pursuant to Section 41 of SIMA or a review of an undertaking under subsection 53(1) SIMA. Therefore, the Agreement allows a panel review of two determinations made by the Deputy Minister which are not presently subject to appeal under SIMA. Further the binational panel is entitled to review a redetermination made by the Deputy Minister which, under the present provisions of SIMA, is appealable to the Tariff Board. An appeal to the Tariff Board or its successor will be available only where the binational panel review process is not invoked. It is anticipated that the appellate function of the Tariff Board will be transferred to a Customs Court.

The review process provides that the panel review will be based upon the administrative record only which would exclude the introduction of any further evidence. The definition of administrative record as defined in Chapter 19 applies both to the final determination made by the Canadian Import Tribunal (CIT) and the Deputy Minister. It provides that the administrative record will include, as well as the final determination and any notices published in the *Canada Gazette*, all documentary or other information presented to or obtained by the competent authority in the course of any proceeding including any governmental memoranda pertaining to the case and any record of *ex parte* meetings as may be required to be kept and all transcripts or records of conferences or hearings. These requirements apply to the United States International Trade Commission and the International Trade Administration of the United States Department of Commerce as well as the Canadian Import Tribunal and the Deputy Minister. It is also provided that the Parties and other persons appearing before a panel can agree to vary the contents of the administrative record. Interested persons will be encouraged to place as much evidence and information as is helpful to their case before the competent investigating authority so that it will form part of the administrative record before the Panel.

In order to give effect to the new provisions concerning panel review and ensure that the process can be initiated by individuals and enterprises, this Chapter of the Agreement provides that either Party on its own initiative may request a panel review of a final determination and must, upon being requested by a person entitled to commence domestic procedures for judicial review, request such a review. By reason of amendments which Canada has undertaken to make to SIMA, the persons or enterprises entitled to request a panel review would include producers of goods subject to an investigation, exporters of the goods and importers of the goods as well as the complainant. Interested persons have the right to appear and be represented by counsel before the panel. The Provinces are not specifically mentioned as an entity which can trigger the panel review process. If the panel procedure is invoked within the time limits provided for in the Agreement, then no recourse may be had to the Courts and it is provided that neither Party will allow an appeal from a panel decision to its domestic courts. However, the panel decision may be reviewed on certain grounds by means of an extraordinary challenge procedure before a panel composed of three judges drawn from a federal court of the United States or a court of superior jurisdiction in Canada. In the case of Canada, this means judges appointed pursuant to Section 96 or 101 of the Constitution Act, 1867. It is further provided that any person intending to have recourse to the courts must first provide sufficient notice to allow other interested parties to invoke the panel procedure if they so wish. Therefore, it is clearly the intention of the Parties that any review of a final decision by a competent authority shall take place before a binational panel rather than the domestic courts. However, as explained earlier, recourse to the domestic courts is not excluded in all circumstances.

¶ 516

An important feature of the Agreement is the composition of the binational panel. The panel will be drawn from a roster of individuals who shall be citizens of Canada or the United States and who "shall be of good character, high standing and repute, and chosen strictly on the basis of objectivity, reliability, sound judgment and general familiarity with international trade law". An equal number of candidates shall be proposed by each Party and a majority of the panelists on each panel shall be lawyers in good standing. The Chairman must be a lawyer. This mixture of persons with legal training and others drawn from the business community is similar to the composition of the Competition Tribunal under Canada's Competition Act. The binational panels established by the Agreement are available to review statutory amendments under Chapter 18 and review final antidumping and countervailing duty determinations under Chapter 19. They are served by a secretariat whose permanent offices are in Washington, D.C. and in the National Capital Region of Canada.

The Agreement states that a panel reviewing a final determination of a competent investigating authority of either Party shall determine whether such final determination was "in accordance with the antidumping or countervailing duty law of the importing party". The standard of review in the case of Canada is the grounds set forth in subsection 28(1) of the Federal Court Act and in the case of the United States is the standards set forth in Section 516A(b)(1)(A) and (B) of the Tariff Act of 1930, as amended. However, the agreement provides that these standards may be amended from time to time by a Party. Therefore, any review of a final determination of a competent authority by a panel will have as its purpose and objective to determine whether the antidumping or countervailing duty law of the importing Party was properly applied, and the standard of review is that specified from time to time in the laws of the importing country.

The standard of review contained in subsection 28(1) of the Federal Court Act which heretofore has been applied to decisions of the CIT will now be extended to final determinations of the Deputy Minister. Subsection 28(1) provides for the following grounds of review:

(a) failure to observe a principle of natural justice or otherwise acting beyond or refusing to exercise its jurisdiction;

(b) error in law in making its decision or order, whether or not the error appears on the face of the record; or

(c) basing its decision or order on an erroneous finding of fact that it made in a perverse or capricious manner or without regard for the material before it.

The standard of review set out in section 516A of the U.S. Tariff Act is whether the decision was arbitrary, capricious, an abuse of discretion, or unsupported by substantial evidence on the record, or otherwise not

¶ 516

in accordance with law. It is to be expected that the jurisprudence developed over the years by the Federal Court of Canada and by the United States Court of International Trade will also be considered by the panel.

An interesting issue will arise when a competent authority, be it the International Trade Commission or the Canadian Import Tribunal, makes a finding of injurious dumping against goods of third countries as well as those of one of the other Party. The panel review is not available with respect to goods originating elsewhere than in Canada or the U.S. The goods subject to the finding which originate or are exported from either Canada or the United States could be the subject of a panel review, which is mandatory if properly invoked; however, the goods of a third country, which were subject to the omnibus finding would not be entitled to a panel review. The finding in respect of these goods could be challenged in the domestic courts. This opens the possibility of conflicting decisions by the panel and the domestic courts on matters arising out of the same proceeding.

The Agreement provides that the decision of a panel reviewing final antidumping and countervailing duty determinations is binding on the parties and that neither Party shall provide in its domestic legislation for an appeal from a panel decision to its domestic courts. The decision of a panel which does not uphold a final determination is remanded to the competent authority for action "not inconsistent with the panel's decision". In such event the panel "shall establish as brief a time as is reasonable for compliance with the remand, taking into account the complexity of the facts and legal issues involved and the nature of the panel's decision". There is no further enforcement mechanism contained in Chapter 19. Presumably, if the competent authority did not take action consistent with the panel's decision, that panel or another panel would again remand the final determination to the competent authority for action consistent with the panel's decision. Another recourse may be to have the dispute concerning the implementation of the panel's recommendation referred to the Commission (Chapter 18).

It has been suggested in the synopsis prepared by the Canadian Government that the panel review process will be more timely and will guarantee the impartial application of antidumping and countervailing duty laws. As to timeliness the review process by panel would normally take up to ten months and could be reviewed by the extraordinary challenge committee which has 90 days to give an initial opinion and a further 30 days to give a final declaratory opinion. The competent authority to which a panel recommendation is remanded is also granted additional time to implement any panel recommendation.

The view that the unique dispute settlement mechanism "guarantees the impartial application of their [the parties] respective antidumping and countervailing duty laws", suggests that it is an improvement over current mechanisms for judicial review.

¶ 516

In assessing this claim, consideration should be given to the nature of the review. The binational panel review will be based on the administrative record of the competent investigating authority, on the basis of existing domestic laws and applying existing standards of review. There is no assurance that the panel's decision will be an improvement over that of the domestic courts or would lead to a different result. The standard of review which the panel is directed to apply is the same standard of review presently applied by the domestic courts. How better equipped than judges are panelists, in particular those with no legal training, to apply legal standards of review. It also places great faith in the ability of a non-national of the importing country and persons who have no legal training from either country to be able to comprehend and apply legal standards of review which heretofore have been applied not only by legally trained persons but by judges in the domestic forum. It is also to be noted that the panel is ad hoc. While there is a roster of fifty persons, there will not necessarily be any continuity of membership on the panels with the result that untrained and inexperienced persons will be called upon to make important legal determinations within a relatively short period of time. This mechanism would be more appropriate if the review was to be based on a homogeneous set of laws and a single standard of review.

The panel decision is not subject to review or appeal except in extraordinary circumstances. This goes against the modern trend of judicial review of statutory tribunals. Will the finality of panel decisions prevail over the inherent jurisdiction of superior courts in Canada to review jurisdictional errors of inferior or statutory tribunals. Although the panels are binational they must be established pursuant to the domestic legislation of each party. Will the panels or competent investigating authories be immune to challenges under the Canadian Charter of Rights or the U.S. Bill of Rights? These issues will undoubtedly be tested in the domestic courts, even in the presence of a privative clause denying further appeal or judicial review.

It has been suggested that the extraordinary challenge procedure would be used sparingly if at all. However, the extraordinary challenge procedure can be invoked by a Party that alleges not only gross misconduct, bias or serious conflict of interest, but also alleges that the panel seriously departed from a fundamental rule of procedure or manifestly exceeded its powers, authority or jurisdiction. The latter grounds are quite broad and may well lead to the extraordinary challenge procedure being invoked more frequently than anticipated.

In Canada, the scope of what is a jurisdictional error has been extended in recent years to include questions of law. In other words there are several types of jurisdictional error and the inclusion of excess of jurisdiction as a ground for review may well result in the extraordinary challenge committee composed of three judges exercising a greater supervisory role over the decisions of review panels.

¶ 518 Provisions Concerning the Development of a Substitute System of Rules in both Countries for Antidumping and Countervailing Duty as Applied to their Bilateral Trade

Chapter 19 also provides that efforts will be made to develop a substitute system of rules in both countries for antidumping and countervailing duties as applied to their bilateral trade. The Parties have established a working group to develop more effective rules and disciplines concerning the use of Government subsidies and to seek to develop a substitute system of rules for dealing with unfair pricing and government subsidization. A major weakness of the agreement is that such an understanding was not reached during the course of the negotiations leading up to the conclusion of the Agreement. Although the Parties have said that the working group shall report as soon as possible it also is clear that the commitment is based on their *best efforts* and that they will seek to implement such substitute system within the next five or seven years. If such a substitute system is not implemented within that time either Party may terminate the Agreement on six months' notice. However, the Agreement itself contains a general termination clause that provides that it can be terminated at any time by either Party upon six months' notice to the other Party.

It is expected that the focus of U.S. trade negotiation efforts will switch to the Uruguay Round and it is likely that any progress in developing a substitute system of rules for dealing with unfair pricing and government subsidization will be tied to events surrounding those multinational negotiations.

Part II

Government Documents

THE CANADA-U.S.
FREE TRADE AGREEMENT

75

Table of Contents

PART THREE: GOVERNMENT PROCUREMENT

Chapter Thirteen: Government Procurement   218

PART FOUR: SERVICES, INVESTMENT AND TEMPORARY ENTRY

Chapter Fourteen: Services   233

Chapter Fifteen: Temporary Entry for Business Persons   251

PART EIGHT: FINAL PROVISIONS

    Article 2101 Statistical Requirements
    Article 2102 Publication of Measures
    Article 2103 Annexes
    Article 2104 Amendments
    Article 2105 Entry into Force
    Article 2106 Duration and Termination

Letters   320

    Standstill
    Implementation of Harmonized System
    Plywood Standards

PREAMBLE

The Government of Canada and the Government of the United States of America, resolved:

TO STRENGTHEN the unique and enduring friendship between their two nations;

TO PROMOTE productivity, full employment, and a steady improvement of living standards in their respective countries;

TO CREATE an expanded and secure market for the goods and services produced in their territories;

TO ADOPT clear and mutually advantageous rules governing their trade;

TO ENSURE a predictable commercial environment for business planning and investment;

TO STRENGTHEN the competitiveness of the United States and Canadian firms in global markets;

TO REDUCE government-created trade distortions while preserving the Parties' flexibility to safeguard the public welfare;

TO BUILD on their mutual rights and obligations under the *General Agreement on Tariffs and Trade* and other multilateral and bilateral instruments of cooperation; and

TO CONTRIBUTE to the harmonious development and expansion of world trade and to provide a catalyst to broader international cooperation;

HAVE AGREED as follows:

PART ONE
OBJECTIVES AND SCOPE

Chapter One

Objectives and Scope

Article 101: Establishment of the Free-Trade Area

The Government of Canada and the Government of the United States of America, consistent with Article XXIV of the *General Agreement on Tariffs and Trade,* hereby establish a free-trade area.

Article 102: Objectives

The objectives of this Agreement, as elaborated more specifically in its provisions, are to:

a) eliminate barriers to trade in goods and services between the territories of the Parties;

b) facilitate conditions of fair competition within the free-trade area;

c) liberalize significantly conditions for investment within this free-trade area;

d) establish effective procedures for the joint administration of this Agreement and the resolution of disputes; and

e) lay the foundation for further bilateral and multilateral cooperation to expand and enhance the benefits of this Agreement.

Article 103: Extent of Obligations

The Parties to this Agreement shall ensure that all necessary measures are taken in order to give effect to its provisions, including their observance, except as otherwise provided in this Agreement, by state, provincial and local governments.

Article 104: Affirmation and Precedence

1. The Parties affirm their existing rights and obligations with respect to each other, as they exist at the time of entry into force of this Agreement, under bilateral and multilateral agreements to which both are party.

2. In the event of any inconsistency between the provisions of this Agreement and such other agreements, the provisions of this Agreement shall prevail to the extent of the inconsistency, except as otherwise provided in this Agreement.

Article 105: National Treatment

Each Party shall, to the extent provided in this Agreement, accord national treatment with respect to investment and to trade in goods and services.

Chapter Two

General Definitions

Article 201: Definitions of General Application

1. For purposes of this Agreement, unless otherwise specified:

covered service means a service as defined in Article 1408;

enterprise means any juridical entity involving a financial commitment for the purpose of commercial gain;

existing means in effect at the time of the entry into force of this Agreement;

goods of a Party means domestic products as these are understood in the *General Agreement on Tariffs and Trade;*

Harmonized System means the Harmonized Commodity Description and Coding System, as amended from time to time, published by the Customs Cooperation Council;

measure includes any law, regulation, procedure, requirement or practice;

national means an individual who is a citizen or permanent resident of a Party and also includes, for the United States of America, "national of the United States" as defined in the existing provisions of the United States *Immigration and Nationality Act;*

new means subsequent to the entry into force of this Agreement;

originating means qualifying under the rules of origin set out in Chapter Three;

person means a national or an enterprise;

person of a Party means a national, or an enterprise constituted under the laws of, or principally carrying on its business within, the territory of the Party;

province means a province of Canada, and includes the Yukon Territory and the Northwest Territories and their successors;

service includes a covered service;

state means a state of the United States of America, and the District of Columbia;

territory means

a) with respect to Canada, the territory to which its customs laws apply, including any areas beyond the territorial seas of Canada within which, in accordance with international law and its domestic laws, Canada may exercise rights with respect to the seabed and subsoil and their natural resources, and,

b) with respect to the United States of America,

   i)   the customs territory of the United States of America which includes the fifty states, the District of Columbia and Puerto Rico,

   ii) the foreign trade zones located in the United States of America and Puerto Rico, and

   iii) any areas beyond the territorial seas of the United States of America within which, in accordance with international law and its domestic laws, the United States of America may exercise rights with respect to the seabed and subsoil and their natural resources;

third country means any country other than Canada or the United States of America or any territory not a part of the territory of the Parties; and

transition period means the period from the date of entry into force of this Agreement to either December 31, 1998 or such earlier date as the Parties may agree.

2.   For purposes of this Agreement, unless otherwise specified, a reference to province or state includes local governments.

PART TWO
TRADE IN GOODS

Chapter Three

Rules of Origin for Goods

Article 301: General Rules

1. Goods originate in the territory of a Party if they are wholly obtained or produced in the territory of either Party or both Parties.

2. In addition, goods originate in the territory of a Party if they have been transformed in the territory of either Party or both Parties so as to be subject to a change in tariff classification as described in Annex 301.2 or to such other requirements as the Annex may provide when no change in tariff classification occurs, and they meet the other conditions set out in that Annex.

3. A good shall not be considered to originate in the territory of a Party pursuant to paragraph 2 merely by virtue of having undergone:

a) simple packaging or, except as expressly provided by the rules of Annex 301.2, combining operations;

b) mere dilution with water or another substance that does not materially alter the characteristics of the good; or

c) any process or work in respect of which it is established, or in respect of which the facts as ascertained clearly justify the presumption, that the sole object was to circumvent the provisions of this Chapter.

4. Accessories, spare parts, or tools delivered with any piece of equipment, machinery, apparatus, or vehicle that form part of its standard equipment shall be deemed to have the same origin as that equipment, machinery, apparatus, or vehicle; provided, that the quantities and values of such accessories, spare parts, or tools are customary for the equipment, machinery, apparatus, or vehicle.

Article 302: Transshipment

Goods exported from the territory of one Party originate in the territory of that Party only if they meet the applicable requirements of Article 301 and are shipped to the territory of the other Party without having entered the commerce of any third country and, if shipped through the territory of a third country, they do not undergo any operations other than unloading, reloading, or any operation necessary to transport them to the territory of the other Party or to preserve them in good condition, and the documents related to their exportation and shipment from the territory of a Party show the territory of the other Party as their final destination.

Article 303: Consultation and Revision

The Parties shall consult regularly to ensure that the provisions of this Chapter are administered effectively, uniformly and consistently with the spirit and intent of this Agreement. If either Party concludes that the provisions of this Chapter require revision to take account of developments in production processes or other matters, the proposed revision along with supporting rationale and any studies shall be submitted to the other Party for consideration and any appropriate action pursuant to Article 2104.

Article 304: Definitions

For purposes of this Chapter:

direct cost of processing or **direct cost of assembling** means the costs directly incurred in, or that can reasonably be allocated to, the production of goods, including:
  a) the cost of all labour, including benefits and on-the-job training, labour provided in connection with supervision, quality control, shipping, receiving, storage, packaging, management at the location of the process or assembly, and other like labour, whether provided by employees or independent contractors;
  b) the cost of inspecting and testing the goods;
  c) the cost of energy, fuel, dies, molds, tooling, and the depreciation and maintenance of machinery and equipment, without regard to whether they originate within the territory of a Party;
  d) development, design, and engineering costs;

    e) rent, mortgage interest, depreciation on buildings, property insurance premiums, maintenance, taxes and the cost of utilities for real property used in the production of the goods; and

    f) royalty, licensing, or other like payments for the right to the goods;

but not including:

    g) costs relating to the general expense of doing business, such as the cost of providing executive, financial, sales, advertising, marketing, accounting and legal services, and insurance;

    h) brokerage charges relating to the importation and exportation of goods;

    i) costs for telephone, mail and other means of communication;

    j) packing costs for exporting the goods;

    k) royalty payments related to a licensing agreement to distribute or sell the goods;

    l) rent, mortgage interest, depreciation on buildings, property insurance premiums, maintenance, taxes and the cost of utilities for real property used by personnel charged with administrative functions; or

    m) profit on the goods;

materials means goods, other than those included as part of the direct cost of processing or assembling, used or consumed in the production of other goods;

value of materials originating in the territory of either Party or both Parties means the aggregate of:

    a) the price paid by the producer of an exported good for materials originating in the territory of either Party or both Parties or for materials imported from a third country used or consumed in the production of such originating materials; and

    b) when not included in that price, the following costs related thereto:

        i) freight, insurance, packing and all other costs incurred in transporting any of the materials referred to in subparagraph (a) to the location of the producer;

        ii) duties, taxes and brokerage fees on such materials paid in the territory of either Party or both Parties;

        iii) the cost of waste or spoilage resulting from the use or consumption of such materials, less the value of renewable scrap or by-product; and

iv) the value of goods and services relating to such materials determined in accordance with subparagraph 1(b) of Article 8 of the *Agreement on Implementation of Article VII of the General Agreement on Tariffs and Trade.*

value of the goods when exported to the territory of the other Party means the aggregate of:

a) the price paid by the producer for all materials, whether or not the materials originate in either Party or both Parties, and, when not included in the price paid for the materials, the following costs related thereto:
   i)   freight, insurance, packing and all other costs incurred in transporting all materials to the location of the producer;
   ii)   duties, taxes and brokerage fees on all materials paid in the territory of either Party or both Parties;
   iii) the cost of waste or spoilage resulting from the use or consumption of such materials, less the value of renewable scrap or by-product; and
   iv)   the value of goods and services relating to all materials determined in accordance with subparagraph 1(b) of Article 8 of the *Agreement on Implementation of Article VII of the General Agreement on Tariffs and Trade;* and
b) the direct cost of processing or the direct cost of assembling the goods;

goods wholly obtained or produced in the territory of either Party or both Parties means:

a) mineral goods extracted in the territory of either Party or both Parties;
b) goods harvested in the territory of either Party or both Parties;
c) live animals born and raised in the territory of either Party or both Parties;
d) goods (fish, shellfish and other marine life) taken from the sea by vessels registered or recorded with a Party and flying its flag;
e) goods produced on board factory ships from the goods referred to in subparagraph (d) provided such factory ships are registered or recorded with that Party and fly its flag;

f) goods taken by a Party or a person of a Party from the seabed or beneath the seabed outside territorial waters, provided that Party has rights to exploit such seabed;

g) goods taken from space, provided they are obtained by a Party or a person of a Party and not processed in a third country;

h) waste and scrap derived from manufacturing operations and used goods, provided they were collected in the territory of either Party or both Parties and are fit only for the recovery of raw materials; and

i) goods produced in the territory of either Party or both Parties exclusively from goods referred to in subparagraphs (a) to (h) inclusive or from their derivatives, at any stage of production.

Annex 301.2

Interpretation

1.   The basis for tariff classification in this Annex is the Harmonized System.

2.   Whenever processing or assembly of goods in the territory of either Party or both Parties results in one of the changes in tariff classification described by the rules set forth in this Annex, such goods shall be considered to have been transformed in the territory of that Party and shall be treated as goods originating in the territory of that Party, provided that they have not subsequently undergone any processing or assembly outside the territory of either Party.

3.   Whenever assembly of goods in the territory of a Party fails to result in a change of tariff classification because

   a) the goods were imported into the territory of the Party in an unassembled or a disassembled form and were classified as unassembled or disassembled goods pursuant to General Rule of Interpretation 2(a) of the Harmonized System, or

   b) the tariff subheading for the goods provides for both the goods themselves and their parts,

such goods shall not be treated as goods originating in the territory of a Party.

4.   Notwithstanding paragraph 3, goods shall nonetheless be considered to have been transformed in the territory of a Party and be treated as goods originating in the territory of the Party; provided, that:

   a) the value of materials originating in the territory of either Party or both Parties used or consumed in the production of the goods plus the direct cost of assembling the goods in the territory of either Party or both Parties constitute not less than 50 percent of the value of the goods when exported to the territory of the other Party, and

b) the goods have not subsequent to assembly undergone processing or further assembly in a third country and they meet the requirements of Article 302.

5.   The provisions of paragraph 4 shall not apply to goods of chapters 61-63 of the Harmonized System.

6.   In making the determination required by subparagraph 4(a), and in making the same or a similar determination when required by the rules of this Annex, where materials originating in the territory of either Party or both Parties and materials obtained or produced in a third country are used or consumed together in the production of goods in the territory of a Party, the value of materials originating in the territory of either Party or both Parties may be treated as such only to the extent that it is directly attributable to the goods under consideration.

Rules

Section I
Live Animals; Animal Products
(Ch. 1-5)

A change from one chapter to another; no changes within chapters.

Section II
Vegetable Products
(Ch. 6-14)

1.   A change from one chapter to another; no changes within chapters except that agricultural and horticultural goods grown in the territory of a Party shall be treated as originating in the territory of that Party even if grown from seed or bulbs imported from a third country.

2.   A change to subheadings 0901.12-0901.40 from any other subheadings, including another subheading within that group.

Section III
Animal or Vegetable Fats and Their Cleavage Products;
Prepared Edible Fats; Animal or Vegetable Waxes
(Ch. 15)

1.   A change to Chapter 15 from any other chapter.

2.   A change to any of the following subheadings from any other subheading: 1507.90, 1508.90, 1511.90, 1512.19, 1512.29, 1513.19, 1513.29, 1514.90, 1515.19, 1515.29.

3.   A change to heading 1516 from any other heading.

4.   A change to heading 1517 from any other heading.

5.   A change to headings 1519-1520 from any other heading outside that group.

6.   A change to subheading 1519.19 from any other subheading.

7.   A change to subheading 1519.20 from any other subheading.

8.   A change to subheading 1520.90 from any other subheading.

Section IV
Prepared Foodstuffs; Beverages, Spirits, and Vinegar; Tobacco and Manufactured Tobacco Substitutes
(Ch. 16-24)

1.   A change from one chapter to another, except for goods of Chapter 20 subject to rule 5.

2.   A change to heading 1704 from any other heading.

3.   A change to heading 1806 from any other heading.

4.   A change to subheading 1806.31 or 1806.90 from any other subheading.

5.   Fruit, nut, and vegetable preparations of Chapter 20 that have been prepared or preserved merely by freezing, by packing (including canning) in water, brine, or in natural juices, or by roasting, either dry or in oil (including processing incidental to freezing, packing, or roasting), shall be treated as a good of the country in which the fresh good was produced.

6.   A change to subheading 2009.90 from any other subheading; provided, that neither a single juice ingredient, nor juice ingredients from a single third country, constitutes in single-strength form more than 60 percent by volume of the product.

7.   A change to headings 2207-2209 from any other heading outside that group.

8.   A change to heading 2309 from any other heading.

9.   A change to headings 2402-2403 (except 2403.91) from any other heading outside that group.

Section V
Mineral Products
(Ch. 25-27)

1.   A change from one chapter to another.

2.   A change to headings 2710-2715 from any other heading outside that group.

3.   A change to heading 2716 from any other heading.

Section VI
Products of the Chemical or Allied Industries
(Ch. 28-38)

1.   A change to Chapters 28-38 from any chapter outside that group.

2.   A change to any subheading of Chapters 28-38 from any other subheading within those chapters; provided, except for the other rules in this section, that the value of materials originating in the territory of either Party or both Parties plus the direct cost of processing performed in the territory of either Party or both Parties constitute not less than 50 percent of the value of the goods when exported to the territory of the other Party.

3.   A change to a heading of Chapter 30 from any other heading, including other headings within that chapter, except a change to heading 3004 from heading 3003.

4.   A change to Chapter 31 from any other chapter.

5.   A change to headings 3208-3215 from any other heading outside that group.

6.   A change to Chapter 33 from any other chapter.

7.   A change to heading 3304-3307 from any heading outside that group.

8.   A change to a heading of Chapter 34 from any other heading, including another heading within that chapter.

9.   A change to subheadings 3402.20 -3402.90 from any other subheading outside that group.

10.   A change to a heading of Chapter 35 from any other heading, including another heading within that chapter.

11.   A change to a heading of Chapter 36 from any other heading, including another heading within that chapter.

12.   A change to Chapter 37 from any other chapter.

13.   A change to heading 3704 from any other heading.

14.   A change to headings 3705-3706 from any other heading outside that group.

15.   A change to heading 3808 from any other heading; provided, that the value of materials originating in the territory of either Party or both Parties plus the direct cost of processing performed in the territory of either Party or both Parties constitute not less than 50 percent of the value of the goods when exported to the territory of the other Party, or, in the case of goods which contain more than one active ingredient, not less than 70 percent of the value of the goods when exported to the territory of the other Party. Any materials that are eligible for duty-free treatment in both Parties on a most-favoured-nation basis, or any materials imported into the territory of either Party which, if imported into the territory of the United States of America, would be free of duty under a trade agreement that is not subject to a competitive need limitation, shall be treated as materials originating in the territory of a Party.

Section VII
Plastics and Articles Thereof; Rubber and Articles Thereof
(Ch. 39-40)

1.   A change to any heading of Chapter 39 from any other heading, including another heading within that chapter; provided, that the value of materials originating in the territory of either Party or both Parties plus the direct cost of processing performed in the territory of either Party or both Parties constitute not less than 50 percent of the value of the goods when exported to the territory of the other Party.

2.   A change to Chapter 40 from any other chapter.

3.   A change to any heading of Chapter 40 from any other heading within that chapter; provided, except for the rules below listed in this section, that the value of materials originating in the territory of either Party or both Parties plus the direct cost of processing performed in the territory of either Party or both Parties constitute not less than 50

percent of the value of the goods when exported to the territory of the other Party.

4.   A change to headings 4007-4008 from any other heading outside that group.

5.   A change to headings 4009-4017 from any other heading outside that group.

6.   A change to subheading 4012.10 from any other subheading.

Section VIII
Raw Hides and Skins, Leather, Furskins and Articles Thereof; Saddlery and Harness, Travel Goods, Handbags, and Similar Containers; Articles of Animal Gut (Other Than Silkworm Gut)
(Ch. 41-43)

1.   A change from one chapter to another.

2.   A change to headings 4104-4111 from any other heading outside that group.

3.   A change to heading 4302 from any other heading.

4.   A change to headings 4303-4304 from any other heading outside that group.

Section IX
Wood and Articles of Wood; Wood Charcoal; Cork and Materials of Cork; Manufactures of Straw, of Esparto or of Other Plaiting Materials; Basketware and Wickerware
(Ch. 44-46)

1.   A change from one chapter to another.

2.   A change between headings in Chapter 44.

3.   A change to any of the following United States tariff items from any other United States tariff item: 4412.11.50, 4412.12.50, 4412.19.50, 4412.29.50, or 4412.99.90. This rule applies only to goods originating in the territory of Canada and imported into the territory of the United States of America.

4.   A change to headings 4503-4504 from any other heading outside that group.

5.   A change to heading 4602 from any other heading.

Section X
Pulp of Wood or of other Fibrous Cellulosic Material; Waste and Scrap of Paper or Paperboard; Paper and Paperboard and Articles Thereof
(Ch. 47-49)

1.   A change from one chapter to another.

2.   A change to heading 4808-4809 from any other heading outside that group.

3.   A change to headings 4814-4823 from any other heading outside that group except a change from heading 4809 to heading 4816.

Section XI
Textiles and Textile Articles
(Ch. 50-63)

Silk

1.   A change to headings 5004-5006 from any heading outside that group.

2.   A change to heading 5007 from any other heading.

Wool

3.   A change to headings 5106-5113 from any heading outside that group.

Cotton

4.   A change to headings 5204-5212 from any heading outside that group.

Flax, Jute, Sisal, Paper Yarn

5.   A change to headings 5306-5311 from any heading outside that group.

Man-Made Filaments

6.   A change to any heading of Chapter 54 from any other chapter.

Man-Made Staple Fibers

7.   A change to headings 5501-5507 from any other chapter.

8.   A change to headings 5508-5516 from any heading outside that group.

Wadding, Felt, Etc.

9.   A change to any heading of Chapter 56 from any heading outside that chapter other than headings 5106-5113, 5204-5212, 5306-5311, or headings of Chapters 54 and 55.

Carpets and Textile Floor, Etc.

10.   A change to any heading of Chapter 57 from any heading outside that chapter other than headings 5106-5113, 5204-5212, 5306-5309, 5311, or 5508-5516.

Special Woven Fabrics, Etc.

11.   A change to any heading of Chapter 58 from any heading outside that chapter other than headings 5106-5113, 5204-5212, 5306-5311, or headings of Chapters 54 and 55.

Impregnated, Coated, Covered, or Laminated Textile Fabrics

12.   A change to any heading of Chapter 59 from any heading outside that chapter other than headings 5111-5113, 5208-5212, 5309-5311, 5407-5408, or 5512-5516.

Knitted or Crocheted Fabrics

13.   A change to any heading of Chapter 60 from any heading outside that chapter other than headings 5106-5113, 5204-5212, 5309-5311, or headings of Chapters 54 and 55.

Apparel - Knitted or Crocheted

14.   A change to any heading of Chapter 61 from any heading outside that chapter other than headings 5111-5113, 5208-5212, 5309-5311, 5407-5408, or 5512-5516; provided, that goods are both cut (or knit to shape) and sewn or otherwise assembled in the territory of either Party or both Parties.

Apparel - Not Knitted or Crocheted

15.   A change to any heading of Chapter 62 from any heading outside that chapter other than headings 5111-5113, 5208-5212, 5309-5311, 5407-5408, or 5512-5516; provided, that goods are both cut and sewn in the territory of either Party or both Parties.

Other Made-Up Articles

16.   A change to any heading of Chapter 63 from any heading outside that chapter other than headings 5106-5113, 5204-5212, 5306-5311, or headings of Chapters 54 and 55; provided, that goods are both cut and sewn in the territory of either Party or both Parties.

17.   Notwithstanding rules 14 and 15, apparel goods provided for in Chapters 61 and 62 that are both cut and sewn in the territory of either Party or both Parties from fabric produced or obtained in a third country, and that meet other applicable conditions for preferred tariff treatment under this Agreement, shall be subject to the rate of duty provided in Annex 401.2, in the annual quantities set forth below, and shall, above those quantities for the remainder of the annual period, be subject to duty at the rates provided for most-favoured nations.

		From Canada	From the United States of America
Non-woolen apparel	50 million SYE	10.5 million SYE	
Woolen apparel	6 million SYE	1.1 million SYE	

SYE- Square Yard Equivalent

Trade in the apparel described in rule 17 shall be monitored by the Parties with a view to adjusting the annual quantity limitations at the request of either Party based on the ability of apparel producers to obtain supplies of particular fabrics originating within the territories of the Parties. Before January 1, 1998, the annual quantity limitations shall be renegotiated to reflect current conditions in the textile and apparel industries located within the territories of the Parties, including the ability of such apparel producers to obtain supplies of particular fabrics originating within the territories of the Parties.

18.   Notwithstanding rules 4, 5, 6, 8, 11, 13 and 16, non-woolen fabric and non-woolen made-up textile articles provided for in Chapters 52-55, 58, 60 and 63 that are woven or knitted in Canada from yarn produced or obtained in a third country, and that meet other applicable conditions for preferred tariff treatment under this Agreement, shall be subject to the rate of duty provided in Annex 401.2, in the annual quantity of 30 million square yards for the period commencing on January 1, 1989 and ending on December 31, 1992, and shall, above this quantity for the remainder of the annual period, be subject to duty at the rates provided for most-favoured nations. The Parties agree to revisit the quantitative element of this agreement two years after its entry into force together with representatives of the industries in order to work out a mutually satisfactory solution, taking into account the availability of yarns in both countries.

Section XII
Footwear, Headgear, Umbrellas, Sun Umbrellas, Walking Sticks, Seatsticks, Whips, Riding Crops and Parts Thereof; Prepared Feathers and Articles Made Therewith; Artificial Flowers; Articles of Human Hair
(Ch. 64-67)

1.   A change from one chapter to another.

2.   A change to subheadings 6401.10-6406.10 from any other subheading outside that group; provided, that the value of materials originating in the territory of either Party or both Parties plus the direct cost of processing performed in the territory of either Party or both Parties constitute not less than 50 percent of the value of the goods when exported to the territory of the other Party.

3.   A change to headings 6503-6507 from any other heading outside that group.

4.   A change to headings 6601-6602 from any other heading outside that group; provided that the value of materials originating in the territory of either Party or both Parties plus the direct cost of processing performed in the territory of either Party or both Parties constitute not less than 50 percent of the value of the goods when exported to the territory of the other Party.

5.   Within heading 6701, goods fabricated from feathers (such as fans, feather dusters, and feather apparel) in which feathers are the material or component that gives the fabricated goods their essential character shall be treated as a good of the country in which fabrication occurred.

6.   A change to heading 6702 from any other heading.

7.   A change to heading 6704 from any other heading.

Section XIII
Articles of Stone, Plaster, Cement, Asbestos, Mica, or Similar Materials
(Ch. 68-70)

1.   A change from one chapter to another.

2.   A change to subheading 6812.20 from any other subheading.

3.   A change to subheading 6812.30-6812.40 from any other subheading outside that group.

4.   A change to subheading 6812.50 from any other subheading.

5.   A change to subheadings 6812.60-6812.90 from any other subheading outside that group.

6.   A change to heading 6813 from any other heading.

7.   A change to headings 7003-7006 from any other heading outside that group.

8. A change to headings 7007-7020 from any other heading outside that group.

9. A change to subheading 7019.20 from any other heading.

Section XIV
Natural or Cultured Pearls, Precious or Semiprecious Stones, Precious Metals, Metals Clad with Precious Metals, and Articles Thereof; Imitation Jewelry; Coin
(Ch. 71)

1. A change from one chapter to another.

2. A change to headings 7113-7118 from any other heading outside that group, except that pearls, temporarily or permanently strung but without the addition of clasps or other ornamental features of precious metals or stones, shall be treated as a good of the country in which the pearls were obtained.

Section XV
Base Metals and Articles of Base Metals
(Ch. 72-83)

1. A change from one chapter to another; provided, that goods subject to rules 9 or 22 meet the conditions set forth therein.

2. A change to headings 7206-7207 from any other heading outside that group.

3. A change to headings 7208-7216 from any other heading outside that group.

4. A change to heading 7217 from any other heading except headings 7213-7215.

5. A change to headings 7218-7222 from any other heading outside that group.

6. A change to heading 7223 from any other heading except headings 7221-7222.

7. A change to headings 7224-7228 from any other heading outside that group.

8.   A change to heading 7229 from any other heading except headings 7227-7228.

9.   A change to heading 7308 from any other heading, except for changes resulting from the following processes performed on angles, shapes, or sections of heading 7216:

   a) drilling, punching, notching, cutting, cambering, or sweeping, whether performed individually or in combination;

   b) adding attachments or weldments for composite construction;

   c) adding of attachments for handling purposes;

   d) adding weldments, connectors, or attachments to H-sections or I-sections; provided, that the maximum cross-sectional dimension of the weldments, connectors, or attachments is not greater than the dimension between the inner surfaces of the flanges of the H-sections or I-sections;

   e) painting, galvanizing, or otherwise coating; or

   f) adding a simple base plate without stiffening elements, individually or in combination with drilling, punching, notching, or cutting, to create an article suitable as a column.

10.   A change to headings 7309-7326 from any other heading outside that group.

11.   A change to headings 7403-7408 from any other heading outside that group; provided, with the exception of a change to subheading 7408.19, that the value of materials originating in the territory of either Party or both Parties plus the direct cost of processing performed in the territory of either Party or both Parties constitute not less than 50 percent of the value of the goods when exported to the territory of the other Party.

12.   A change to heading 7409 from any other heading.

13.   A change to headings 7410-7419 from any other heading outside that group; provided, that with respect to a change to heading 7413, the

value of materials originating in the territory of either Party or both Parties plus the direct cost of processing performed in the territory of either Party or both Parties constitute not less than 50 percent of the value of goods when exported to the territory of the other Party.

14. A change to heading 7505 from any other heading.

15. A change to heading 7506 from any other heading.

16. A change to United States tariff item 7506.20.50 from any other United States tariff item. This rule applies only to goods originating in the territory of Canada and imported into the territory of the United States of America.

17. A change to headings 7507-7508 from any other heading outside that group.

18. A change to headings 7604-7606 from any other heading outside that group.

19. A change to heading 7607 from any other heading.

20. A change to headings 7608-7609 from any other heading outside that group.

21. A change to headings 7610-7616 from any other heading outside that group.

22. A change to headings 7801 or 7901 from headings of other chapters; provided, that the value of materials originating in the territory of either Party or both Parties plus the direct cost of processing performed in the territory of either Party or both Parties constitute not less than 50 percent of the value of the goods when exported to the territory of the other Party.

23. A change to headings 7803-7806 from any other heading, including another heading within that group; provided, that the value of materials originating in the territory of either Party or both Parties plus the direct cost of processing performed in the territory of either Party or both Parties constitute not less than 50 percent of the value of the goods when exported to the territory of the other Party.

NOTE: see rule 22 regarding 7901.

24.   A change to headings 7904-7907 from any other heading, including another heading within that group; provided, that the value of materials originating in the territory of either Party or both Parties plus the direct cost of processing performed in the territory of either Party or both Parties constitute not less than 50 percent of the value of the goods when exported to the territory of the other Party.

25.   A change to headings 8003-8004 from any other heading outside that group.

26.   A change to headings 8005-8007 from any other heading outside that group.

27.   A change to any of the following subheadings from any other subheading: 8101.92, 8101.99, 8102.92, 8102.99, 8103.90, 8104.90, 8105.90, 8108.90, 8109.90.

28.   A change to subheading 8107.90 from any other subheading; provided, that the value of materials originating in the territory of either Party or both Parties plus the direct cost of processing performed in the territory of either Party or both Parties constitute not less than 50 percent of the value of the goods when exported to the territory of the other Party.

29.   A change to United States tariff item 8111.00.60 from any other United States tariff item. This rule applies only to goods originating in the territory of Canada and imported into the territory of the United States of America.

Section XVI
Machinery and Mechanical Appliances; Electrical Equipment; Parts Thereof; Sound Recorders and Reproducers, and Parts and Accessories of Such Articles
(Ch. 84-85)

1.   A change from one chapter to another, other than a change to heading 8544.

2.   A change from one heading (other than a parts heading) to another heading, other than heading 8528 or 8529.

3.   A change to heading 8407 from any other heading; provided, that the value of materials originating in the territory of either Party

or both Parties plus the direct cost of processing performed in the territory of either Party or both Parties constitute not less than 50 percent of the value of the goods when exported to the territory of the other Party

4.   A change to heading 8528 or 8529 from any other heading, a change from a parts heading to a heading other than a parts heading, or a change from a parts subheading to a subheading other than a parts subheading; provided, with the exception of a change to subheading 8471.92, that the value of materials originating in the territory of either Party or both Parties plus the direct cost of processing performed in the territory of either Party or both Parties constitute not less than 50 percent of the value of the goods when exported to the territory of the other Party.

5.   A change to subheadings 8471.20-8471.91 from any sub-headings outside that group.

6.   A change to subheadings 8516.10-8516.79 from subheading 8516.80.

7.   A change to heading 8524 from any other heading. Goods subject to classification under headings 8523 or 8524 shall remain classified in those headings, whether or not they are entered with the apparatus for which they are intended.

NOTE: see rule 4 regarding headings 8528 and 8529.

8.   A change to heading 8544 from any other heading; provided, that the value of materials originating in the territory of either Party or both Parties plus the direct cost of processing performed in the territory of either Party or both Parties constitute not less than 50 percent of the value of the goods when exported to the territory of the other Party.

Section XVII
Vehicles, Aircraft, Vessels and Associated Transport Equipment
(Ch. 86-89)

1.   A change from one chapter to another.

2.   A change to any heading of this Section (other than a heading within the groups 8701-8705 or 8901-8905) from another heading other than a parts heading.

3.   A change to any heading of this Section from a parts heading; or within any heading, a change to any subheading from a parts subheading; provided, that the value of materials originating in the territory of either Party or both Parties plus the direct cost of processing performed in the territory of either Party or both Parties constitute not less than 50 percent of the value of the goods when exported to the territory of the other Party.

4.   A change to headings 8701-8705 from any other heading; provided, that the value of materials originating in the territory of either Party or both Parties plus the direct cost of processing performed in the territory of either Party or both Parties constitute not less than 50 percent of the value of the goods when exported to the territory of the other Party.

5.   A change to headings 8901-8905 from any other headings; provided, that the value of materials originating in the territory of either Party or both Parties plus the direct cost of processing performed in the territory of either Party or both Parties constitute not less than 50 percent of the value of the goods when exported to the territory of the other Party.

Section XVIII
Optical, Photographic, Cinematographic, Measuring, Checking, Precision, Medical or Surgical Instruments and Apparatus, Clocks and Watches; Musical Instruments; Parts and Accessories Thereof
(Ch. 90-92)

1.   A change from one chapter to another.

2.   A change to any heading of this Section from a parts heading, or to any subheading from a parts subheading; provided, with the exception of a change to heading 9009, that the value of materials originating in the territory of either Party of both Parties plus the direct cost of processing performed in the territory of either Party or both Parties constitute not less than 50 percent of the value of the goods when exported to the territory of the other Party.

3.   A change to any heading within the group 9005-9032 from any other heading (including another heading within that group), except that a change from a parts heading shall be subject to rule 2 of this Section.

4.   Notwithstanding rule 2, goods subject to classification within headings 9101-9107 shall be treated as products of the country in which the movement subject to classification under headings 9108-9110 was produced.

5.   A change to headings 9108-9113 from any other heading, including another heading within that group; provided, that the value of materials originating in the territory of either Party or both Parties plus the direct cost of processing performed in the territory of either Party or both Parties constitute not less than 50 percent of the value of the goods when exported to the territory of the other Party.

Section XIX
Arms and Ammunition; Parts and Accessories Thereof
(Ch. 93)

1.   A change to this chapter from any other chapter.

2.   A change to any heading of this Section from a parts heading, or to any subheading from a parts subheading; provided, that the value of materials originating in the territory of either Party or both Parties plus the direct cost of processing performed in the territory of either Party or both Parties constitute not less than 50 percent of the value of the goods when exported to the territory of the other Party.

Section XX
Miscellaneous Manufactured Articles
(Ch. 94-96)

1.   A change from one chapter to another, except a change to subheading 9404.90 from headings 5007, 5111-5113, 5208-5212, 5309-5311, 5407-5408, and 5512-5516.

2.   A change to any heading of this Section from a parts heading, or to any subheading from a parts subheading; provided, that the value of materials originating in the territory of either Party or both Parties plus the direct cost of processing performed in the territory of either Party or both Parties constitute not less than 50 percent of the value of the goods when exported to the territory of the other Party.

3.   A change to a subheading within the group 9608.10-9608.39 from a subheading within the group 9608.91-9608.99; provided, that the value of materials originating in the territory of either Party or both Parties plus the direct cost of processing performed in the territory of either Party or both Parties constitute not less than 50 percent of the value of the goods when exported to the territory of the other Party.

4.   A change to subheading 9614.20 from subheading 9614.10.

Section XXI
Works of Art, Collectors' Pieces and Antiques
(Ch. 97)

1.   A change to this chapter from any other chapter.

Chapter Four

Border Measures

Article 401: Tariff Elimination

1.   Neither Party shall increase any existing customs duty, or introduce any customs duty, on goods originating in the territory of the other Party, except as otherwise provided in this Agreement.

2.   Except as otherwise provided in this Agreement, each Party shall progressively eliminate its customs duties on goods originating in the territory of the other Party in accordance with the following schedule:

   a) duties on goods provided for in each of the items designated as staging category A in each Party's Schedule contained in Annex 401.2 shall be eliminated entirely and such goods shall be free of duty, effective January 1, 1989;

   b) duties on goods provided for in each of the items designated as staging category B in each Party's Schedule contained in Annex 401.2 shall be removed in five equal annual stages commencing on January 1, 1989, and such goods shall be free of duty, effective January 1, 1993; and

   c) duties on goods provided for in each of the items designated as staging category C in each Party's Schedule contained in Annex 401.2 shall be removed in ten equal annual stages commencing on January 1, 1989, and such goods shall be free of duty, effective January 1, 1998.

3.   The base rate of duty for purposes of determining the interim stages of reduction for a tariff item under subparagraphs (b) and (c) of paragraph 2 is the rate indicated for the item in each Party's Schedule contained in Annex 401.2.

4.   Except as otherwise provided in this Agreement, goods originating in the territory of the other Party that are provided for in each of the items designated as staging category D in each Party's Schedule contained in Annex 401.2 shall continue to receive the existing duty-free treatment indicated therein for such goods.

113

5.   At the request of either Party, the Parties shall consult to consider acceleration of the elimination of the duty on specific items in the Schedule of each Party. An agreement between the Parties on such accelerated implementation of duty-free treatment shall be considered a part of this Agreement and the accelerated implementation schedule for an item shall replace and supersede the prior implementation schedule contained in this Agreement for the item.

6.   Canada shall continue to exempt from customs duties certain machinery and equipment considered "not available" from Canadian production and certain repair and replacement parts originating in the territory of the United States of America, in accordance with Annex 401.6.

7.   Canada shall not increase the rate of customs duty on goods originating in the territory of the United States of America that are set out in the Schedule of Statutory and Temporary Concessionary Provisions in the Canadian Tariff Schedule Converted to the Harmonized System, with the exception of the goods set out in Annex 401.7.

8.   The United States of America shall not impose a customs duty on goods originating in the territory of Canada that were subject to a temporary suspension of the duty on October 3, 1987, and which are listed with a base rate of free in subchapter II of chapter 99 of the Schedule of the United States of America contained in Annex 401.2, except as noted in that subchapter and as listed in Annex 401.7.

Article 402:   Rounding of Interim Rates

To simplify application of interim staged rates in the removal of duties in accordance with subparagraphs 2(b) and (c) of Article 401, such rates shall be rounded down, with the limited exceptions set out in each Party's Schedule in Annex 401.2, to the nearest 0.1 percent ad valorem or, if the rate of duty is expressed in monetary units, to the nearest 0.1 cent. In no case shall a rate be rounded up.

Article 403:   Customs User Fees

1.   Neither Party shall introduce customs user fees with respect to goods originating in the territory of the other Party.

2.   Subject to paragraph 3, the United States of America may change the level of existing customs user fees.

3.   The United States of America shall eliminate existing customs user fees on goods originating in the territory of Canada according to the following schedule:

a) with respect to goods entered or withdrawn from warehouse for consumption on or after January 1, 1990, the user fee shall be 80 percent of the user fee otherwise applicable on that date;

b) with respect to goods entered or withdrawn from warehouse for consumption on or after January 1, 1991, the user fee shall be 60 percent of the user fee otherwise applicable on that date;

c) with respect to goods entered or withdrawn from warehouse for consumption on or after January 1, 1992, the user fee shall be 40 percent of the user fee otherwise applicable on that date;

d) with respect to goods entered or withdrawn from warehouse for consumption on or after January 1, 1993, the user fee shall be 20 percent of the user fee otherwise applicable on that date; and

e) with respect to goods entered or withdrawn from warehouse for consumption on or after January 1, 1994, there shall be no customs user fee.

Article 404: Drawback

1.   Goods imported into the territory of a Party (including goods imported in bond or qualifying for benefit under a foreign trade zone, inward processing, or similar program) and subsequently exported to the territory of the other Party, or incorporated into, or directly consumed in the production of, goods subsequently exported to the territory of the other Party, shall be subject to the customs duties of the Party applicable to goods entered for consumption in the customs territory of that Party prior to their export to the territory of the other Party. Such duties shall not be reduced, eliminated or refunded by reason of such exportation, and their payment shall not be deferred upon such exportation.

2.   The prohibition set out in paragraph 1 also applies where the imported goods are substituted by domestic or other imported goods

exported to the territory of the other Party, or incorporated into or directly consumed in the production of goods subsequently exported to the territory of the other Party.

3.   Goods exported to the territory of the other Party from a foreign trade zone or similar area shall be subject to the applicable customs duties of the Party maintaining the foreign trade zone or similar area as though the goods were withdrawn for domestic consumption.

4.   Paragraphs 1, 2 and 3 do not apply to:

   a) goods under bond for transportation and exportation to the territory of the other Party or exported to the territory of the other Party in the same condition as when imported into the territory of the Party (testing, cleaning, repacking or inspecting the goods, preserving them in their same condition, or other like process, shall not, for the purposes of this Article, be a process that would change the condition of the goods);

   b) goods deemed to be exported from the territory of a Party or goods incorporated into, or directly consumed in the production of, such goods, by reason of:

      i)   delivery to a duty-free shop,

      ii)   use as stores or supplies for ships or aircraft, or

      iii) use in joint undertakings of the Parties and that will subsequently become the property of the other Party; or

   c) dutiable goods originating in the territory of the other Party that are imported into the territory of the Party and subsequently re-exported to the territory of the other Party, or are incorporated into, or directly consumed in the production of, goods subsequently exported to the territory of the other Party.

5.   Paragraphs 1, 2 and 3 do not apply to a refund of customs duties imposed by a Party on particular goods imported into its territory and subsequently exported to the territory of the other Party, where that refund is granted by reason of the failure of such goods to conform to

sample or specification, or by reason of the shipment of such goods without the consent of the consignee.

6.   Solely for the purposes of this Article, the term "customs duties" includes the charges referred to in subparagraphs (b), (d) and (e) in the definition of customs duties contained in Article 410.

7.   Except as the Parties may agree to delay the application of this Article, this Article shall apply to customs duties imposed on imported goods that are:

   a) exported to the territory of the other Party on or after January 1, 1994, or that are substituted by domestic or other imported goods exported to the territory of the other Party on or after January 1, 1994; or

   b) incorporated into, or directly consumed in the production of, goods subsequently exported to the territory of the other Party on or after January 1, 1994, or that are substituted by domestic or other imported goods incorporated into, or directly consumed in the production of, goods exported to the territory of the other Party on or after January 1, 1994.

8.   Unless otherwise agreed by the Parties, this Article shall not apply to:

   a) imported citrus products; and

   b) fabric not originating in the territory of either Party or both Parties and made into apparel that is subject to the most-favoured-nation tariff when exported to the territory of the other Party.

Article 405: Waiver of Customs Duties

1.   Neither Party shall, after the later of June 30, 1988 or the date of approval of this Agreement by the Congress of the United States of America, introduce any new program, expand with respect to then-existing recipients or extend to any new recipient the application of a program existing prior to such date that waives otherwise applicable customs duties on any goods imported from any country, including the territory of the other Party, where the waiver is conditioned,

explicitly or implicitly, upon the fulfillment of performance requirements.

2.   Neither Party shall, explicitly or implicitly, condition upon the fulfillment of performance requirements the continuation of any program existing on the date referred to in paragraph 1 that provides for the waiver of customs duties on any goods imported from any country, including the territory of the other Party, and entered or withdrawn from warehouse for consumption on or after January 1, 1998.

3.   Whenever the other Party can show that a waiver or a combination of waivers of customs duties granted with respect to goods for commercial use by a designated person has an adverse impact on the commercial interests of a person of the other Party, or of a person owned or controlled by a person of the other Party that is located in the territory of the Party granting the waiver of customs duties, or on the other Party's economy, the Party granting the waiver either shall cease to grant it or shall make it generally available to any importer.

4.   The provisions of paragraph 2 shall not apply with respect to the granting of waivers of customs duties conditioned, explicitly or implicitly, upon the fulfillment of performance requirements, to the manufacturers of automotive goods listed in Part One of Annex 1002.1 in accordance with the headnote to that Part. Nothing in this Agreement affects the rights of either Party under any agreement, other than this Agreement, with respect to the granting of such waivers of customs duties.

Article 406: Customs Administration

The Parties' respective Customs Administrations shall cooperate as specified in Annex 406 (Customs Administration).

Article 407: Import and Export Restrictions

1.   Subject to the further rights and obligations of this Agreement, the Parties affirm their respective rights and obligations under the *General Agreement on Tariffs and Trade* (GATT) with respect to prohibitions or restrictions on bilateral trade in goods.

2. The Parties understand that the GATT rights and obligations affirmed in paragraph 1 prohibit, in any circumstances in which any other form of quantitative restriction is prohibited, minimum export-price requirements and, except as permitted in enforcement of countervailing and antidumping orders and undertakings, minimum import-price requirements.

3. In circumstances where a Party imposes a restriction on importation from or exportation to a third country of a good, nothing in this Agreement shall be construed to prevent the Party from:

   a) limiting or prohibiting the importation from the territory of the other Party of such good of the third country; or

   b) requiring as a condition of export of such good of the Party to the territory of the other Party, that the good be consumed within the territory of the other Party.

4. In the event that either Party imposes a restriction on imports of a good from third countries, the Parties, upon request of either Party, shall consult with a view to avoiding undue interference with or distortion of pricing, marketing and distribution arrangements in the other Party.

5. The Parties shall eliminate the restrictions as set out in Annex 407.6.

Article 408: Export Taxes

Neither Party shall maintain or introduce any tax, duty, or charge on the export of any good to the territory of the other Party, unless such tax, duty, or charge is also maintained or introduced on such good when destined for domestic consumption.

Article 409: Other Export Measures

1. Either Party may maintain or introduce a restriction otherwise justified under the provisions of Articles XI:2(a) and XX(g), (i) and (j) of the GATT with respect to the export of a good of the Party to the territory of the other Party, only if:

   a) the restriction does not reduce the proportion of the total export shipments of the specific good made available to the other Party relative to the total supply of that good of the Party maintaining the restriction as compared to the proportion prevailing in the most recent 36-month period for which data are available prior to the imposition of the measure, or in such other representative period on which the Parties may agree;

b) the Party does not impose a higher price for exports of a good to the other Party than the price charged for such good when consumed domestically, by means of any measure such as licences, fees, taxation and minimum price requirements. The foregoing provision does not apply to a higher price which may result from a measure taken pursuant to subparagraph (a) that only restricts the volume of exports; and

c) the restriction does not require the disruption of normal channels of supply to the other Party or normal proportions among specific goods or categories of goods supplied to the other Party.

2.   With respect to the implementation of the provisions of this Article, the Parties shall cooperate in the maintenance and development of effective controls on the export of each other's goods to third countries.

Article 410: Definitions

For purposes of this Chapter:

consumed means transformed so as to qualify under the rules of origin set out in Chapter Three, or actually consumed;

Customs Administration means, in Canada, that part of the Department of National Revenue for which the Deputy Minister of National Revenue for Customs and Excise, or any successor thereof, is responsible, and, in the United States of America, the United States Customs Service, Department of the Treasury, or any successor thereof;

customs duty includes any customs or import duty and charge of any kind imposed in connection with the importation of goods, including any form of surtax or surcharge on imports, with the exception of:

a) a charge equivalent to an internal tax imposed consistently with the provisions of paragraph 2 of Article III of the GATT in respect of like domestic goods or in respect of goods from which the imported good has been manufactured or produced in whole or in part,

b) any antidumping or countervailing duty applied pursuant to either Party's domestic law consistent with the provisions of Chapter Nineteen,

c) fees or other charges in connection with importation commensurate with the cost of services rendered, subject to Article 403;

d) premiums offered or collected on imported goods arising out of any tendering system in respect of the administration of quantitative import restrictions or tariff quotas, and

e) fees applied pursuant to section 22 of the United States *Agricultural Adjustment Act* of 1933, as amended, subject to the provisions of Chapter Seven (Agriculture);

existing customs duty means a duty, the rate of which is set out as the base rate for a tariff item in each Party's schedule contained in Annex 401.2;

performance requirement means a requirement that:

a) a given level or percentage of goods or services be exported,

b) domestic goods or services of the Party granting the waiver of customs duties be substituted for imported goods,

c) a person benefitting from the waiver of customs duties purchase other goods or services in the territory of the Party granting the waiver of customs duties, or accord a preference to domestically produced goods or services, or

d) a person benefitting from the waiver of customs duties produce, in the territory of the Party granting the waiver of customs duties, goods or services with a given level or percentage of domestic content;

restriction means any limitation, whether made effective through quotas, licenses, permits, minimum price requirements or any other means;

total export shipments means the total shipments from total supply to users located in the territory of the other Party;

total supply means shipments to domestic users and foreign users from:

    a) domestic production,
    b) domestic inventory, and
    c) other imports as appropriate; and

waiver of customs duties means relief by any means from customs duties on goods imported into the territory of a Party.

Annex 401.2

A. Schedule of CANADA

attached

B. Schedule of the UNITED STATES OF AMERICA

attached

Annex 401.6

Machinery and Equipment

1.   Canada shall continue to exempt from customs duties the machinery and equipment listed as "not available" from Canadian production in Column I of Schedule I of Appendix A to Memorandum D8-5-1 of March 11, 1987, published by the Department of National Revenue, Customs and Excise (the Memorandum), with the exception of the following (identified by the product code used in connection with such machinery and equipment in Column I of Schedule I of Appendix A to the Memorandum):

02 BC L.	02 BC M.	02 BC N.
02 BC P.	02 BC Q.	04 FE B.
04 FK ..	04 FN ..	07 CA ..
07 EC ..	07 FD ..	07 MA ..
07 LA ..	17 DH ..	18 B. ..
18 FD ..	41 CD A.	45 GB ..
59 BN ..	61 AC ..	61 AD ..
61 AE ..	61 AG ..	61 AH B.
61 DB A.	61 DF A.	61 DF B.
63 AS ..	69 D. ..	71 CD ..
71 JE A.	71 JE C.	71 JF C.

2.   Canada shall also continue to exempt from customs duties repair and replacement parts for the machinery and equipment that it exempts from customs duties, as set out in paragraph 1, with the exception of repair and replacement parts listed as "available" from Canadian production in column II of Schedule I, or listed as not eligible for remission of customs duty in Schedule II, of Appendix A to the Memorandum.

3.   Canada shall review, by January 1, 1989, for the purpose of exempting from customs duties, the machinery and equipment set out as exceptions in paragraph 1, as well as the machinery and equipment not listed as either "available" or "not available" in Schedule I of Appendix A to the Memorandum.

Annex 401.7

Treatment of Concessionary Duty Provisions

Canada

1. Canada may exempt the following goods (identified by the code for them in the Schedule of Statutory and Temporary Concessionary Provisions in the Canadian Tariff Schedule Converted to the Harmonized System) from the undertaking in paragraph 7 of Article 401:

1695	3175	4205
4210	4211	4212
4220	4225	4300
4305	4315	4380
4381	4382	4780
4865	5175	5180
5960	6235	6335
6340	6600	6650
6655	6850	6851
6852	6945	7520
7862	7866	7938

United States of America

2. The United States of America may exempt the following goods (identified by the code for them in the Harmonized System) from the undertaking in paragraph 8 of Article 401:

9902.2937	Terfenadine
9902.2938	Flecainide
9902.2939	Mepenzolate Bromide
9902.3808	Mixtures of Potassium
9902.3823	Mixtures of 5-Chloro-2-Methyl-4-Isothiazolin ... magnesium nitrate

Annex 406

Customs Administration

A. Declaration of Origin

Imported Goods

1.   Subject to paragraph 3, each Party may:

   a) require that an importer who represents that goods imported
      from the territory of the other Party meet the rules of origin set
      out in Chapter Three (Rules of Origin) make a written
      declaration to that effect and base such declaration on the
      exporter's written certification to the same effect;

   b) require that, upon request, such importer provide the Customs
      Administration of the Party with proof of the exporter's written
      certification of the origin of the goods; and

   c) make mandatory the declaration required by subparagraph (a)
      and the provision of proof thereof required by subparagraph
      (b), and may further provide that failure to comply with such
      mandatory requirements shall have the same legal consequences
      as a violation of its laws with respect to making a false statement
      or representation.

Exported Goods

2.   Each Party shall:

   a) require that an exporter who certifies in writing that goods it
      exports to the territory of the other Party meet the rules of
      origin set out in Chapter Three provide, upon request, the
      Customs Administration of that Party with a copy of that
      certification; and

   b) make it unlawful to certify falsely that goods exported to the
      territory of the other Party meet the rules of origin set out in
      Chapter Three, and shall further provide that such unlawful act
      shall have the same legal consequences as a violation of its laws
      with respect to making a false statement or representation.

Exceptions

3.   Either Party may provide for exemptions from compliance with paragraph 1.

B. Administration and Enforcement

Records and Audit

4.   Each Party shall ensure that records are kept with respect to the goods subject to paragraphs 1 and 2, and shall ensure that such records are subject to whatever audit or other statutory requirements apply to importers' records.

Cooperation

5.   In furtherance of their mutual interest in ensuring the effective administration of paragraphs 1 and 2, and in the prevention, investigation and repression of unlawful acts, the Parties shall cooperate fully in the enforcement of their respective laws in accordance with this Agreement and other treaties, agreements and memoranda of understanding between them.

C. Rules of Origin

Consultation on Uniform Application

6.   The Parties, through their Customs Administrations, shall consult with each other concerning the uniform application of the principles set out in Chapter Three.   Each Party shall make its precedential decisions applying these principles available to the other Party.

Appeals Relating to Origin

7.   Each Party shall provide the same rights of review and appeal with respect to a decision relating to the origin of imported goods represented as meeting the requirements of Chapter Three as are provided with respect to the tariff classification of imported goods.

D. Flow of Trade

Facilitation

8.   The Parties shall cooperate, to the extent possible, in customs matters in order to facilitate the flow of trade between them, particularly in matters relating to the collection of statistics with respect to the importation and exportation of goods, the harmonization of documents used in trade, and the exchange of information.

Notification and Consultation Prior to Major Changes

9.   The Parties shall notify and consult with each other with respect to and, where possible, in advance of, major proposed changes in customs administration that would affect the flow of bilateral trade, such as:

a) the closing of a port or customs office;

b) the hours of service at a port or customs office;

c) the re-routing of the natural flow of trade;

d) resources, including personnel, facilities, and equipment, allocated to commercial processing and inspection;

e) trade documentation required by the Customs Administration or another agency of a Party;

f) customs procedures followed to implement the requirements of other agencies of a Party; and

g) the processing of travellers.

Annex 407.6
Elimination of Quantitative Restrictions

1.   Canada shall eliminate, as of January 1, 1989, the embargo (set out in Tariff Item 99216-1 of Schedule C of the *Customs Tariff,* or its successor) on used or second-hand aeroplanes and aircraft of all kinds.

2.   The United States of America shall eliminate, as of January 1, 1993, the embargo set out in 19 U.S.C. § 1305 on any

a) lottery ticket,

b) printed paper that may be used as a lottery ticket, or

c) advertisement,

for a United States lottery, printed in Canada.

Chapter Five

National Treatment

Article 501: Incorporation of GATT Rule

1.   Each Party shall accord national treatment to the goods of the other Party in accordance with the existing provisions of Article III of the *General Agreement on Tariffs and Trade* (GATT), including its interpretative notes, and to this end the provisions of Article III of the GATT and its interpretative notes are incorporated into and made part of this Part of this Agreement.

2.   For purposes of this Agreement, the provisions of this Chapter shall be applied in accordance with existing interpretations adopted by the Contracting Parties to the GATT.

Article 502: Provincial and State Measures

The provisions of this Chapter regarding the treatment of like, directly competitive or substitutable goods shall mean, with respect to a province or state, treatment no less favourable than the most favourable treatment accorded by such province or state to any like, directly competitive or substitutable goods, as the case may be, of the Party of which it forms a part.

Chapter Six
Technical Standards

Article 601: Scope

1.   The provisions of this Chapter shall apply to technical standards related to goods other than agricultural, food, beverage and certain related goods as defined in Chapter Seven (Agriculture).

2.   The provisions of this Chapter shall not apply to any measure of a provincial or state government. Accordingly, the Parties need not ensure the observance of these provisions by state or provincial governments.

Article 602: Affirmation of GATT Agreement

The Parties affirm their respective rights and obligations under the GATT *Agreement on Technical Barriers to Trade.*

Article 603: No Disguised Barriers to Trade

Neither Party shall maintain or introduce standards-related measures or procedures for product approval that would create unnecessary obstacles to trade between the territories of the Parties. Unnecessary obstacles to trade shall not be deemed to be created if:

a) the demonstrable purpose of such measure or procedure is to achieve a legitimate domestic objective; and

b) the measure or procedure does not operate to exclude goods of the other Party that meet that legitimate domestic objective.

Article 604: Compatibility

1.   To the greatest extent possible, and taking into account international standardization activities, each Party shall make compatible its standards-related measures and procedures for product approval with those of the other Party.

2.   Each Party shall, upon request of the other Party, take such reasonable measures as may be available to it to promote the objectives

of paragraph 1 with respect to specific standards-related measures that are developed or maintained by private standards-related organizations within its territory.

Article 605: Accreditation

1.   Each Party shall provide for recognition of the accreditation systems for testing facilities, inspection agencies and certification bodies of the other Party.

2.   Neither Party shall require as a condition for accreditation that testing facilities, inspection agencies or certification bodies be located or established in or make decisions within its territory.

3.   Either Party may charge a reasonable fee, limited in amount to the approximate cost of the services rendered, to testing facilities, inspection agencies or certification bodies seeking accreditation, provided that such fees shall be charged on an equal basis to the testing facilities, inspection agencies or certification bodies of either Party. Where a Party charges such fees during the transition period, they need not be charged to domestic testing facilities, inspection agencies or certification bodies.

Article 606: Acceptance of Test Data

Each Party shall provide, upon request, a written explanation whenever any of its federal government bodies is unable to accept from bodies located in the territory of the other Party test results that are needed to obtain certification or product approval.

Article 607: Information Exchange

1.   Each Party shall promptly provide the other Party with full texts of proposed federal government standards-related measures and product approval procedures published in official journals in sufficient time to provide persons of the other Party with at least 60 days to develop comments and discuss them with the appropriate regulating authority prior to submitting the comments.

2.   Either Party may, in urgent circumstances where delay would frustrate the achievement of a legitimate domestic objective, proceed without prior provision of a text under paragraph 1. In such instances, the texts shall be provided expeditiously after issuance in final form.

3.   Where feasible, each Party shall:

   a) notify the other Party of proposed standards-related measures
      of state and provincial authorities that may significantly affect
      bilateral trade; if such notice cannot be provided in advance, it
      should be provided as expeditiously as possible;

   b) provide a full text of such proposed state and provincial
      standards-related measures;

   c) take such reasonable steps as may be available to it to provide
      persons of the other Party with information that would facilitate
      their provision of comments to, and discussions of comments
      with, appropriate state or provincial authorities; and

   d) take such reasonable steps as may be available to it to notify the
      other Party of standards-related measures of major national
      private organizations.

Article 608: Further Implementation

The Parties shall, as may be appropriate to further the objectives
of this Chapter, undertake additional negotiations with respect to:

   a) making compatible standards-related measures and product
      approval procedures;

   b) accreditation; and

   c) acceptance of test data.

Article 609: Definitions

For purposes of this Chapter:

accreditation means a formal recognition of competence to carry out
specific tests or specific types of tests, including authorization to
certify conformity with standards or technical specifications, by means
of a certificate of conformity or mark of conformity;

legitimate domestic objective means an objective whose purpose is to protect health, safety, essential security, the environment, or consumer interests;

make compatible means the process by which differing standards, technical regulations or certification systems of the same scope which have been approved by different standardizing bodies are recognized as being either technically identical or technically equivalent in practice;

product approval means a federal government declaration that a set of published criteria has been fulfilled and therefore that goods are permitted to be used in a specific manner or for a specific purpose;

standards-related measures include technical specifications, technical regulations, standards and rules for certification systems that apply to goods, and processes and production methods; and

testing facility means a facility that inspects, measures, examines, tests, calibrates or otherwise determines the characteristics or performance of materials or goods.

Chapter Seven

Agriculture

Article 701:   Agricultural Subsidies

1.   The Parties agree that their primary goal with respect to agricultural subsidies is to achieve, on a global basis, the elimination of all subsidies which distort agricultural trade, and the Parties agree to work together to achieve this goal, including through multilateral trade negotiations such as the Uruguay Round.

2.   Neither Party shall introduce or maintain any export subsidy on any agricultural goods originating in, or shipped from, its territory that are exported directly or indirectly to the territory of the other Party.

3.   Neither Party, including any public entity that it establishes or maintains, shall sell agricultural goods for export to the territory of the other Party at a price below the acquisition price of the goods plus any storage, handling or other costs incurred by it with respect to those goods.

4.   Each Party shall take into account the export interests of the other Party in the use of any export subsidy on any agricultural good exported to third countries, recognizing that such subsidies may have prejudicial effects on the export interests of the other Party.

5.   Canada shall exclude from the transport rates established under the *Western Grain Transportation Act* agricultural goods originating in Canada and shipped via west coast ports for consumption in the United States of America.

Article 702: Special Provisions for Fresh Fruits and Vegetables

1. a) Notwithstanding Article 401, for a period of 20 years from the entry into force of this Agreement, each Party reserves the right to apply a temporary duty on fresh fruits or vegetables originating in the territory of the other Party and imported into its territory, when

135

    i) for each of five consecutive working days the import price of such fruit or vegetable for each such day is below 90 percent of the average monthly import price, for the month in which that day falls, over the preceding five years, excluding the years with the highest and lowest average monthly import price; and

    ii) the planted acreage in the importing Party for the particular fruit or vegetable is no higher than the average acreage over the preceding five years, excluding the years with the highest and lowest acreage.

b) The temporary duty referred to in subparagraph (a) may be applied on a regional or national basis, and the import prices and planted acreage will then be determined on a regional or national basis, as appropriate.

c) For purposes of calculating the planted acreage referred to in subparagraph (a)(ii), any acreage increase attributed directly to a reduction in wine grape planted acreage existing on October 4, 1987 shall be excluded.

2.   Any temporary duty applied under this Article together with any other duty in effect for the particular fresh fruit or vegetable shall not exceed the lesser of:

a) the applicable most-favoured-nation (MFN) rate of duty that was in effect for the particular fresh fruit or vegetable prior to the date of entry into force of this Agreement determined with reference to the same season in which the temporary duty is applied; or

b) the MFN rate of duty in effect for imports of that particular fresh fruit or vegetable at the time the temporary duty is applied.

3.   Any temporary duty shall only be applied either once per twelve-month period per good nationally or once per twelve-month period per good in each region. If a temporary duty is initially applied in one or more regions, any later application in a different region during that twelve-month period shall be based on a later five consecutive working day period under subparagraph 1(a)(i). No

temporary duty shall apply to goods in transit at the time the duty is applied.

4.   Such a temporary duty shall be removed when, for a period of five consecutive working days, the representative F.O.B point of shipment price in the exporting Party exceeds 90 percent of the average monthly import price referred to in subparagraph 1(a)(i), adjusted to an F.O.B point of shipment price, if necessary, and in any event shall be removed after 180 days.

5.   Prior to the application of the temporary duty, the importing Party shall provide to the exporting Party two working days notice and an opportunity to consult during those two working days.

6.   No Party may introduce or maintain any action under this Article on a particular good during such time as an action is maintained under Chapter Eleven (Emergency Action) on the same good.

7.   For purposes of this Article, fresh fruit or vegetable shall mean any good classified within the following tariff headings of the Harmonized System (HS):

HS Tariff Heading	Description
07.01	potatoes, fresh or chilled
07.02	tomatoes, fresh or chilled
07.03	onions, shallots, garlic, leeks and other alliaceous vegetables, fresh or chilled
07.04	cabbages, cauliflowers, kohlrabi, kale and similar edible brassicas, fresh or chilled
07.05	lettuce (lactuca sativa) and chicory (cichorium spp.), fresh or chilled
07.06	carrots, salad beets or beetroot, salsify, celeriac, radishes and similar

	edible roots (excluding turnips), fresh or chilled
07.07	cucumbers and gherkins, fresh or chilled
07.08	leguminous vegetables, shelled or unshelled, fresh or chilled
07.09	other vegetables (excluding truffles), fresh or chilled
08.06.10	grapes, fresh
08.08.20	pears and quinces, fresh
08.09	apricots, cherries, peaches (including nectarines), plums and sloes, fresh
08.10	other fruit (excluding cranberries and blueberries), fresh.

8.   The Parties shall, upon the request of either Party, consult concerning removal of any temporary duty applied under paragraph 1.

9.   For purposes of this Article, a region in Canada means:

   a) British Columbia, Alberta, Saskatchewan, Manitoba, and that part of Ontario west of 89° 19' longtitude (Thunder Bay);

   b) Quebec and that part of Ontario east of 89° 19' longtitude (Thunder Bay); or

   c) New Brunswick, Nova Scotia, Prince Edward Island and Newfoundland.

Article 703: Market Access for Agriculture

In order to facilitate trade in agricultural goods, the Parties shall work together to improve access to each other's markets through the elimination or reduction of import barriers.

Article 704: Market Access for Meat

1. Neither Party shall introduce, maintain or seek any quantitative import restriction or any other measure having equivalent effect on meat goods originating in the territory of the other Party except as otherwise provided in this Agreement.

2. If a Party imposes any quantitative import restriction on meat goods from all third countries, or negotiates agreements limiting exports from third countries, and if the other Party does not take equivalent action, then the first Party may impose quantitative import restrictions on meat goods originating in the territory of the other Party only to the extent and only for such period of time as is sufficient to prevent frustration of the action taken on imports of the meat goods from third countries. The Party contemplating the action shall notify the other Party and provide an opportunity to consult prior to taking action pursuant to this paragraph.

Article 705: Market Access for Grain and Grain Products

1. Commencing at such time as the level of government support for any of the grains wheat, oats, or barley in the United States of America becomes equal to or less than the level of government support for that grain in Canada, Canada shall eliminate any import permit requirements for wheat and wheat products, oats and oat products, or barley and barley products, as the case may be, originating in the territory of the United States of America, except that Canada may require that the grain be:

a) accompanied by an end-use certificate which has been completed by the importer of record declaring that it is imported for consumption in Canada and is consigned directly to a milling, manufacturing, brewing, distilling or other processing facility for consumption at that facility;

b) denatured if for feed use; or

c) accompanied by a certificate issued by Agriculture Canada, or its successors, if for seed use.

2. The Canadian Grain Commission, or its successors, shall be responsible for monitoring compliance with subparagraphs 1(a) and

(b) and shall freely provide the end-use certificate required in subparagraph 1(a).

3.   For purposes of paragraph 1, wheat, oat and barley products shall be defined as processed or manufactured substances which contain alone or in combination more than 25 percent by weight of such grain or grains.   Any grain for which import permit requirements have been eliminated in accordance with paragraph 1 shall be excluded from this definition.

4.   The method for calculating the level of government support referred to in paragraph 1 is set out in Annex 705.4.

5.   Each Party shall, for purposes of restricting the importation of a grain or of a grain product due to its content of that grain, retain the right, to the extent consistent with other provisions of this Agreement, to introduce or, where they have been eliminated, reintroduce quantitative import restrictions or import fees on imports of such grain or grain products originating in the territory of the other Party if such imports increase significantly as a result of a substantial change in either Party's support programs for that grain. For purposes of this paragraph, grain means wheat, oats, barley, rye, corn, triticale and sorghum.

Article 706: Market Access for Poultry and Eggs

If Canada maintains or introduces quantitative import restrictions on any of the following goods, Canada shall permit the importation of such goods as follows:

a) the level of global import quota on chicken and chicken products, as defined in Annex 706, for any given year shall be no less than 7.5 percent of the previous year's domestic production of chicken in Canada;

b) the level of global import quota on turkey and turkey products, as defined in Annex 706, for any given year shall be no less than 3.5 percent of that year's Canadian domestic turkey production quota; and

c) the level of global import quotas on eggs and egg products for any given year shall be no less than the following percentages of the previous year's Canadian domestic shell egg production:

    i)   1.647 percent for shell eggs;

    ii) 0.714 percent for frozen, liquid and further processed eggs; and

    iii) 0.627 percent for powdered eggs.

Article 707: Market Access for Sugar-Containing Products

The United States of America shall not introduce or maintain any quantitative import restriction or import fee on any good originating in Canada containing ten percent or less sugar by dry weight for purposes of restricting the sugar content of such good.

Article 708: Technical Regulations and Standards for Agricultural, Food, Beverage and Certain Related Goods

1.   Consistent with the legitimate need for technical regulations and standards to protect human, animal and plant life and to facilitate commerce between the Parties, the Parties shall seek an open border policy with respect to trade in agricultural, food, beverage and certain related goods and shall be guided in the regulation of such goods and in the implementation of this Article and the Schedules contained in Annex 708.1 by the following principles:

    a) to harmonize their respective technical regulatory requirements and inspection procedures, taking into account appropriate international standards, or, where harmonization is not feasible, to make equivalent their respective technical regulatory requirements and inspection procedures;

    b) to apply any import or quarantine restriction on the basis of regional rather than national distribution of diseases or pests in the territory of the exporting Party, where such diseases or pests are distributed regionally rather than nationally;

    c) to establish equivalent accreditation procedures for inspection systems and inspectors;

    d) to establish reciprocal training programs and, where appropriate, to utilize each other's personnel for testing and inspection of agricultural, food, beverage and certain related goods; and

e) to establish, where possible, common data and information requirements for submissions relating to the approval of new goods and processes.

2.   The Parties shall, with respect to agricultural, food, beverage and certain related goods:

a) work toward the elimination of technical regulations and standards that constitute, and prevent the introduction of technical regulations and government standards that would constitute, an arbitrary, unjustifiable or disguised restriction on bilateral trade;

b) exchange information, subject to considerations of confidentiality, related to technical regulations, standards and testing; and

c) notify and consult with each other during the development or prior to the implementation or change in the application of any technical regulation or government standard that may affect trade in such goods.

3.   Where, for agricultural, food, beverage and certain related goods other than animals:

a) the Parties have harmonized or accepted the equivalence of each other's inspection systems, certification procedures or testing requirements, and

b) the exporting Party has, pursuant to such systems, procedures or requirements, determined or certified, as the case may be, that such goods meet the standards or technical regulations of the importing Party,

the importing Party may examine such goods imported from the territory of the exporting Party only to ensure that (b) has occurred. This provision shall not preclude spot checks or similar verifying measures necessary to ensure compliance with the importing Party's standards or technical regulations provided that such spot checks or similar verifying measures, including any conducted at the border, are conducted no more frequently than those conducted by the importing Party under similar circumstances with respect to its goods.

4. To further the implementation of this Article and the Schedules contained in Annex 708.1:

a) the Parties shall establish the following working groups, each with equal representation from each Party:

i) Animal Health,
ii) Plant Health, Seeds and Fertilizers,
iii) Meat and Poultry Inspection,
iv) Dairy, Fruit, Vegetable and Egg Inspection,
v) Veterinary Drugs and Feeds,
vi) Food, Beverage and Colour Additives and Unavoidable Contaminants,
vii) Pesticides, and
viii) Packaging and Labelling of Agricultural, Food, Beverage and Certain Related Goods for Human Consumption;

b) these working groups shall:

i) meet at the request of either Party, but in any event not less than once a year unless the Parties otherwise agree, to further the implementation of this Article and the Schedules contained in Annex 708.1 or to address other issues as they arise, and

ii) inform the joint monitoring committee of their work; and

c) the Parties shall establish a joint monitoring committee, with equal representation from each Party, which shall meet at least annually and which shall:

i) monitor the progress of the working groups to ensure the timely implementation of this Article and the Schedules contained in Annex 708.1, and

ii) report the progress of the working groups to the Minister of Agriculture for Canada and the Secretary of Agriculture for the United States of America and such other Ministers or Cabinet-level officers as may be appropriate and to the

Commission referred to in Chapter Eighteen (Institutional Provisions).

Article 709: Consultations

The Parties shall consult on agricultural issues semi-annually and at such other times as they may agree.

Article 710: International Obligations

Unless otherwise specifically provided in this Chapter, the Parties retain their rights and obligations with respect to agricultural, food, beverage and certain related goods under the *General Agreement on Tariffs and Trade* (GATT) and agreements negotiated under the GATT, including their rights and obligations under GATT Article XI.

Article 711: Definitions

For purposes of this Chapter:

agricultural goods means all goods classified within chapters 1, 2, 4, 6, 7, 8, 9, 10, 11, 12, 13, 14, 15, 17, 18, 19, 20, 21 and 24 of the Harmonized System and all goods classified within the following specific tariff headings of the Harmonized System:
05.02 to 05.11.10 inclusive
05.11.99
16.01
16.02
16.03 (extracts and juices of meats only)
22.01
22.02
22.09
23.01.10
23.02 to 23.09 inclusive
33.01
33.02
35.01 to 35.05 inclusive
40.01
41.01 to 41.03 inclusive
43.01
51.01 to 51.05 inclusive
52.01 to 52.03 inclusive

53.01 to 53.05 inclusive;

agricultural, food, beverage and certain related goods means
all agricultural goods, all goods classified within chapter 3 of the
Harmonized System, and all goods classified within the following
specific tariff headings of the Harmonized System:

16.03 (other than extracts and juices of meat)
16.04 to 16.05 inclusive
22.03 to 22.08 inclusive
23.01.20
29.36
29.37
29.40 to 29.42 inclusive
30.01 to 30.04 inclusive
31.01 to 31.05 inclusive
32.03
32.04 (food, drug or cosmetic dyes and preparations only)
38.08
39.17.10
44.01 to 44.18 inclusive;

animal means any living being other than a human or a plant;

equivalent means having the same effect;

export subsidy means a subsidy that is conditional upon the
exportation of agricultural goods. An illustrative list of such export
subsidies is found in paragraphs (a) to (1) of the Annex to the
*Agreement on Interpretation and Application of Articles VI, XVI and
XXIII of the General Agreement on Tariffs and Trade;*

harmonization means making identical;

import fee means a fee on imports, including a fee applied pursuant
to Section 22 of the United States *Agricultural Adjustment Act* of
1933, as amended, but excluding a customs duty as defined in Chapter
Four (Border Measures);

import price means the value for imports into a Party determined
for customs purposes by the customs authorities in that Party, except
that, in the case of imports sold on a consignment basis, a Party may

use the price reported for such sales adjusted to the same pricing basis as the value determined for customs purposes;

meat goods means meat of cattle (including veal), goats, and sheep (except lambs), whether fresh, chilled or frozen;

standard means a technical specification approved by a recognized standardizing body for repeated or continuous application, with which compliance is not mandatory;

sugar means sugar derived from sugar cane or sugar beets;

technical regulation means a technical specification, including the applicable administrative provisions, with which compliance is mandatory; and

technical specification means a specification contained in a document that lays down characteristics of a good such as levels of quality, performance, safety or dimensions. It may include, or deal exclusively with, terminology, symbols, testing and test methods, packaging, marking or labelling requirements as they apply to a good.

Annex 705.4

Levels of Government Support for Wheat, Oats and Barley

I. Formula and Rules for Computation

1.   This Annex shall apply to each of the grains wheat, oats and barley until such time as import permit requirements have been eliminated for that grain pursuant to Article 705.

2.   This Annex shall apply only to the calculation referred to in Article 705 and shall not be construed as a statement by either Party of the support it provides for any other purpose.

3.   For purposes of paragraph 1 of Article 705, where the level of government support in a Party for wheat, oats or barley is compared to the level of government support in the other Party for that grain, the level of government support in a Party shall be the average of the percentages, computed in accordance with paragraph 4, for the two most recent crop years for which data are available.

4.   Government support for wheat, oats or barley for a crop year shall be determined in accordance with the following formula, expressed as a percentage:

$$\text{Government Support} = \frac{\text{Total Government Support}}{\text{Adjusted Producer Value}}$$

where:

Adjusted Producer Value means the value of production for wheat, oats or barley for that crop year plus direct government payments for that crop year;

Direct Government Payments means payments that are directly made to producers of wheat, oats or barley and that are associated with the production of that grain for that crop year, excluding any such payment to reduce the costs of production;

Total Government Support means all government programs or other means of government support directed towards affecting the income of producers of wheat, oats or barley from that grain for that crop year.

5.   For purposes of Article 705, Schedules 1 and 2 set forth all government programs and other means of providing support for wheat, oats or barley as of October 4, 1987 and the method for computing the levels of government support as of that date.

6.   The computation referred to in paragraph 5 may be adjusted to reflect modifications to government programs or means of support, new programs or means of support, and the availability of new types of data.

7.   a) Where government support is measured on the basis of a calendar year and cannot be attributed to a crop year, it shall be attributed to the crop year beginning in that calendar year.

  b) Where government support is measured on the basis of a fiscal year and cannot be attributed to a crop year, it shall be attributed:

   i) for Canada, to the crop year beginning in that fiscal year;

   ii) for the United States of America, to the crop year ending in that fiscal year.

  c) All government expenditures shall exclude user contributions.

8.   For purposes of this Annex, government data published or otherwise made officially available shall be used, unless clearly inappropriate.

9.   All computations shall be done on the basis of the currency of the Party providing support.

II. Institutional Procedures

10.   The Parties shall establish a Working Group with three representatives from each Party.

11.   The Working Group shall:

   a) exchange information related to government programs for wheat, oats or barley; and

   b) discuss the computation of the level of government support in each Party for wheat, oats or barley.

12.   Each Party shall, by January 1 of each year unless the Parties otherwise agree, forward to the other Party all available relevant data for the computation of the forwarding Party's level of support for wheat, oats and barley for the two most recent crop years for which data are available. Each Party shall forward to the other Party all other relevant data when available.

13.   Each Party shall, by April 1 of each year unless the Parties otherwise agree, determine its level of support for wheat, oats and barley pursuant to paragraph 3 and immediately forward such determination and supporting computations to the other Party.

14.   The Parties shall, upon request of either Party, consult regarding such determination.

15.   Each Party shall notify the other Party of its acceptance or rejection of the other Party's determination within 30 days of receipt of such determination.

16.   If a Party does not accept the other Party's determination, either Party may refer the matter to an arbitration panel pursuant to Article 1806.

17.   The panel shall be established upon the date of such referral and shall establish its own rules and procedure.

18.   The panel shall be appointed pursuant to paragraph 3 of Article 1807.

19.   The panel shall issue its written decision within 30 days of the date the chairman is appointed. The Parties mutually agree that such decision shall be binding.

Schedule 1

United States Government Support Programs

A. Direct Payments

1. Payments of the Commodity Credit Corporation (CCC)

Support from payments made by CCC to wheat, oats, and barley producers pursuant to the *Agricultural Act of 1949,* as amended, consists of any deficiency, disaster and paid land diversion payments for that crop. Support is computed as the total amount of payments for wheat, oats or barley for that crop year made in cash, commodities and the total face value of any payments made in certificates.

2. CCC Storage Payments: Farmer-Owned Reserve Program and Special Producer Loan Storage Program

Under the Farmer-Owned Reserve (FOR) Program and Special Producer Loan Storage Program, CCC provides support by paying producers for storing their own commodities. Support from these programs for a crop year is the total amount of payments, computed for each month in the crop year in accordance with the following formula:

$$[\tfrac{1}{12} \times A \times B] + [\tfrac{1}{12} \times C \times D]$$

where:

A =   the annual storage payment rate for wheat, oats or barley in the Farmer-Owned Reserve Program

B =   the amount of wheat, oats or barley in the Farmer-Owned Reserve Program for that month

C =   the annual storage payment rate for wheat, oats or barley in the Special Producer Loan Storage Program

D =   the amount of wheat, oats or barley in the Special Producer Loan Storage Program for that month.

3.   Conservation Reserve Program

The support provided for a crop year by the Conservation Reserve Program (CRP) is one-half of the total annual rental payments made pursuant to the CRP by CCC for acreage taken out of production for wheat, oats or barley.

4.   Acreage Reduction Program

The support provided to producers of wheat, oats or barley is adjusted to take account of income foregone from reduced production as a result of the acreage reduction program. The support is reduced by the income foregone for a crop year, computed in accordance with the following formula:

$$(0.9 \times A \times B \times C) - (0.9 \times A) \times (D - E)$$

where:

A =   acreage idled under the acreage reduction program
B =   yield per acre on idled acreage in bushels

where:

$$B = \frac{[(G + 0.85 \times A) \times (H - \frac{0.85 \times A \times J}{I})] - F}{0.85 \times A}.$$

and

F =   total quantity produced in bushels
G =   total acreage harvested
H =   United States average yield per harvested acre in bushels per acre
I =   10 million for wheat and 1 million for barley or oats
J =   1.1 for wheat, 1 for barley, and 1.2 for oats
C =   export price in dollars per bushel

where:

$$C = K - \frac{L}{M}$$

and

    K =   season average farm price in dollars per bushel
    L =   total value of Export Enhancement Program bonuses for wheat and wheat products, oats and oat products, or barley and barley products in dollars
    M =   total quantity of wheat, oats or barley exported as grain and the grain equivalent of wheat, oat or barley products exported in bushels

or
if L = 0, then C = K

    D =   national average variable cash expenses per acre as reported by the Economic Research Service in dollars
    E =   expenses incurred to maintain conserving uses, deemed to be \$15 per acre for wheat and \$20 per acre for barley and oats.

Support shall only be adjusted when the income foregone, computed in accordance with this formula, exceeds zero.

5.   Certificate Premiums and Discounts

CCC generic certificates provide support in addition to the face value of the certificates to the extent that producers obtain a premium for the certificates in the market above their face value. In the same manner, support provided by certificates would be reduced to the extent that certificate values are discounted in the market. The support for a crop year is computed in accordance with the following formula:

$$A \times (B - C)$$

where:

    A =   the weighted average premium or discount for the crop year
    B =   the total face value of generic certificates issued to wheat, oats or barley producers for the programs specified in paragraph A.1 for that crop year
    C =   the total face value of generic certificates returned to CCC by producers for cash.

For purposes of paragraph 5, the average monthly premium or discount shall be derived from the most representative survey available of premiums or discounts realized in the market and shall be weighted by the monthly value of total certificates exchanged for CCC commodities.

B. Other Support

6. CCC Loan Forfeiture Benefits

The forfeiture to CCC on a non-recourse basis of wheat, oats or barley, pledged as collateral for a commodity loan, provides support to the extent that the price paid by CCC for the grain exceeds the market price of that grain. Support for a crop year is computed by multiplying the quantity of grain forfeited by the difference between the season average farm price for the grain and the unit value of CCC collateral acquisitions of that grain.

7. Price Enhancing Aspects of Government Programs

Government acreage control programs, inventory actions, import tariffs on wheat, oats or barley, and export programs provide support to the extent that they enhance prices received by producers in the domestic market above the prices received on the world market. The price enhancing effect is measured by the difference between the season average farm price for the grain and the world price for that grain. The support for a crop year for wheat, oats or barley is computed in accordance with the following formula:

$$\frac{A}{B} \times C$$

where:

A = total value of Export Enhancement Program (EEP) bonuses for wheat, oats or barley
B = volume of exports for wheat, oats or barley
C = volume of production for wheat, oats or barley.

For purposes of paragraph 7, EEP bonus means the face value of commodity certificates issued by CCC for export sales of wheat, oats or barley.

8.   Advance Payments

Advance payments provide support to the extent that the government pays the interest costs on funds advanced. The total support provided for a crop year by advance payments made by CCC for wheat, oats or barley is computed for each month in accordance with the following formula:

$$A \times \frac{B}{12} \times C$$

where:

A =   advance payments made by CCC for wheat, oats or barley in a month

B =   the CCC interest rate at the time the advance payments are made

C =   the number of months that the payments precede the crop year for which they are made.

9.   Crop Insurance Programs

The support provided through crop insurance programs is the difference between crop insurance payments made to producers under Federal Crop Insurance Programs for wheat, oats or barley for a crop year and premiums paid by producers in respect thereof. The amount of support may be a positive or negative number.

10.   Government Service Programs For Agriculture

Government service programs consist of the Federal Grain Inspection Service (FGIS) weighing and inspection programs; Agricultural Research Service (ARS); Cooperative State Extension Service programs (CSES); irrigation programs under the Bureau of Reclamation (BR); Corps of Engineers (CE) inland waterway programs; conservation programs of the Soil Conservation Service (SCS) and the Agricultural Stabilization and Conservation Service (ASCS); the freight-related program expenditures and the freight-related low-interest loan program of the Federal Railway Administration (FRA); the cooperator programs of the Foreign Agricultural Service (FAS); the market news service, seed plant protection, and product standards and grading programs of the Agricultural Marketing Service (AMS); the plant disease and pest control programs of the Animal and Plant Health Inspection Service (APHIS); and projects for the promotion of wheat, oats or barley under the Targeted Export Assistance Program. Support provided for a crop year for wheat, oats or barley by these programs is determined as follows:

i) net expenditures in a fiscal year for the weighing and inspection programs of the Federal Grain Inspection Service, computed for wheat, oats or barley in accordance with the following formula:

$$A \times \frac{B}{C}$$

where:

A = net expenditures by the Federal Grain Inspection Service for weighing and inspection programs
B = value of production of wheats, oats or barley
C = total value of production of all grains and oilseeds;

ii) net expenditures in a fiscal year by the Agricultural Research Service and the Cooperative State Extension Service, computed in accordance with the following formula:

$$A \times \frac{B}{C}$$

where:

A = net expenditures for ARS & CSES
B = value of production of wheat, oats or barley
C = total value of agricultural production;

iii) net expenditures in a fiscal year by the Bureau of Reclamation for irrigation programs, computed in accordance with the following formula:

$$A \times \frac{B}{C}$$

where:

A = net expenditures by the Bureau of Reclamation for irrigation programs

B = value of production of wheat, oats or barley using the irrigation programs

C = value of production of all crops using the irrigation programs;

iv) net expenditures in a fiscal year by the Corps of Engineers for the operation, maintenance and construction of inland waterways, computed in accordance with the following formula:

$$A \times \frac{B}{C}$$

where:

A = net expenditures for the operation, maintenance and construction of inland waterways

B = ton-miles travelled on inland waterways by wheat, oats or barley

C = total ton-miles travelled by all commodities on inland waterways;

v) net expenditures in a fiscal year for conservation programs under the Soil Conservation Service and the Agricultural Stabilization and Conservation Service, computed for wheat, oats or barley in accordance with the following formula:

$$A \times \frac{B}{C}$$

where:

A= net expenditures by the Agricultural Stabilization and Conservation Service and the Soil Conservation Service for conservation programs

B = value of production of wheat, oats or barley

C = total value of agricultural production;

vi) expenditures in a fiscal year by the Federal Railway Administration for freight-related programs, computed in accordance with the following formula:

$$A \times \frac{B}{C}$$

where:

A= expenditures by the Federal Railway Administration for freight-related programs
B = ton-miles travelled by wheat, oats or barley on railways
C = the ton-miles travelled by all commodities on railways;

vii) support provided in a fiscal year for wheat, oats or barley by the Federal Railway Administration through low-interest loans for rail freight, computed in accordance with the following formula:

$$(A - B) \times \frac{C}{D}$$

where:

A = the commercial lending rate
B= the interest rate charged by the Federal Railway Administration on loans for rail freight
C = ton-miles travelled by wheat, oats or barley on railways
D= ton-miles travelled by all commodities on railways;

viii) net expenditures in a fiscal year by the Foreign Agricultural Service (FAS), computed in accordance with the following formula:

$$A \times \frac{B}{C}$$

where:

A = net expenditures for cooperator programs of FAS
B = value of production of wheat, oats or barley
C = total value of agricultural production;

ix) net expenditures in a fiscal year for the Agricultural Marketing Service computed in accordance with the following formula:

$$(A \times \frac{B}{C}) + (D + E) \times \frac{B}{F}$$

where:

A =   net expenditures for market news service
B =   value of production for wheat, oats or barley
C =   total value of agricultural production
D =   net expenditures for seed plant protection
E =   net expenditure for product standard and grading programs
F =   total value of crop production;

x) net expenditures in a fiscal year for plant disease and pest control programs of the Animal and Plant Health Inspection Service (APHIS), computed for wheat, oats or barley in accordance with the following formula:

$$A \times \frac{B}{C}$$

where:

A =   net expenditures for the plant disease and pest control programs of the Animal and Plant Health Inspection Service
B =   value of production of wheat, oats or barley
C =   total value of agricultural production; and

xi) net expenditures in a fiscal year under the Targeted Export Assistance Program for projects promoting wheat, oats or barley.

11. CCC Commodity Loans

The support provided by CCC commodity loans, including regular loans, Farmer-Owned Reserve loans, and Special Producer Loan Storage Program loans, is the difference between the commercial rate of interest and the rate of interest paid by a producer. Support for a crop year is the total of the amounts computed in accordance with the following formula, for each loan:

i) for regular commodity loans, loans under the Special Producer Loan Storage Program and Farmer-Owned Reserve loans not exceeding 1 year:

$$(A - B) \times (C \times D)$$

where:

A = the rate of interest reported by agricultural banks for non-real estate loans
B = the interest rate charged by CCC
C = the value of the loan
D = the proportion of the year the loan is in effect;

ii) for Farmer-Owned Reserve loans exceeding 1 year:

$$A \times B \times C$$

where:

A = the rate of interest reported by agricultural banks for non-real estate loans
B = the value of the loan
C = the proportion of that crop year the loan is in effect; and

iii) the amount of interest forgiven by CCC in a crop year on CCC commodity loans for wheat, oats or barley, computed in accordance with the following formula:

$$A \times B \times C$$

where for each loan:

A = the CCC interest rate for the loan
B = value of the loan for which interest has been forgiven
C = the proportion of the crop year the loan was in effect.

12. State Budget Outlays

The support provided by state governments for a crop year is the agricultural expenditures by such governments for support programs for wheat, oats or barley, computed in accordance with the following formula:

$$(A - B) \times \frac{C}{D}$$

where:

A= agricultural expenditures by state governments as compiled by the United States Bureau of the Census

B= transfers, if any, by the federal government for those expenditures

C = the value of production for wheat, oats or barley

D = the total value of agricultural production.

13. Farm Credit Programs

The support provided for a crop year by farm credit programs shall be included in the computation of the level of support. The Parties shall develop a mutually agreed methodology for computing such support by January 31, 1989.

C. Adjustments

The computation of the level of United States government support in this Annex shall reflect spending reductions resulting from a sequestration order pursuant to the *Balanced Budget and Emergency Deficit Control Act of 1985* or any other budget reduction provision.

Schedule 2

Canadian Government Support Programs

A. Direct Payments

1.   Payments made pursuant to the *Agricultural Stabilization Act*

The support provided by the federal government pursuant to the *Agricultural Stabilization Act* is the total amount of payments to producers of wheat, oats or barley for that crop year.

2.   Payments made pursuant to the *Western Grain Stabilization Act*

The support provided by the federal government is its share of the cost of financing the Western Grain Stabilization Program. The support is computed in accordance with the following formula:

$$[\frac{A}{A+B} \times C + \frac{B}{A+B} \times D] \times \frac{E}{F}$$

where:

A =   the total amount of levy contributions made by the federal government to the Western Grain Stabilization Account in the five crop years ending in the crop year for which the computation is being made for all grains and oilseeds eligible for support under the *Act*

B =   the total amount of levies paid by producers in the Western Grain Stabilization Account in the five crop years ending in the crop year for which the computation is being made for all grains and oilseeds eligible for support under the *Act*.

C =   the total amount of stabilization payments made pursuant to the *Act* , for all grains and oilseeds eligible for support under the *Act,* for the crop year for which the computation is being made

D =   any government funds, other than levies, to make up any Western Grain Stabilization Account deficit incurred in that crop year

E = the value of marketings in that crop year of wheat, oats or barley eligible for support under the *Act*

F = total value of marketings in that crop year of all grains and oilseeds eligible for support under the *Act*.

3. Payments pursuant to the Special Canadian Grains Program

The support provided by the federal government to producers of wheat, oats or barley through the Special Canadian Grains Program is the total amount paid to producers of such grain for the crop year.

4. Stabilization payments made by provincial governments

The support provided by provincial governments as stabilization payments is computed by subtracting producer levies from the total amount of payments made to producers of wheat, oats or barley for the crop year.

5. Income Foregone Adjustment

The support provided to producers of wheat, oats or barley is adjusted to take account of income foregone from reduced production, as a result of restrictive Canadian Wheat Board delivery quotas. The support is reduced by the income foregone for a crop year, computed in accordance with the following formula:

$$[(A - B - C) \times D - E + F] \times (G - 13) \times \frac{H}{I}$$

where:

$$E = \frac{J - K - (G \times F)}{I}$$

and where:

A = the Canadian Wheat Board final realized price, in store Thunder Bay, for No.1 CWRS wheat, No.1 Feed oats or No. 1 Feed barley in dollars per tonne

B = the average freight rate for wheat, oats and barley paid by producers in Western Canada in dollars per tonne

C = the average elevation and handling tariffs in Western Canada for wheat, oats or barley in dollars per tonne

D = the average yields in Western Canada for wheat, oats or barley in tonnes per acre

E = variable cash expenses for wheat, oats or barley in dollars per acre

F = variable cash expenses of summerfallow, deemed to be $15 per acre

G = the summerfallow area in millions of acres

H= the areas planted to wheat, oats or barley in Western Canada in millions of acres

I = the total planted area in Western Canada of crops eligible for coverage under the *Western Grain Stabilization Act* in millions of acres

J = the gross grain expenses used to calculate payments pursuant to the *Western Grain Stabilization Act,* in millions of dollars

K= the non-variable cash expenses included in J (taxes, tools, building maintenance, utilities, insurance, interest and miscellaneous) in millions of dollars.

Support shall only be adjusted when the income foregone, computed in accordance with this formula, exceeds zero.

B. Other Support

6.   Expenditures of the Canadian Grain Commission

The Canadian Grain Commission (Commission) provides grading and inspection services for grains and oilseeds. The support provided by the Commission is the net expenditures in a fiscal year by the Commission for wheat, oats or barley, computed in accordance with the following formula:

$$(A - B) \times \frac{C}{D}$$

where:

A= total expenditures by the Canadian Grain Commission for all grains and oilseeds

B= user fees paid for services performed by the Canadian Grain Commission for all grains and oilseeds

C = farm cash receipts for wheat, oats or barley

D = farm cash receipts for all grains and oilseeds.

7.   Wheat Board Pool Deficit

The federal government provides support to the extent that initial payments made by the Canadian Wheat Board (CWB) to producers for wheat, oats or barley exceed net returns realized by the CWB in the market. This support is computed as follows:

i) **for wheat:**

1) where, at the end of the crop year, farm stocks of wheat in Western Canada exceed 1,128,000 tonnes, support is the amount paid to the Canadian Wheat Board for that crop year by the federal government pursuant to the *Canadian Wheat Board Act* to offset any deficit in pool accounts for wheat; or

2) where at the end of the crop year, farm stocks of wheat in Western Canada do not exceed 1,128,000 tonnes, the support provided by the federal goverment for wheat for that crop year is computed in accordance with the following formula:

$$\frac{A}{B} \times (C - D + E)$$

where:

A = Canadian Wheat Board pool deficits for wheat for that crop year
B = volume of wheat delivered to the Canadian Wheat Board by eligible producers in that crop year
C = production of wheat in Western Canada in that crop year
D = farm stocks of wheat in Western Canada at the end of that crop year
E = farm stocks of wheat in Western Canada at the end of the previous crop year;

ii) **for oats or barley**: the amount paid to the Canadian Wheat Board for the crop year by the federal government pursuant to the *Canadian Wheat Board Act* to offset any deficit in pool accounts for oats or barley.

8.   Domestic Wheat Pricing

Support is provided by the Domestic Wheat Pricing Policy to the extent that the domestic price for wheat exceeds the world market price. The support provided to producers of wheat by the Domestic Wheat Pricing Policy is computed in accordance with the following formula:

(A - B) x C

where:

A = the average domestic selling price for wheat milled in Canada for domestic human consumption
B = the average export price for wheat
C = the volume of wheat milled in Canada for domestic human consumption.

For purposes of this paragraph,

i) the average domestic selling price for wheat milled in Canada for domestic human consumption is computed in accordance with the following formula:

D - (0.5 x (E + F))

where:

D = the average domestic selling price for a crop year for No. 1 Canada Western Red Spring (CWRS) wheat of 13.5% protein
E = the difference between the Canadian Wheat Board final realized prices for that crop year for No. 1 CWRS wheat of 13.5% protein and No. 1 CWRS wheat
F = the aggregate of E and the difference between the Canadian Wheat Board final realized prices for that crop year for No. 1 CWRS wheat and No. 2 CWRS wheat;

For purposes of this subparagraph, all prices are basis in-store Thunder Bay;

ii) the value of domestic sales is computed by multiplying the average domestic selling price for wheat milled in Canada for domestic human consumption by the volume of sales from the pool account for wheat;

iii) the value of export sales is computed by subtracting the value of sales for domestic human consumption from the value of total sales from the pool account for wheat; and

iv) the average export price is computed by dividing the total value of export sales for wheat by the total volume of export sales from the pool account for wheat.

9.   Domestic Price Gap: Oats or Barley

Support is provided to producers of oats or barley to the extent that the domestic price for oats or barley exceeds the world market price for that grain. The support is computed in accordance with the following formula:

$$[D - (A - B - C)] \times E$$

where:

$A =$ the Canadian Wheat Board final realized prices for No. 1 Feed oats or No. 1 Feed barley, in store Thunder Bay

$B =$ the average elevation and handling tariffs in Western Canada for oats or barley

$C =$ the average freight rate paid by producers in Western Canada for oats or barley

$D =$ the off-Board prices of oats or barley in the Prairies derived from *Western Grain Stabilization Act* data and published by the Canadian Grain Commission

$E =$ the consumption in Western Canada of oats or barley for feed.

The amount computed in accordance with the formula is included in the computation of support only when it exceeds zero.

10.   Advance Payments

Advance payments provide support to producers of wheat, oats or barley to the extent that the federal government pays interest costs on funds advanced to producers pursuant to the *Prairie Grain Advance*

Payments Act. The support is computed in accordance with the following formula:

$$\frac{A}{B} \times C$$

where:

A =   value of advances made in the fiscal year for wheat, oats or barley

B =   value of advances made in the fiscal year for all eligible crops

C =   interest cost of the funds advanced in the fiscal year to producers for all eligible crops.

11. Crop Insurance

The amount of support provided through crop insurance is the difference between crop insurance payments made to producers for wheat, oats or barley for a crop year and crop insurance premiums paid by producers in respect thereof, computed as follows:

i) in the case of provinces other than Ontario, the total amount of crop insurance payments made for wheat, oats or barley less crop insurance premiums paid by producers in respect thereof;

ii) in the case of Ontario

1) for winter wheat, the total crop insurance payments for winter wheat less crop insurance premiums paid by producers for that crop.

For purposes of this subparagraph, any crop insurance payments made for winter wheat are to be attributed to the crop year in which the crop was harvested;

2) for spring wheat, oats or barley, the crop insurance payment for such grain, determined in accordance with the following formula:

$$(A - B) \times \frac{C}{D}$$

where:

A =   total crop insurance payments for spring wheat, oats, barley, spring rye and mixed grains

B=   total crop insurance premiums paid by producers for spring wheat, oats, barley, spring rye and mixed grains

C =   total area in Ontario planted to spring wheat, oats or barley

D =   total area in Ontario planted to spring wheat, oats, barley, spring rye and mixed grains.

The amount of support provided through crop insurance may be a positive or negative number.

12.   Western Grain Transportation Act

The federal government through the *Western Grain Transportation Act* provides support for the rail transportation of wheat, oats or barley produced in Western Canada by sharing the cost of transportation of such grain. The support provided pursuant to the *Act* to wheat, oats or barley producers is computed as follows:

where, at the end of the crop year,

i) farm stocks in Western Canada exceed 1,128,000 tonnes for wheat, 950,000 tonnes for barley or 500,000 tonnes for oats, the government support provided under the *Act* for wheat, oats or barley is computed by multiplying the shipments in a crop year of wheat, oats or barley which are eligible for statutory rates under the *Act* by the government share of the average cost per tonne of moving wheat, oats or barley for that crop year, as determined by the Canadian Transportation Commission or its successors prior to the start of that crop year pursuant to Part II of the *Act*; or

ii) farm stocks in Western Canada do not exceed 1,128,000 tonnes for wheat, 950,000 tonnes for barley or 500,000 tonnes for oats, government support provided for that crop year under the *Act* for wheat, oats or barley is computed in accordance with the following formula:

$$A \times (B - C + D)$$

where:

A =   the government share of the average cost per tonne of
        moving wheat, oats or barley, for that crop year, as
        determined by the Canadian Transportation Commission
        or its successor, prior to the start of that crop year
        pursuant to Part II of the *Act*

B =   production of wheat, oats or barley in Western Canada in
        that crop year

C =   farm stocks of wheat, oats or barley in Western Canada at
        the end of that crop year

D =   farm stocks of wheat, oats or barley in Western Canada at
        the end of the previous crop year.

13. Prairie Branch Line Rehabilitation Program

The federal government provides support through the Prairie
Branch Line Rehabilitation Program by paying for the rehabilitation
of rail lines and for the purchase of rail cars in Western Canada. The
support provided in a fiscal year for wheat, oats or barley is computed
in accordance with the following formula:

$$\frac{A}{B} \times [(C \times \frac{B}{D}) + E + F]$$

where:

A =   total annual shipments of wheat, oats or barley on the
        rehabilitated branch lines

B =   total annual shipments of all grains and oilseeds on the
        rehabilitated branch lines

C =   expenditures made under the Prairie Branch Line
        Rehabilitation Program during the fiscal year

D =   total annual tonnage shipped over the rehabilitated branch
        lines

E =   expenditures during the fiscal year by the federal
        government for the purchase or lease of hopper cars
        intended for the transport of grains and oilseeds

F =   expenditures during the fiscal year by the federal
        government for the rehabilitation of boxcars intended for
        the transport of grains and oilseeds.

14.   Research Expenditures

The support provided by the federal government for research for wheat, oats or barley is the research expenditure made in a fiscal year for that grain, or where otherwise not ascertainable, the amount computed in accordance with the following formula:

$$\frac{\underline{A} \times C}{B}$$

where:

A =   farm cash receipts for wheat, oats or barley
B =   total farm cash receipts
C =   the aggregate of expenditures of the Research Branch of Agriculture Canada, the New Crop Development Program, the agriculture share of the Industrial Research Program and federal contributions to the Biotechnology Institute.

15.   General Support Programs of the Federal Government

The *Prairie Farm Rehabilitation Act*, the *Agriculture and Rural Development Act* (ARDA), and the Economic and Rural Development Agreements (ERDA) provide general support to producers of wheat, oats or barley. The support is the expenditures by the federal government under the *Prairie Farm Rehabilitation Act* , ARDA and ERDA in a fiscal year for wheat, oats or barley, computed in accordance with the following formula:

$$\frac{A \times \underline{B}}{C}$$

where:

A =   the expenditure under the program
B =   farm cash receipts for wheat, oats or barley
C =   total farm cash receipts.

16. General Provincial Government Expenditures for Agriculture

The support provided for a crop year by each provincial department or ministry responsible for agriculture is the net expenditure for wheat, oats or barley or, where otherwise not ascertainable, the amount computed in accordance with the following formula:

$$(A \times 0.926) \times \frac{B}{C}$$

where:

A = expenditures for agricultural purposes by the provincial department or ministry responsible for agriculture in that province less all crop insurance and crop stabilization payments

B = farm cash receipts for wheat, oats or barley in that province

C = total farm cash receipts in that province.

For purposes of this paragraph, the ministry or department responsible for agriculture means:

1) in Newfoundland, the Department of Rural, Agricultural and Northern Development
2) in Prince Edward Island, the Department of Agriculture
3) in Nova Scotia, the Department of Agriculture and Marketing
4) in New Brunswick, the Department of Agriculture
5) in Ontario, the Ministry of Agriculture and Food
6) in Manitoba, the Department of Agriculture
7) in Saskatchewan, the Department of Agriculture
8) in Alberta, the Department of Agriculture
9) in British Columbia, the Ministry of Agriculture and Fisheries
10) in Quebec, the Ministry of Agriculture, Fisheries and Food.

17. Farm Credit Programs

Support provided for a crop year by farm credit programs shall be included in the computation of the level of support. The Parties shall develop a methodology for computing such support by January 31,1989

C. Definitions

For purposes of this Schedule:

grains and oilseeds means wheat, oats, barley, canola, flaxseed, rye, mustard seed, grain corn, soybeans, mixed grain, buckwheat, sunflower seed, peas and beans.

Western Canada means the provinces of Manitoba, Saskatchewan, Alberta, and British Columbia.

Eastern Canada means the provinces of Ontario, Quebec, New Brunswick, Nova Scotia, Prince Edward Island, Newfoundland.

farm cash receipts means receipts derived from the sale of products excluding direct government payments associated with such sales.

value of production means the level of production for wheat, oats or barley multiplied by the producer price for any such grain.

the producer price of wheat is computed as the price per tonne realized by the Canadian Wheat Board, basis in-store Thunder Bay, for No. 1 Canada Western Red Spring Wheat less the aggregate of:

a) the average per tonne elevation and handling tariffs paid by producers in Western Canada; and
b) the average per tonne transportation charges paid by producers in Western Canada.

the producer price of barley is computed as the price per tonne realized by the Canadian Wheat Board, basis in-store Thunder Bay, for No. 1 Feed barley less the aggregate of:

a) the average per tonne elevation and handling tariffs paid by producers in Western Canada; and
b) the average per tonne transportation charges paid by producers in Western Canada.

the producer price of oats is computed as the price per tonne realized by the Canadian Wheat Board, basis in-store Thunder Bay, for No. 1 Feed oats less the aggregate of:

a) the average per tonne elevation and handling tariffs paid by producers in Western Canada; and

b) the average per tonne transportation charges paid by producers in Western Canada.

Annex 706

Market Access for Poultry

1.   For purposes of Article 706:

   a) chicken and chicken products means chicken and chicken capons, live or eviscerated, chicken parts, whether breaded or battered, and chicken products manufactured wholly thereof, whether breaded or battered;

   b) turkey and turkey products means turkey, live or eviscerated, turkey parts, whether breaded or battered, and turkey products, manufactured wholly thereof, whether breaded or battered.

2.   Without limiting the generality of subparagraph 1(a), chicken and chicken products does not include chicken cordon bleu, breaded breast of chicken cordon bleu, chicken Kiev, breaded breast of chicken Kiev, boneless Rock Cornish with rice, stuffed Rock Cornish; boneless chicken with apples and almonds, chicken Romanoff Regell, chicken Neptune breast, boneless chicken Panache, chicken TV dinners, old roosters, and "spent fowl" commonly called "stewing hen".

3.   Without limiting the generality of subparagraph 1(b), turkey and turkey products does not include turkey cordon bleu, breaded breast of turkey cordon bleu, turkey Kiev, breaded breast of turkey Kiev, boneless turkey with apples and almonds, turkey Romanoff Regell, turkey Neptune breast, boneless turkey Panache, and turkey TV dinners.

Annex 708.1

Technical Regulations and Standards for Agricultural, Food, Beverage and Certain Related Goods

For purposes of the Schedules contained in this Annex:

feed means a product intended for consumption by animals, including a medicated feed, but not a product regulated by either Party as a veterinary drug;

fertilizer means any good supplying nutrients for plant growth; soil and plant amendments; agricultural liming and acidifying agents and mixtures of fertilizers and pesticides;

means of conveyance means any material, equipment, carrier, container, article or other thing that may contain or carry a plant pest;

pest, for purposes of Schedule 7 only, means any injurious, noxious or troublesome insect, fungus, bacterial organism, virus, weed, rodent or other plant or animal pest, and includes any injurious, noxious or troublesome organic function of a plant or animal;

pesticide, for purposes of Schedule 7 only, means any product, device, organism or substance manufactured, represented or sold to control or mitigate actions of any pest;

plant means any plant or part thereof, plant material and plant product;

plant pest means any form of plant or animal life or any pathogenic agent, injurious or potentially injurious to plants; and

veterinary drug means any substance applied or administered to an animal, whether for therapeutic, prophylactic, or diagnostic purposes, or for the modification of physiological functions or behavior, but excluding veterinary biologics such as vaccines, bacterins, antisera or toxoids and analogous products.

SCHEDULE 1: Feeds

1.   For purposes of this Schedule, technical regulations do not include grading requirements.

2.   The Parties shall, with respect to feeds:

   a) work toward the harmonization or equivalence of federal government requirements for:

   i) labelling, content guarantees, testing requirements, and exemptions from specified regulations, and

   ii) source, type, level, directions for use, withdrawal times, compatibility, cautions and warnings for additives and drugs that are allowed in feeds;

   b) work, through the National Association of State Departments of Agriculture and the Association of American Feed Control Officials, or any successor entities, toward the harmonization or equivalence of Canadian federal and United States federal and state requirements with respect to labelling, content guarantees, packaging, testing requirements, tonnage fees, registration and exemptions from specified regulations;

   c) adopt procedures to exchange, and grant reciprocal recognition of, feed mill inspection results;

   d) work toward the establishment of equivalent manufacturing practice regulations for medicated feeds;

   e) work toward the harmonization of procedures to validate feed assay methods for measuring drugs, additives and contaminants in feeds; and

   f) work toward the harmonization of tolerances and action levels of contaminants and drug residues in feeds.

SCHEDULE 2: Fertilizers

The Parties shall, with respect to fertilizers:

a) work toward equivalent federal government requirements for:

   i) labelling, content guarantees, testing requirements, and exemptions from specified regulations for soil and plant amendments, and

   ii) source, type, level, directions for use, withdrawal times, compatibility, cautions and warnings for pesticides that are allowed in fertilizers;

b) work, through the National Association of State Departments of Agriculture, the Association of American Plant Food Control Officials, or any successor entities, toward the harmonization or equivalence of Canadian federal and United States state requirements for registration, labelling, content guarantees, packaging, tonnage fees and exemptions from specified regulations;

c) work toward the adoption of procedures to harmonize sampling and analytical test methods (such as those adopted by the Association of Official Analytical Chemists) for determining the guarantees with respect to content and contaminants; and

d) work toward harmonizing tolerances and action levels.

SCHEDULE 3: Seeds

The Parties shall, with respect to seeds:

a) not maintain or introduce origin-staining requirements for alfalfa or clover seed originating in the territory of the other Party;

b) work, through the National Association of State Departments of Agriculture and the American Association of Seed Control Officials, or any successor entities, toward allowing seeds grown in the territory of Canada and imported into the United States of America to be governed by uniform regulatory requirements within the United States of America; and

c) maintain mutual recognition of variety certification standards and procedures, and seed testing methods and procedures, established by members of the Association of Seed Certifying Agencies and the Association of Official Seed Analysts or any successor entities.

SCHEDULE 4: Animal Health

1.   The Parties shall, with respect to animal health:

a) make equivalent and, where equivalent, accept the equivalence of, export certifications issued by private veterinarians accredited by the federal governments of either Party;

b) exchange test protocols and reagents to assist in the harmonization of test methods;

c) work toward equivalent technical regulations, testing and certification procedures for veterinary biologics;

d) work toward equivalent and, where possible, harmonized animal disease test methods and procedures for animal disease control, eradication and certification;

e) work toward procedures and conditions for the importation of animals, including embryos, without disease testing or with minimal testing and certification, when the territory of, or a region within, the exporting Party attains an agreed acceptable status for specified diseases;

f) work toward the development of procedures and conditions to reduce the embargo period following eradication of outbreaks of foot and mouth disease, rinderpest, or other diseases exotic to Canada and the United States of America;

g) work toward an agreement delineating the criteria for recognizing that a region is free from specified diseases;

h) maintain a current agenda of animal health issues and develop a specific timetable for their resolution; and

i) work toward eliminating state and provincial restrictions related to the importation of animals, including embryos, animal products and by-products.

2.   In accordance with procedures and conditions to be agreed, the United States of America shall not prohibit the importation of animals, including embryos, and animal products, from Canadian regions because of foot and mouth disease or rinderpest, when:

a) the Parties have negotiated an agreement in accordance with subparagraph 1(g) of this Schedule; and

b) Canada has certified that those regions are free of foot and mouth disease or rinderpest.

3.   In accordance with procedures and conditions to be agreed, Canada shall permit the direct importation, without quarantine, of:

a) in the case of bluetongue, United States breeding cattle based on a single test from states where an effective insect vector does not exist and from a group of states during a specified vector-free winter period; and

b) in the case of pseudorabies, live swine from the United States of America for immediate slaughter.

SCHEDULE 5: Veterinary Drugs

1.   The Parties recognize that:

   a) veterinary drugs should be safe for the target animal;

   b) veterinary drugs should be effective for their intended use; and

   c) in the case of veterinary drugs for food-producing animals, the residue of the drug remaining in the edible product of the animal should be safe for animal and human consumption.

2.   The Parties shall, with respect to veterinary drugs:

   a) make equivalent and, where equivalent, accept the equivalence of, health and safety regulatory requirements, definitions, claims, warning and caution statements, procedures for establishing tolerances, methods of risk assessment and investigational new veterinary drug requirements within twenty-four months of entry into force of this Agreement;

   b) examine published tolerances for veterinary drug residues in food and classify them into those tolerances that are harmonized and those that are different;

   c) adopt, where both Parties agree to their use, CODEX standards on residues of veterinary drugs in foods;

   d) make equivalent and, where equivalent, accept the equivalence of, pharmaceutical assay methods, drug residue screening, and food monitoring assay methods;

   e) make equivalent and, where equivalent, accept the equivalence of, emergency drug use authorizations and veterinary prescriptions for the medication of feeds;

   f) adopt procedures to harmonize tissue assay methods within twelve months of entry into force of this Agreement; and

g) work toward developing a minimum threshold for compounds that do not have a published tolerance, for purposes of removing from regulation such compounds found in food at levels below that threshold. This policy will only apply to compounds where there is no indication that the substance is a carcinogen.

SCHEDULE 6: Plant Health

1.   The Parties shall, with respect to plant health:

   a) work toward equivalent and, where possible, harmonized quarantine procedures for plants that are produced or grown in the territories of both Parties;

   b) work toward equivalent and, where possible, harmonized regulations regarding the importation of plants, particularly from third countries;

   c) work toward an agreement on the qualifications to be met by accredited plant health inspectors of either Party who issue phytosanitary certificates for shipments between the Parties. Once the Parties so agree, any such inspector shall be required to meet the agreed qualifications and each Party shall accept certificates issued by those inspectors; and

   d) notify the other Party, as soon as possible, of action taken within their respective territories to monitor and control plant pests or the importation of plants, whether from the other Party or from a third country.

2.   When a plant capable of carrying a plant pest is produced or grown in the territory of one Party but not in that of the other, the non-producing or non-growing Party shall:

   a) inform the public of the dangers of unauthorized transborder movement of such plants and of the necessity to control the export of these plants and means of conveyance into the territory of the producing or growing Party; and

   b) provide such controls on, and phytosanitary certification of, such plants by inspectors accredited by the federal government of either Party, as are required to protect the health of plants in the producing or growing Party.

SCHEDULE 7: Pesticides

The Parties shall, with respect to pesticides:

a) exchange analytical residue methodology and provide crop residue data for the use, including minor uses, of pesticides;

b) cooperate regarding regulatory reviews of data on registered older chemicals;

c) work toward equivalent guidelines, technical regulations, standards and test methods;

d) work toward equivalent residue monitoring programs;

e) work toward equivalent technical regulations, standards or certifications for those pesticides selected by the Parties; and

f) work toward equivalence in:

    i)   the process for risk-benefit assessment,

    ii) tolerance setting, and

    iii) the setting of regulatory policies with respect to oncogenic pesticides.

SCHEDULE 8: Food, Beverage and Colour Additives

The Parties shall, with respect to food, beverage and colour additives, work toward the development of:

a) a uniform policy, with respect to compounds that migrate to foods and beverages, for removing those compounds from regulation where found below certain thresholds; and

b) uniform methods of risk assessment and health hazard evaluation systems.

SCHEDULE 9: Packaging and Labelling of Agricultural, Food, Beverage and Certain Related Goods for Human Consumption

1.   The Parties shall, with respect to packaging and labelling of agricultural, food, beverage and certain related goods for human consumption:

    a) work toward the acceptance of dual declarations of content where the net quantity can be expressed in metric and United States units of measure, regardless of the order of the declaration;

    b) work toward equivalent requirements for matters such as:

        i) nutrition labelling,

        ii) ingredient listing or declaration,

        iii) labelling terminology and definitions,

        iv) grading declarations; and

    c) review container sizes, including can sizes.

2.   The Parties shall accept the use of the terms "canola oil" and "low erucic acid rapeseed oil" as synonymous. Canola oil means the oil extracted from canola seed, which oil contains less than two percent erucic acid.

SCHEDULE 10:   Meat, Poultry and Egg Inspection

1.   The Parties shall work toward making equivalent and, where equivalent, accepting the equivalence of:

a) each other's reviews of mutually recognized meat and poultry inspection systems and facilities of third countries;

b) each other's internal review systems with respect to meat, poultry, egg and egg product inspection;

c) each other's meat, poultry, egg and egg product inspection systems;

d) each other's laboratory system procedures, and the results from each others' federally accredited and approved laboratories with respect to meat and poultry; and

e) specific testing methods and procedures with respect to eggs and egg products.

2.   Consistent with paragraph 3 of Article 708, where:

a) the Parties have harmonized or accepted the equivalence of each other's inspection systems or certification procedures for meat, poultry, or eggs, and

b) the exporting Party has, pursuant to such systems or procedures, determined or certified that such meat, poultry, or eggs meet the standards or technical regulations of the importing Party,

the importing Party may examine such goods imported from the territory of the exporting Party only to ensure that (b) has occurred. This provision shall not preclude spot checks or similar verifying measures necessary to ensure compliance with the importing Party's standards or technical regulations provided that such spot checks or similar verifying measures, including any conducted at the border and including any unloading requirement, are conducted no more frequently than those conducted by the importing Party, under similar circumstances, with respect to its goods.

SCHEDULE 11: Dairy, Fruit and Vegetable Inspection

The Parties shall:

a) make equivalent and, where equivalent, accept the equivalence of, each Party's inspection systems for fresh fruits and vegetables;

b) work toward equivalent inspection systems for dairy products; and

c) make equivalent and, where equivalent, accept the equivalence of, laboratory system results from each other's federally accredited or approved laboratories for dairy inspection.

SCHEDULE 12:   Unavoidable Contaminants in Foods and Beverages

The Parties shall, with respect to unavoidable contaminants in foods and beverages, work toward:

a) harmonizing their regulatory requirements;

b) making equivalent test methods used to determine acceptable levels of contaminants in foods and beverages;

c) harmonizing the process for setting tolerance or action levels for unavoidable contaminants through the following procedures:

   i) determining to what extent the contaminant is unavoidable,

   ii) determining the toxicity of the contaminant,

   iii) estimating the likely exposure for humans,

   iv) using risk assessment to establish an action level or tolerance, and

   v) determining the extent to which analytical methods are available to measure contaminants in foods and beverages; and

d) developing uniform methods of assessing risk and evaluating health hazards.

Chapter Eight

Wine and Distilled Spirits

Article 801: Coverage

1.   This Chapter applies to any measure related to the internal sale and distribution of wine and distilled spirits.

2.   Except as otherwise provided in this Chapter, Chapter Five (National Treatment) shall not apply to:

   a)   a non-conforming provision of any existing measure;

   b)   the continuation or prompt renewal of a non-conforming provision of any existing measure; or

   c)   an amendment to a non-conforming provision of any existing measure to the extent that the amendment does not decrease its conformity with any of the provisions of Chapter Five.

3.   The Party asserting that paragraph 2 applies to one of its measures shall have the burden of establishing the validity of such assertion.

Article 802: Listing

1.   Any measure related to listing of wine and distilled spirits of the other Party shall:

   a) conform with Chapter Five;

   b) be transparent, non-discriminatory and provide for prompt decision on any listing application, prompt written notification of such decision to the applicant and, in the case of a negative decision, provide for a statement of the reason for refusal;

   c) establish administrative appeal procedures for listing decisions that provide for prompt, fair and objective rulings;

   d) be based on normal commercial considerations;

e) not create disguised barriers to trade; and

f) be published and made generally available to persons of the other Party.

2. Notwithstanding paragraph 1 and Chapter Five, and provided that listing measures of British Columbia otherwise conform with the provisions of paragraph 1 and Chapter Five, automatic listing measures in the province of British Columbia may be maintained provided they apply only to estate wineries existing on October 4, 1987, producing less than 30,000 gallons of wine annually and meeting the then-existing content rule.

Article 803: Pricing

1. Where the distributor is a public entity, the entity may charge the actual cost-of-service differential between wine or distilled spirits of the other Party and domestic wine or distilled spirits. Any such differential shall not exceed the actual amount by which the audited cost of service for the wine or distilled spirits of the exporting Party exceeds the audited cost of service for the wine or distilled spirits of the importing Party.

2. Nothing in paragraph 1 and Chapter Five shall prohibit a differential in price mark-ups for wine in excess of that referred to in paragraph 1 prior to January 1, 1995, provided that any such excess does not exceed:

a) as of January 1, 1989, 75 percent of the base differential referred to in paragraph 3;

b) as of January 1, 1990, 50 percent of such base differential;

c) as of January 1, 1991, 40 percent of such base differential;

d) as of January 1, 1992, 30 percent of such base differential;

e) as of January 1, 1993, 20 percent of such base differential;

f) as of January 1, 1994, 10 percent of such base differential; and

g) as of January 1, 1995 and beyond, 0 percent of such base differential.

3. For purposes of paragraph 2, the base differential shall be calculated by subtracting the permissible cost-of-service differential referred to in paragraph 1 from the mark-up differential applied by the competent authority as of October 4, 1987.

4. All discriminatory mark-ups on distilled spirits shall be eliminated immediately upon the entry into force of this Agreement. Cost-of-service differential mark-ups as described in paragraph 1 above shall be permitted.

5. Any other discriminatory pricing measure shall be eliminated upon entry into force of this Agreement.

Article 804: Distribution

1. Any measure related to distribution of wine or distilled spirits of the other Party shall conform with Chapter Five.

2. Notwithstanding paragraph 1, and provided that distribution measures otherwise ensure conformity with Chapter Five, a Party may:

a) maintain or introduce a measure limiting on-premise sales by a winery or distillery to those wines or distilled spirits produced on its premises; or

b) maintain a measure requiring private wine store outlets in existence on October 4, 1987 in the provinces of Ontario and British Columbia to discriminate in favour of wine of those provinces to a degree no greater than the discrimination required by such existing measure.

3. Nothing in this Agreement shall prohibit the Province of Quebec from requiring that any wine sold in grocery stores in Quebec be bottled in Quebec, provided that alternative outlets are provided in Quebec for the sale of wine of the United States of America, whether or not such wine is bottled in Quebec.

Article 805: Blending Requirement

Canada shall eliminate any measure requiring that distilled spirits imported in bulk from the United States of America for bottling be blended with any distilled spirits of Canada.

Article 806: Distinctive Products

1.   Solely for purposes of standards and labelling, Canada shall recognize the standard for Bourbon Whiskey, including straight Bourbon Whiskey, as described in the laws and regulations of the United States of America. Accordingly, Canada shall not permit the sale of any product as Bourbon Whiskey, including straight Bourbon Whiskey, unless the product has been manufactured in the United States of America and complies with the prescribed standards of the United States of America.

2.   Solely for purposes of standards and labelling, the United States of America shall recognize Canadian Whiskey as a distinctive product of Canada. Accordingly, the United States of America shall not permit the sale of any product as Canadian Whiskey unless it has been manufactured in Canada in accordance with the laws and regulations of Canada governing the manufacture of Canadian Whiskey for consumption in Canada.

Article 807: International Obligation

Unless otherwise specifically provided in this Chapter, the Parties retain their rights and obligations under the *General Agreement on Tariffs and Trade* (GATT) and agreements negotiated under the GATT.

Article 808: Definitions

For purposes of this Chapter:

distilled spirits include distilled spirits and distilled spirit-containing beverages;

existing measure means a measure in force as of October 4, 1987;

in existence on October 4, 1987 means, with respect to wine store outlets referred to in subparagraph 2(b) of Article 804, those, that on October 4, 1987, were in operation, were in the process of being built, or for which an application to operate had been approved by the Ontario or British Columbia liquor controlling authority, as the case may be; and

wine includes wine and wine-containing beverages.

Chapter Nine

Energy

Article 901: Scope

1.   This Chapter applies to measures related to energy goods originating in the territory of either Party.

2.   For purposes of this Chapter, energy goods refer to those goods classified in the Harmonized System under:

a) Chapter 27 (except headings 2707 and 2712);

b) subheading 2612.10;

c) subheadings 2844.10 through 2844.50 (only with respect to uranium compounds classified under those subheadings); and

d) subheading 2845.10.

Article 902: Import and Export Restrictions

1.   Subject to the further rights and obligations of this Agreement, the Parties affirm their respective rights and obligations under the *General Agreement on Tariffs and Trade* (GATT) with respect to prohibitions or restrictions on bilateral trade in energy goods.

2.   The Parties understand that the GATT rights and obligations affirmed in paragraph 1 prohibit, in any circumstances in which any other form of quantitative restriction is prohibited, minimum export-price requirements and, except as permitted in enforcement of countervailing and antidumping orders and undertakings, minimum import-price requirements.

3.   In circumstances where a Party imposes a restriction on importation from or exportation to a third country of an energy good, nothing in this Agreement shall be construed to prevent the Party from:

a) limiting or prohibiting the importation from the territory of the other Party of such energy good of the third country; or

b) requiring as a condition of export of such energy good to the territory of the other Party, that the good be consumed within the territory of the other Party.

4.   In the event that either Party imposes a restriction on imports of an energy good from third countries, the Parties, upon request of either Party, shall consult with a view to avoiding undue interference with or distortion of pricing, marketing and distribution arrangements in the other Party.

5.   The Parties shall implement the provisions of Annex 902.5.

Article 903: Export Taxes

Neither Party shall maintain or introduce any tax, duty, or charge on the export of any energy good to the other Party, unless such tax, duty, or charge is also maintained or introduced on such energy good when destined for domestic consumption.

Article 904: Other Export Measures

Either Party may maintain or introduce a restriction otherwise justified under the provisions of Articles XI:2(a) and XX(g), (i) and (j) of the GATT with respect to the export of an energy good of the Party to the territory of the other Party, only if:

a) the restriction does not reduce the proportion of the total export shipments of a specific energy good made available to the other Party relative to the total supply of that good of the Party maintaining the restriction as compared to the proportion prevailing in the most recent 36-month period for which data are available prior to the imposition of the measure, or in such other representative period on which the Parties may agree;

b) the Party does not impose a higher price for exports of an energy good to the other Party than the price charged for such energy good when consumed domestically, by means of any measure such as licences, fees, taxation and minimum price requirements. The foregoing provision does not apply to a higher price which may result from a measure taken pursuant to subparagraph (a) that only restricts the volume of exports; and

c) the restriction does not require the disruption of normal channels of supply to the other Party or normal proportions among specific energy goods supplied to the other Party such as, for example, between crude oil and refined products and among different categories of crude oil and of refined products.

Article 905: Regulatory and Other Measures

1.   If either Party considers that energy regulatory actions by the other Party would directly result in discrimination against its energy goods or its persons inconsistent with the principles of this Agreement, that Party may initiate direct consultations with the other Party. For purposes of this Article, an "energy regulatory action" shall include any action, in the case of Canada, by the National Energy Board, or its successor, and in the case of the United States of America, by either the Federal Energy Regulatory Commission or the Economic Regulatory Administration or their successors. Consultations with respect to the actions of these agencies shall include, in the case of Canada, the Department of Energy, Mines, and Resources and, in the case of the United States of America, the Department of Energy. With respect to a regulatory action of another agency, at any level of government, the Parties shall determine which agencies shall participate in the consultations.

2.   In addition, the Parties shall implement the provisions of Annex 905.2.

Article 906: Government Incentives for Energy Resource Development

Both Parties have agreed to allow existing or future incentives for oil and gas exploration, development and related activities in order to maintain the reserve base for these energy resources.

Article 907: National Security Measures

Neither Party shall maintain or introduce a measure restricting imports of an energy good from, or exports of an energy good to, the other Party under Article XXI of the GATT or under Article 2003 (National Security) of this Agreement, except to the extent necessary to:

a) supply a military establishment of a Party or enable fulfillment of a critical defense contract of a Party;

b) respond to a situation of armed conflict involving the Party taking the measure;

c) implement national policies or international agreements relating to the non-proliferation of nuclear weapons or other nuclear explosive devices; or

d) respond to direct threats of disruption in the supply of nuclear materials for defense purposes.

Article 908:   International Obligations

The Parties intend no inconsistency between the provisions of this Chapter and the *Agreement on an International Energy Program* (IEP). In the event of any unavoidable inconsistency between the IEP and this Chapter, the provisions of the IEP shall prevail to the extent of that inconsistency.

Article 909: Definitions

For purposes of this Chapter:

consumed means transformed so as to qualify under the rules of origin set out in Chapter Three, or actually consumed;

restriction means any limitation, whether made effective through quotas, licenses, permits, minimum price requirements or any other means;

total export shipments means the total shipments from total supply to users located in the territory of the other Party; and

total supply means shipments to domestic users and foreign users from

a) domestic production,
b) domestic inventory, and
c) other imports, as appropriate.

Annex 902.5

Import Measures

1.   The United States of America shall exempt Canada from any restriction on the enrichment of foreign uranium under section 161v of the *Atomic Energy Act.*

Export Measures

2.   Canada shall exempt the United States of America from the Canadian Uranium Upgrading Policy as announced by the Minister of State for Mines on October 18, 1985.

3.   The United States of America shall exempt Canada from the prohibition on the exportation of Alaskan oil under section 7(d) of the *Export Administration Act of 1979,* as amended, up to a maximum volume of 50 thousand barrels per day on an annual average basis, subject to the condition that such oil be transported to Canada from a suitable location within the lower 48 states.

Annex 905.2

Regulatory and Other Measures

<u>Canada</u>

1.   Of the tests set out under subparagraph 6(2)(z) of the *National Energy Board Part VI Regulations* on the export of energy goods to the United States of America, Canada shall eliminate the "least cost alternative test", described in subparagraph 6(2)(z)(iii).

<u>United States of America</u>

2.   The United States of America shall cause the Bonneville Power Administration to modify its Intertie Access Policy so as to afford British Columbia Hydro treatment no less favourable than the most favourable treatment afforded to utilities located outside the Pacific Northwest.

3.   No other policy of the Bonneville Power Administration or law authorizing such policy need be changed insofar as such law or policy concerns energy sales, transmission of energy and related business arrangements between the Bonneville Power Administration and British Columbia Hydro.

<u>General</u>

4.   It is understood that the implementation of this Chapter includes the administration of any "surplus tests" on the export of any energy good to the other Party in a manner consistent with the provisions of Articles 902, 903 and 904.

5.   The Parties fully expect that the Bonneville Power Administration and British Columbia Hydro will continue to negotiate mutually beneficial arrangements consistent with the objectives of this Agreement and separately to seek any additional authorities that may be needed.

Chapter Ten

Trade in Automotive Goods

Article 1001: Existing Arrangement

Each Party shall endeavour to administer the *Agreement Concerning Automotive Products between the Government of Canada and the Government of the United States of America* that entered into force definitively on September 16, 1966 in the best interests of employment and production in both countries.

Article 1002: Waiver of Customs Duties

1.   Neither Party shall grant a waiver of otherwise applicable customs duties to a recipient other than those recipients listed in Annex 1002.1, nor shall either Party expand the extent or application of, or extend the duration of, any waiver granted to any such recipient with respect to:

  a) automotive goods imported into its territory from any country where such waiver is conditioned, explicitly or implicitly, upon the fulfillment of performance requirements applicable to any goods; or

  b) any goods imported from any country where such waiver is conditioned, explicitly or implicitly, upon the fulfillment of performance requirements applicable to automotive goods.

2.   Waivers of customs duties granted to the recipients listed in Part Two of Annex 1002.1, where the amount of duty waived depends on exports, shall:

  a) after January 1, 1989 exclude exports to the territory of the other Party in calculating the duty waived; and

  b) terminate on or before January 1, 1998.

3.   Waivers of customs duties granted to the recipients listed in Part Three of Annex 1002.1, where the amount of duty waived depends on Canadian value added contained in production in Canada, shall terminate not later than:

201

a) January 1, 1996; or

b) such earlier date specified in existing agreements between Canada and the recipient of the waiver.

4.   Whenever the other Party can show that a waiver or combination of waivers of customs duties granted with respect to automotive goods for commercial use by a designated person has an adverse impact on the commercial interests of a person of the other Party, or of a person owned or controlled by a person of the other Party that is located in the territory of the Party granting the waiver of customs duties, or on the other Party's economy, the Party granting the waiver either shall cease to grant it or shall make it generally available to any importer. The provisions of this paragraph shall not apply to the waivers of customs duties to those recipients listed in Part One of Annex 1002.1 in accordance with the headnote to that Part or to the waivers of customs duties referred to in paragraphs 2 and 3 for the periods during which such waiver of customs duties may be conditioned upon the fulfillment of performance requirements set forth in paragraphs 2 and 3.

Article 1003: Import Restrictions

Canada shall phase out the import restriction on used automobiles set out in tariff item 99215-1 of Schedule C to the *Customs Tariff,* or its successor, in five annual stages commencing on January 1, 1989 in accordance with the following schedule:

a) in the first year, used automobiles that are eight years old or older;

b) in the second year, used automobiles that are six years old or older;

c) in the third year, used automobiles that are four years old or older;

d) in the fourth year, used automobiles that are two years old or older; and

e) in the fifth year and thereafter, no restrictions.

Article 1004:   Select Panel

The Parties recognize the continued importance of automotive trade and production for the respective economies of the two countries and the need to ensure that the industry in both countries should prosper in the future. As the worldwide industry is evolving very rapidly, the Parties shall establish a select panel consisting of a group of informed persons to assess the state of the North American industry and to propose public policy measures and private initiatives to improve its competitiveness in domestic and foreign markets. The Parties shall also cooperate in the Uruguay Round of multilateral trade negotiations to create new export opportunities for North American automotive goods.

Article 1005: Relationship to Other Chapters

1.   Chapter Three (Rules of Origin) applies to:

   a) automotive goods imported into the territory of the United States of America; and

   b) automotive goods imported into the territory of Canada under this Agreement.

2.   In determining whether a vehicle originates in the territory of either Party or both Parties under paragraph 4 of Section XVII of Annex 301.2, instead of a calculation based on each vehicle, the manufacturer may elect to average its calculation over a 12 month period on the same class of vehicles or sister vehicles (station wagons and other body styles in the same car line), assembled in the same plant.

3.   The provisions of Article 405 apply to the waivers of customs duties affecting automotive goods except where otherwise provided in this Chapter.

4.   The list of recipients in Annex 1002.1 and the definition "class of vehicles" may be modified by agreement between the Parties.

Article 1006: Definitions

For purposes of this Chapter:

automotive goods means motor vehicles and those goods used or intended for use in motor vehicles;

Canadian manufacturer means a person who manufactures automotive goods within the territory of Canada;

class of vehicles means any one of the following:

    a) minicompact automobiles - less than 85 cubic feet of passenger and luggage volume,

    b) subcompact automobiles - between 85 and 100 cubic feet of passenger and luggage volume,

    c) compact automobiles - between 100 and 110 cubic feet of passenger and luggage volume,

    d) midsize automobiles - between 110 and 120 cubic feet of passenger and luggage volume,

    e) large automobiles - 120 or more cubic feet of passenger and luggage volume,

    f) trucks, or

    g) buses.

NOTE: A vehicle that may have more than one possible use (e.g., vans, jeeps) would be defined as either an automobile or truck based on whether it is designed and marketed principally for the transport of passengers or the transport of cargo.

comparable arrangement means arrangements whereby waivers of customs duties are granted to Canadian manufacturers upon the fulfillment of conditions comparable to those described in the agreement referred to in Article 1001;

customs duty has the same meaning as in Article 410;

performance requirements has the same meaning as in Article 410;

used automobiles means used or second-hand automobiles and used or second-hand motor vehicles of all kinds that are manufactured prior to the calendar year in which importation into the territory of Canada is sought to be made; and

waiver of customs duties has the same meaning as in Article 410.

Annex 1002.1

Part One: Waivers of Customs Duties

The following Canadian manufacturers have qualified under the agreement referred to in Article 1001 and comparable arrangements or, on the basis of available information and projections, may be reasonably expected to qualify by the 1989 model year. The final list of those companies covered by the list below that so qualify will be provided by Canada to the United States of America within 90 days after the end of the 1989 model year.[1]

AMI Stego Limited
Advance Engineered Products Ltd.
Alforge Metals Corporation Limited
Almac Industries Ltd.
Amalgamated Metal Industries
American Motors (Canada) Inc.
American Motors (Canada) Limited
American Motors (Canada) Ltd.
Amertek Inc.
Atelier Gérard Laberge Inc.
Atlantic Truck and Trailer Limited
Atlas 2,000 Inc.
Atlas Hoist and Body Inc.
Aurora Cars Limited
Aurora Cars, a Division of Grove Ridge Industries Limited
B.K. & B. Truck Bodies Limited
B.T.L. Body Inc.
Babcock Motor Bodies Limited
Back Motor Bodies Ltd.
Belgium Standard Industries, A Division of Amertek Inc.

---

[1] Waivers of customs duties shall cease being granted to any recipient listed in Part One of Annex 1002.1 if:

a) effective control of the conduct and operation of the recipient's business or substantial ownership of its assets is acquired, directly or indirectly, by a manufacturer of motor vehicles that is not a listed recipient; and

b) the fundamental nature, scope or size of the business of the recipient is significantly altered from the business of the recipient as carried on immediately prior to the acquisition of control or change in ownership.

Bevcam Inc.
Boîtes de Camion Alco Inc.
Boîtes de Camion GAM Inc.
Boîtes de Camion Saguenay (1987) Inc.
Bombardier Inc., Logistic Equipment Division
Bricklin Canada Limited
Burke Canada Inc.
CAMI Automotive Inc.
Canadian Blue Bird Coach Ltd.
Canadian Disposal Equipment Co. Ltd.
Canadian Kenworth Ltd.
Canassen Limited
Capital Disposal Equipment Inc.
Capital Truck Bodies
Care Equipment Manufacturing Co. Ltd.
Central Truck Body Co. Ltd.
Champion Truck Bodies Limited
Childs Truck Bodies Ltd.
Chrysler Canada Ltd.
Collins Manufacturing Company Limited
Commercial Truck Bodies
Commercial Vans Inc.
Consolidated Dynamics Limited
Contran Manufacturing Ltd.
County Truck & Trailer, a Division of Peterson Vans Inc.
Cusco Industries, Division of Cusco Fabricators Ltd.
D. & C. Roussy Industries Ltd.
DEL Equipment Limited, Division of Diesel Equipment Limited
Deluxe Van & Body Ltd.
Dempster Systems Limited
Dependable Truck and Tank Repairs Ltd.
Diesel Equipment Limited
Dominion Truck Bodies Ltd.
Dresser Canada, Inc.
Durabody & Trailer Limited
Dynamic Fiber Ltd.
Dynatel Inc.
Eastern Steel Products/ Frink Canada, Division of Compro Limited
Eastway Tank, Pump and Meter Co. Ltd.
Edmonton Truck Body Ltd.
Elcombe Engineering Ltd.
Equipement Labrie Ltée
F.A.D. Industries Inc.

F.W.D. Corporation
Fabricants de Boîtes de Camions BEL (1986) Inc.
Fanotech Industries Inc.
Fawcett Van & Stake Ltd.
Fleet Truck Bodies
Ford Motor Company of Canada Limited
Forman Tank & Welding, Ltd.
Fort Garry Industries Ltd.
Freightliner of Canada Ltd.
G. G. Cargo Trailer Industries Ltd.
G. & G. Welding
G.R. Patstone Ltd.
General Motors of Canada Limited
George C. Doerr Body and Trailer Co.
Girardin Corporation
Greyhound Canada Inc.
H.E. Brown Supply Co.
Hal-Vey Industries Ltd.
Hayes Manufacturing Company Limited
Hutchinson Industries
Ideal Body Limited
IMT Cranes Canada, Ltd.
Intercontinental Truck Body B.C. Inc.
Intercontinental Truck Body Ltd.
Intermeccanica International Inc.
J.H. Corbeil Inc.
Jauvin Truck Bodies Limited
Jean-Marc Vigeant Inc.
Kaiser Jeep of Canada Limited
Kamloops Allweld Aluminum Service Limited
L. Knight & Co. Ltd.
Lennoxvan (1986) Inc.
Les Carrosseries Fontaine (1979) Ltée
Les Entreprises Michel Corbeil Inc.
Les Industries Savard Inc.
Mack Trucks Manufacturing Company of Canada Limited
Marathon Electric Vehicles Inc.
McEwan-Tougard Industries Limited
MCI Limited
Minoru Truck Bodies Ltd.
Mond Industries Limited
Morrison & Co. Ltd.
Motor Coach Industries Limited

Multi-Vans Inc.
Navistar International Corporation Canada
New Flyer Industries Limited
Off-Highway Vehicles: Ceco Sales Limited
Off-Highway Vehicles: Cypress Equipment Ltd.
Off-Highway Vehicles: Euclid Canada
Off-Highway Vehicles: General Motors of Canada Limited
Off-Highway Vehicles: General Motors of Canada Limited, Diesel
    Division
Off-Highway Vehicles: Mack Trucks Manufacturing Company of
    Canada Limited
Off-Highway Vehicles: Paccar Canada Ltd.
Off-Highway Vehicles: Pacific Truck & Trailer Ltd.
Off-Highway Vehicles: Ume Canada
Off-Highway Vehicles: Unit Rig & Equipment Co. (Canada) Ltd.
Off-Highway Vehicles: Wabco Equipment of Canada
Ontario Bus Industries Limited
Ontario Fiberglass Production O/B 536794 Ont. Ltd.
Ottawa Truck Bodies Ltée/Ltd.
Paccar Canada Ltd.
Parco-Hesse Corporation Inc.
Peabody Myers (Canada), Division of Peabody International
    Canada Ltd.
Pettibone Canada Limited
Phil Larochelle (1977)
Phil Larochelle Equipment Inc.
Philwood Industries Ltd.
Pitman Manufacturing Co. Inc.
PK Welding & Fabricators Limited
Pollock Truck Bodies, Division of Pollock Rentals Limited
Prevost Car Inc.
Québec Truck Bodies Boîtes de Camions Inc.
R & M Manufacturing Ltd.
Raytel Equipment Ltd.
Rebel Steel Industries Ltd.
Red Top Equipment Company Limited
Réfrigération Thermo King Montréal Inc.
Reliance Truck and Equipment
Remtec Inc.
Roberts Truck Equipment Ltd.
Rubber Railway Company Ltd.
Sentinal Vehicles Limited
Sheller-Globe of Canada Limited

Sicard Inc.
SMI Industries Canada Ltd.
SMI Industries Limited
Soudure G. & G. Ltée
Sturdy Truck Body (1972) Limited
Superior Bus Mfg. Ltd.
Supravan Ltée
Swartz Motor Bodies Limited
Teal Manufacturing Ltd.
The Electric & Gas Welding Co. Limited
Thermo King Western (Calgary) Ltd.
Thermo King Western Ltd.
Thomas Built Buses of Canada Limited
Tipping Motor Bodies Limited
Toronto Kitchen Equipment Limited
Tor Truck Corporation
Trailmobile Group of Companies Ltd.
Transit Van Bodies Inc.
Triangle Truck Equipment Ltd.
Triple E Industries Ltd.
Truck Equipment & Service Co. Ltd.
UTDC Inc.
Universal Carrier Manufacturing Ltd.
Universal Handling Equipment Co.
Universal Sales Limited
Universal Truck Body Ltd.
Univision Industries Limited
V. Lacasse Ltée
Vennes Boîte de Camion Inc.
Volvo Canada Ltd.
Vulcan Equipment Company Limited
W.H. Olsen Manufacturing Co. Ltd.
Wajax UEC Limited
Walinga Body & Coach Limited
Walter Canada Inc.
Walter Motor Trucks of Canada Limited
Welles Corporation Limited
Westank-Willock, a Division of Willock Industries Ltd.
Western Rock Bit Company Limited
Western Star Trucks Inc.
Western Utilities Equipment Co. Ltd.
Wheels, Brakes and Equipment Limited
White Motor Corporation of Canada Limited

Wilcox Bodies Limited
Wilson Motor Bodies Ltd.
Wilson's Truck Bodies, a Division of L & A Machine (N.S.) Limited
Wilson's Truck Body Shop Ltd.
Wiltsie Truck Bodies Ltd.

Part Two: Export-Based Waivers of Customs Duties

The following Canadian manufacturers have qualified for export-based waivers of customs duties or, on the basis of available information and projections, may be reasonably expected to qualify by the date of entry into force of this Agreement. Canada shall provide the United States of America with the final list of those companies on this list that have qualified as of the date of entry into force of this Agreement.

BMW Canada Inc.
Fiat Canada
Honda Canada Inc.
Hyundai Auto Canada Inc.
Jaguar Canada Inc.
Mazda Canada Inc.
Mercedes-Benz of Canada Inc.
Nissan Automobile Company (Canada) Ltd.
Peugeot Canada Ltée/Ltd.
Saab-Scania Canada Inc.
Subaru Auto Canada Limited
Toyota Canada Inc.
Volkswagen Canada Inc.

Part Three: Production-Based Waivers of Customs Duties

The following Canadian manufacturers have qualified for production-based waivers of customs duties or, on the basis of available information and projections, may be reasonably expected to qualify by the date of entry into force of this Agreement. The final list of those companies covered by the list below that so qualify will be provided by Canada to the United States of America within 90 days after the end of the 1989 model year.

CAMI Automotive Inc. [2]
Honda Canada Inc./Honda of Canada Mfg., Inc.
Hyundai Auto Canada Inc.
Toyota Motor Manufacturing Canada Inc.

---

[2] If it fails to qualify under Part One.

Chapter Eleven

Emergency Action

Article 1101: Bilateral Actions

1.   Subject to paragraphs 2 and 4, and during the transition period only, if a good originating in the territory of one Party is, as a result of the reduction or elimination of a duty provided for in Chapter Four, being imported into the territory of the other Party in such increased quantities, in absolute terms, and under such conditions so that the imports of such good from the exporting Party alone constitute a substantial cause of serious injury to a domestic industry producing a like or directly competitive good, the importing Party may, to the extent necessary to remedy the injury:

   a) suspend the further reduction of any rate of duty provided for under this Agreement on such good;

   b) increase the rate of duty on such good to a level not to exceed the lesser of:

      i) the most-favoured-nation (MFN) rate of duty in effect at that time; or

      ii) the MFN rate of duty in effect on the day immediately preceding the date of the entry into force of this Agreement; or

   c) in the case of a duty applied to a good on a seasonal basis, increase the rate of duty to a level not to exceed the MFN rate of duty that was in effect on such good for the corresponding season immediately prior to the date of entry into force of this Agreement.

2.   The following conditions and limitations shall apply to an action authorized by paragraph 1:

   a) notification and consultation shall precede the action;

b) no action shall be maintained for a period exceeding three years or, except with the consent of the other Party, have effect beyond the expiration of the transition period;

c) no action shall be taken by either Party more than once during the transition period against any particular good of the other Party; and

d) upon the termination of the action, the rate of duty shall be the rate which would have been in effect but for the action.

3.   A Party may institute a bilateral emergency action after the expiration of the transition period to deal with cases of serious injury to a domestic industry arising from the operation of this Agreement only with the consent of the other Party.

4.   The Party taking an action pursuant to this Article shall provide to the other Party mutually agreed trade liberalizing compensation in the form of concessions having substantially equivalent trade effects to the other Party or equivalent to the value of the additional duties expected to result from the action. If the Parties are unable to agree upon compensation, the exporting Party may take tariff action having trade effects substantially equivalent to the action taken by the importing Party under paragraph 1.

Article 1102: Global Actions

1.   With respect to an emergency action taken by a Party on a global basis, the Parties shall retain their respective rights and obligations under Article XIX of the *General Agreement on Tariffs and Trade* subject to the requirement that a Party taking such action shall exclude the other Party from such global action unless imports from that Party are substantial and are contributing importantly to the serious injury or threat thereof caused by imports. For purposes of this paragraph, imports in the range of five percent to ten percent or less of total imports would normally not be considered substantial.

2.   A Party taking an emergency global action, from which the other Party is initially excluded pursuant to paragraph 1, shall have the right subsequently to include the other Party in the global action in the event of a surge in imports of such good from the other Party that undermines the effectiveness of such action.

3.   A Party shall, without delay, provide notice to the other Party of the institution of a proceeding that may result in an emergency action under paragraphs 1 or 2.

4.   In no case shall a Party take an action authorized under paragraphs 1 or 2, imposing restrictions on a good:

a) without prior notice and consultation; and

b) that would have the effect of reducing imports of such good of the other Party below the trend of imports over a reasonable recent base period with allowance for growth.

5.   The Party taking an action pursuant to this Article shall provide to the other Party mutually agreed trade liberalizing compensation in the form of concessions having substantially equivalent trade effects to the other Party or equivalent to the value of the additional duties expected to result from the action. If the Parties are unable to agree upon compensation, the exporting Party may take action having trade effects substantially equivalent to the action taken by the importing Party under paragraph 1.

Article 1103: Arbitration

Articles 1806 (Arbitration) and 1807 (Panel Procedures) shall not apply with respect to proposed actions under this Chapter. Any dispute with respect to actual actions not resolved by consultation shall be referred to arbitration under Article 1806.

Article 1104: Definitions

For purposes of this Chapter:

contribute importantly means an important cause, but not necessarily the most important cause, of serious injury from imports;

emergency action means any emergency action taken after the entry into force of this Agreement; and

surge means a significant increase in imports over the trend for a reasonable recent base period for which data are available.

Chapter Twelve

Exceptions for Trade in Goods

Article 1201: GATT Exceptions

Subject to the provisions of Articles 409 and 904, the provisions of Article XX of the *General Agreement on Tariffs and Trade* (GATT) are incorporated into and made a part of this Part of this Agreement.

Article 1202: Protocol of Provisional Application

Any measure of either Party that remains exempt from the obligations of the GATT by virtue of subparagraph 1(b) of the Protocol of Provisional Application of the GATT, shall to the same extent be exempt from the obligations of this Part of this Agreement.

Article 1203: Miscellaneous Exceptions

The provisions of this Part shall not apply to:

a) controls by the United States of America on the export of logs of all species;

b) controls by Canada on the export of logs of all species; and

c) controls by Canada on the export of unprocessed fish pursuant to the following existing statutes:

   (i) *New Brunswick Fish Processing Act,* 1982 and *Fisheries Development Act,* 1977;
   (ii) *Newfoundland Fish Inspection Act,* 1970;
   (iii) *Nova Scotia Fisheries Act,* 1977;
   (iv) *Prince Edward Island Fish Inspection Act,* 1956; and
   (v) *Quebec Marine Products Processing Act,* No. 38, 1987.

Article 1204: Beer and Malt Containing Beverages

1.   With respect to measures related to the internal sale and distribution of beer and malt containing beverages, Chapter Five shall not apply to:

  a)   a non-conforming provision of any existing measure;

  b)   the continuation or prompt renewal of a non-conforming provision of any existing measure; or

  c)   an amendment to a non-conforming provision of any existing measure to the extent that the amendment does not decrease its conformity with any of the provisions of Chapter Five.

2.   The Party asserting that paragraph 1 applies shall have the burden of establishing the validity of such assertion.

3.   Existing measure in paragraph 1 refers to a measure in force as of October 4, 1987.

Article 1205: GATT Rights

The Parties retain their rights and obligations under GATT and agreements negotiated under the GATT with respect to matters exempt from this Part under Articles 1203 and 1204.

PART THREE
GOVERNMENT PROCUREMENT

Chapter Thirteen

Government Procurement

Article 1301: Objective

1.   In the interest of expanding mutually beneficial trade opportunities in government procurement based on the principles of non-discrimination and fair and open competition for the supply of goods and services, the Parties shall actively strive to achieve, as quickly as possible, the multilateral liberalization of international government procurement policies to provide balanced and equitable opportunities.

2.   As a further step toward multilateral liberalization and improvement of the GATT *Agreement on Government Procurement,* which includes the annexes thereto (the Code), the Parties shall undertake the obligations of this Chapter.

Article 1302: Reaffirmation of Existing Obligations

The Parties reaffirm their rights and obligations under the provisions of the Code.

Article 1303: Scope

1.   For procurements covered by this Chapter, the Code, as modified or supplemented by this Chapter, is incorporated into and made a part of this Chapter.

2.   Any modifications to the Code shall automatically be incorporated into, and made a part of, this Chapter on the date that these modifications take effect for the Parties unless the Parties otherwise agree.

3.   In the event of any inconsistency between the provisions of the Code and the obligations of this Chapter, the obligations of this Chapter shall prevail to the extent of the inconsistency.

Article 1304: Coverage

1. The obligations of this Chapter shall apply only to procurements specified in Code Annex I, including the general notes thereto, for the United States of America and Canada respectively, that are above a threshold of twenty-five thousand US dollars and the equivalent in Canadian dollars, as the case may be, and below the Code threshold.

2. Canada will calculate, and convert the value of the threshold of (US)$25,000 into its own national currency and notify the value to the United States of America, it being understood that these calculations will be based on the official conversion rates of the Bank of Canada. The conversion rates, for purposes of this Chapter, will be the average of the weekly values of the Canadian dollar in terms of the US dollar over the two-year period preceding October 1, with effect from January 1. The threshold in Canadian currency will be fixed for January 1, 1989, on the basis of calculations for the preceding one-year period, and thereafter it will be fixed for two-year periods, on the basis of calculations for the preceding two-year period.

3. Code Annex I is incorporated into and made a part of this Chapter and is reproduced in Annex 1304.3. Any further modifications to Annex I shall automatically be incorporated into and made a part of Annex 1304.3 on the date that such modifications take effect for the Parties unless the Parties otherwise agree.

Article 1305: Expanded Procedural Obligations

1. With respect to all measures regarding government procurement covered by this Chapter, each Party shall accord to eligible goods treatment no less favourable than the most favourable treatment accorded to its own goods.

2. Each Party shall, for its procurements covered by this Chapter:

    a) provide all potential suppliers equal access to pre-solicitation information and with equal opportunity to compete in the pre-notification phase;

    b) provide all potential suppliers equal opportunity to be responsive to the requirements of the procuring entity in the tendering and bidding phase;

c) use decision criteria in the qualification of potential suppliers, evaluation of bids and awarding of contracts, that:

    i)   best meet the requirements specified in the tender documentation,

    ii) are free of preferences in any form in favour of its own goods, and

    iii) are clearly specified in advance; and

d) promote competition by making available information on contract awards in the post-award phase.

3.   Each Party shall introduce and maintain, in accordance with the principles contained in Annex 1305.3, equitable, timely, transparent and effective bid challenge procedures for potential suppliers of eligible goods.

4.   In implementing its procedural obligations under this Chapter, each Party shall provide sufficient transparency in the procurement process to ensure that the bid challenge system operates effectively. Accordingly, each Party shall ensure that complete documentation and records, including a written record of all communications substantially affecting each procurement, are maintained in order to allow verification that the procurement process was carried out in accordance with the obligations of this Chapter.

5.   Potential suppliers of either Party shall have reasonable access to information substantially affecting the procurement, subject to laws and regulations of either Party relating to confidentiality.

6.   Each Party shall take all necessary steps to ensure the efficient administration of the obligations under this Chapter.

7.   Each Party shall use the publications it has specified in the Code, or other publications as mutually agreed, to comply with the publication requirements of this Chapter.

Article 1306: Monitoring and Exchange of Information

1.   The Parties shall cooperate in monitoring the implementation, administration and enforcement of the obligations of this Chapter.

2.   In addition to the information requirements of the Code, the Parties shall collect and exchange annual statistics on the procurements covered by this Chapter. Statistics and other information shall be reported on the basis of the eligible goods. Such reports shall identify the country of origin of the goods covered under this Chapter and contain the following information with respect to contracts awarded:

a) total government procurement by procuring entity and product category, according to their respective federal goods identification schedules; and

b) single tendering statistics for each entity. Single tendering information on product categories shall be supplied upon request.

3.   Each Party shall give sympathetic consideration to a request from the other Party for the exchange of additional information on a reciprocal basis.

Article 1307: Further Negotiations

The Parties shall undertake bilateral negotiations with a view to improving and expanding the provisions of this Chapter, not later than one year after the conclusion of the existing multilateral renegotiations pursuant to Article IX:6(b) of the Code, taking into account the results of these renegotiations.

Article 1308: National Security

Notwithstanding Article 2003 (National Security), for purposes of this Chapter the provisions of Article VIII of the Code shall apply.

Article 1309: Definitions

For purposes of this Chapter:

eligible goods means unmanufactured materials mined or produced in the territory of either Party and manufactured materials manufactured in the territory of either Party if the cost of the goods originating outside the territories of the Parties and used in such materials is less than 50 percent of the cost of all the goods used in such materials; and

territory of a Party means

a) for the United States of America, the United States, its possessions, Puerto Rico, and any other place subject to its jurisdiction, including its foreign trade zones, but does not include trust territories or leased bases, and

b) for Canada, the territory to which its customs laws apply.

Annex 1304.3+

Entities Covered++

Canada

1. Department of Agriculture
2. Department of Consumer and Corporate Affairs
3. Department of Energy, Mines and Resources including:
   Atomic Energy Control Board
   Energy Supplies Allocation Board
   National Energy Board
4. Department of Employment and Immigration including:
   Immigration Appeal Board
   Canada Employment and Immigration Commission
5. Department of External Affairs
6. Department of Finance including:
   Department of Insurance
   Anti-Dumping Tribunal
   Municipal Development and Loan Board
   Tariff Board
7. Department of the Environment
8. Department of Indian Affairs and Northern Development
9. Department of Regional Industrial Expansion including:
   Machinery Equipment Advisory Board
10. Department of Justice including:
    Canadian Human Rights Commission
    Statute Revision Commission
    Supreme Court of Canada
11. Department of Labour including:
    Canada Labour Relations Board
12. Department of National Defence* including:
    Defence Construction (1951) Limited

+ This Annex reproduces verbatim the annexes for Canada and the United States of America in the Code. All references are those in the Code except for the footnotes marked with + symbols that are not contained in the Code but are added for explanatory purposes.

++ The entities in this Annex listed for Canada and their successor entities are included in the coverage of this Agreement.

13.   Department of National Health and Welfare including:
          Medical Research Council
          Office of the Coordinator, Status of Women
14.   Department of National Revenue
15.   Department of Post Office [1]
16.   Department of Public Works
17.   Department of Secretary of State of Canada including:
          National Library
          National Museums of Canada
          Public Archives
          Public Service Commission
18.   Department of Solicitor General including:
          Royal Canadian Mounted Police*
          Correctional Service of Canada
          National Parole Board
19.   Department of Supply and Services (on its own account)
      including:
          Canadian General Standards Board
          Statistics Canada
20.   Department of Veterans Affairs including:
          Veterans Land Administration
21.   Auditor General of Canada
22.   National Research Council
23.   Privy Council Office including:
          Canada Intergovernmental Conference Secretariat
          Commissioner of Official Languages
          Economic Council
          Public Service Staff Relations Board
          Federal Provincial Relations Office
          Office of the Governor General's Secretary
24.   National Capital Commission
25.   Ministry of State for Science and Technology including:
          Science Council
26.   National Battlefields Commission
27.   Office of the Chief Electoral Office
28.   Treasury Board
29.   Canadian International Development Agency (on its own
      account)
30.   Natural Sciences and Engineering Research Council

---

[1] The Department of the Post Office is on this List of entities on the
understanding that, should it cease to be a governed department, the
provisions of Article IX, paragraph 5(b) would not apply.

31.   Social Sciences and Humanities Research Council
32.   Fisheries Price Support Board

* The following products purchased by the Department of National Defence and the RCMP are included in the coverage of this Agreement, subject to the application of paragraph 1 of Article VIII.

(Numbers refer to the Federal Supply Classification Code)

22.   Railway Equipment
23.   Motor vehicles, trailers and cycles (except buses in 2310, military trucks and trailers in 2320 and 2330 and tracked combat, assault and tactical vehicles in 2350)
24.   Tractors
25.   Vehicular equipment components
26.   Tyres and Tubes
29.   Engine accessories
30.   Mechanical power transmission equipment
32.   Woodworking machinery and equipment
34.   Metal working machinery
35.   Service and trade equipment
36.   Special industry machinery
37.   Agricultural machinery and equipment
38.   Construction, mining, excavating and highway maintenance equipment
39.   Materials handling equipment
40.   Rope, cable, chain and fittings
41.   Refrigeration and air conditioning equipment
42.   Fire fighting, rescue and safety equipment (except 4220 Marine life-saving and diving equipment 4230 Decontaminating and impregnating equipment)
43.   Pumps and compressors
44.   Furnace, steam plant, drying equipment and nuclear reactors
45.   Plumbing, heating and sanitation equipment
46.   Water purification and sewage treatment equipment
47.   Pipe, tubing, hose and fittings
48.   Valves
49.   Maintenance and repair shop equipment
52.   Measuring tools
53.   Hardware and abrasives
54.   Prefabricated structures and scaffolding
55.   Lumber, millwork, plywood and veneer
56.   Construction and building materials

61. Electric wire and power and distribution equipment
62. Lighting fixtures and lamps
63. Alarm and signal systems
65. Medical, dental and veterinary equipment and supplies
66. Instruments and Laboratory equipment
   except (6615: Automatic pilot mechanisms and airborne gyro
                          components
              6665: Hazard-detecting instruments and apparatus)
67. Photographic equipment
68. Chemicals and chemical products
69. Training aids and devices
70. General purpose automatic data processing equipment,
   software, supplies and support equipment (except 7010 ADPE
   configurations)
71. Furniture
72. Household and commercial furnishings and appliances
73. Food preparation and serving equipment
74. Office machines, visible record equipment and automatic data
   processing equipment
75. Office supplies and devices
76. Books, maps and other publications
   (except 7650: Drawings and specifications)
77. Musical instruments, phonographs and home-type radios
78. Recreational and athletic equipment
79. Cleaning equipment and supplies
80. Brushes, paints, sealers and adhesives
81. Containers, packaging and packing supplies
85. Toiletries
87. Agricultural supplies
88. Live animals
91. Fuels, lubricants, oils and waxes
93. Non-metallic fabricated materials
94. Non-metallic crude materials
96. Ores, minerals and their primary products
99. Miscellaneous

General Note:

Notwithstanding the above, this Agreement does not apply to contracts
set aside for small businesses.

United States

The following entities+++ are included in the coverage of this Agreement by the United States:

1. Department of Agriculture (This Agreement does not apply to procurement of agricultural products made in furtherance of agricultural support programmes or human feeding programmes)
2. Department of Commerce
3. Department of Education
4. Department of Health and Human Services
5. Department of Housing and Urban Development
6. Department of Interior (excluding the Bureau of Reclamation)
7. Department of Justice
8. Department of Labour
9. Department of State
10. United States International Development Co-operation Agency
11. Department of the Treasury
12. General Services Administration (Purchases by the National Tools Center are not included; purchases by the Regional 9 Office of San Francisco, California are not included)
13. National Aeronautics and Space Administration (NASA)
14. Veterans Administration
15. Environmental Protection Agency
16. United States Information Agency
17. National Science Foundation
18. Panama Canal Company and Canal Zone Government
19. Executive Office of the President
20. Farm Credit Administration
21. National Credit Union Administration
22. Merit Systems Protection Board
23. ACTION
24. United States Arms Control and Disarmament Agency
25. Civil Aeronautics Board
26. Federal Home Loan Bank Board
27. National Labour Relations Board
28. National Mediation Board
29. Railroad Retirement Board
30. American Battle Monuments Commission

+++ and their successor entities.

31.   Federal Communications Commission
32.   Federal Trade Commission
33.   Inter-State Commerce Commission
34.   Securities and Exchange Commission
35.   Office of Personnel Management
36.   United States International Trade Commission
37.   Export-Import Bank of the United States
38.   Federal Mediation and Conciliation Service
39.   Selective Service System
40.   Smithsonian Institution
41.   Federal Deposit Insurance Corporation
42.   Consumer Product Safety Commission
43.   Equal Employment Opportunity Commission
44.   Federal Maritime Commission
45.   National Transportation Safety Board
46.   Nuclear Regulatory Commission
47.   Overseas Private Investment Corporation
48.   Administrative Conference of the United States
49.   Board for International Broadcasting
50.   Commission on Civil Rights
51.   Commodity Futures Trading Commission
52.   The Maritime Administration of the Department of
      Transportation
53.   The Peace Corps
54.   Department of Defense (excluding Corps of Engineers)

This Agreement will not apply to the following purchases of the DOD:

(a)   Federal Supply Classification (FSC) 83 - all elements of
      this classification other than pins, needles, sewing kits,
      flagstaffs, flagpoles, and flagstaff trucks;
(b)   FSC 84 - all elements other than sub-class 8460 (luggage);
(c)   FSC 89 - all elements other than sub-class 8975
      (tobacco products)
(d)   FSC 2310 - (buses only);
(e)   Specialty metals, defined as steels melted in steel
      manufacturing facilities located in the United States or its
      possessions, where the maximum alloy content exceeds
      one or more of the following limits, must be used in
      products purchased by DOD: (1) manganese, 1.65 per
      cent; silicon, 0.60 per cent; or copper, 0.06 per cent; or
      which contains more than 0.25 per cent of any of the

following elements: aluminium, chromium, cobalt, columbium, molybdenum, nickel, titanium, tungsten, or vanadium;   (2) metal alloys consisting of nickel, iron-nickel,and cobalt base alloys containing a total of other alloying metals (except iron) in excess of 10 per cent; (3) titanium and titanium alloys; or, (4) zirconium base alloys;

(f)   FSC 19 and 20 - that part of these classifications defined as naval vessels or major components of the hull or superstructure thereof;

(g)   FSC 51;

(h)   Following FSC categories are not generally covered due to application of Article VIII, paragraph 1:

10, 12, 13, 14, 15, 16, 17, 19, 20, 28, 31, 58, 59, 95

This Agreement will generally apply to purchases of the following FSC categories subject to United States Government determinations under the provisions of Article VIII, paragraph 1 .

22.	Railway Equipment
23.	Motor Vehicles, Trailers, and Cycles (except buses in 2310)
24.	Tractors
25.	Vehicular Equipment Components
26.	Tyres and Tubes
29.	Engine Accessories
30.	Mechanical Power Transmission Equipment
32.	Woodworking Machinery and Equipment
34.	Metalworking Machinery
35.	Service and Trade Equipment
36.	Special Industry Machinery
37.	Agricultural Machinery and Equipment
38.	Construction, Mining, Excavating, and Highway Maintenance Equipment
39.	Materials Handling Equipment
40.	Rope, Cable, Chain and Fittings
41.	Refrigeration and Air Conditioning Equipment
42.	Fire Fighting, Rescue and Safety Equipment
43.	Pumps and Compressors
44.	Furnace, Steam Plant, Drying Equipment and Nuclear Reactors
45.	Plumbing, Heating and Sanitation Equipment
46.	Water Purification and Sewage Treatment Equipment
47.	Pipe, Tubing, Hose and Fittings
48.	Valves
49.	Maintenance and Repair Shop Equipment

52. Measuring Tools
53. Hardware and Abrasives
54. Prefabricated Structures and Scaffolding
55. Lumber, Millwork, Plywood and Veneer
56. Construction and Building Materials
61. Electric Wire, and Power and Distribution Equipment
62. Lighting Fixtures and Lamps
63. Alarm and Signal Systems
65. Medical, Dental, and Veterinary Equipment and Supplies
66. Instruments and Laboratory Equipment
67. Photographic Equipment
68. Chemicals and Chemical Products
69. Training Aids and Devices
70. General Purpose ADPE, Software, Supplies and Support
     Equipment
71. Furniture
72. Household and Commercial Furnishings and Appliances
73. Food Preparation and Serving Equipment
74. Office Machines, Visible Record Equipment and ADP
     Equipment
75. Office Supplies and Devices
76. Books, Maps and Other Publications
77. Musical Instruments, Phonographs, and Home Type Radios
78. Recreational and Athletic Equipment
79. Cleaning Equipment and Supplies
80. Brushes, Paints, Sealers and Adhesives
81. Containers, Packaging and Packing Supplies
85. Toiletries
87. Agricultural Supplies
88. Live Animals
91. Fuels, Lubricants, Oils and Waxes
93. Non-metallic Fabricated Materials
94. Non-metallic Crude Materials
96. Ores, Minerals and their Primary Products
99. Miscellaneous

General Notes

1.   Notwithstanding the above, this Agreement will not apply to set asides on behalf of small and minority businesses.

2.   Pursuant to Article I, paragraph 1(a), transportation is not included in services incidental to procurement contracts.

Annex 1305.3

Principles Guiding Bid Challenge Procedures

In order to promote fair, open and impartial procurement procedures, the Parties shall maintain bid challenge procedures for procurements covered by this Chapter in accordance with the principles that follow.

a) Bid challenges may concern any aspect of the procurement process covered by this Chapter leading up to and including the contract award.

b) Prior to initiating a bid challenge, a supplier should be encouraged to seek a resolution of any complaint with the contracting authority.

c) Whether or not a supplier has resorted to subparagraph (b) or upon unsuccessful resolution of a complaint pursuant to subparagraph (b), the supplier shall be allowed to submit a bid challenge or seek any other relief available to such supplier.

d) The procurement body for each entity covered by this Chapter, with respect to its covered procurements, shall accord impartial and timely consideration to any complaint or bid challenge by any supplier.

e) A reviewing authority with no substantial interest in the outcome of the procurement shall have responsibility for receiving and deciding bid challenges.

f) Upon receipt of a bid challenge, the reviewing authority shall expeditiously proceed to investigate the challenge and may delay the proposed award pending resolution of the bid challenge except in cases of urgency or where the delay would be prejudicial to the public interest. The reviewing authority shall determine the appropriate remedy, which may include re-evaluating offers, recompeting the contract, or terminating the contract.

g) The reviewing authority should be authorized to make recommendations in writing to contracting authorities respecting all facets of the procurement process, including recommendations for changes in procedures in order to bring them into conformity with the obligations of this Chapter. The procurement body or covered entities shall normally follow such recommendations.

h) Decisions of the reviewing authority respecting bid challenges shall be provided in writing in a timely fashion and made available to the Parties and all interested persons.

i) Each Party shall specify in writing and shall make generally available to all potential suppliers, all bid challenge procedures, including general time frames maintained or introduced by the procurement body for each entity with respect to bid challenge procedures.

j) Each Party may modify its bid challenge procedures from time to time provided such modifications are in conformity with this Chapter.

PART FOUR
SERVICES, INVESTMENT
AND TEMPORARY ENTRY

Chapter Fourteen

Services

Article 1401: Scope and Coverage

1.   This Chapter shall apply to any measure of a Party related to the provision of a covered service by or on behalf of a person of the other Party within or into the territory of the Party.

2.   In this Chapter, provision of a covered service includes:

   a) the production, distribution, sale, marketing and delivery of a covered service and the purchase or use thereof;

   b) access to, and use of, domestic distribution systems;

   c) the establishment of a commercial presence (other than an investment) for the purpose of distributing, marketing, delivering, or facilitating a covered service; and

   d) subject to Chapter Sixteen (Investment), any investment for the provision of a covered service and any activity associated with the provision of a covered service.

Article 1402: Rights and Obligations

1.   Subject to paragraph 3, each Party shall accord to persons of the other Party treatment no less favourable than that accorded in like circumstances to its persons with respect to the measures covered by this Chapter.

2.   The treatment accorded by a Party under paragraph 1 shall mean, with respect to a province or a state, treatment no less favourable than the most favourable treatment accorded by such province or state in like circumstances to persons of the Party of which it forms a part.

3.   Notwithstanding paragraphs 1 and 2, the treatment a Party accords to persons of the other Party may be different from the treatment the Party accords its persons provided that:

   a) the difference in treatment is no greater than that necessary for prudential, fiduciary, health and safety, or consumer protection reasons;

   b) such different treatment is equivalent in effect to the treatment accorded by the Party to its persons for such reasons; and

   c) prior notification of the proposed treatment has been given in accordance with Article 1803.

4.   The Party proposing or according different treatment under paragraph 3 shall have the burden of establishing that such treatment is consistent with that paragraph.

5.   Paragraphs 1, 2, and 3 of this Article and Article 1403 shall not apply to:

   a)   a non-conforming provision of any existing measure;

   b)   the continuation or prompt renewal of a non-conforming provision of any existing measure; or

   c)   an amendment to a non-conforming provision of any existing measure to the extent that the amendment does not decrease its conformity with any of the provisions of paragraphs 1, 2 or 3 or of Article 1403.

6.   The Party asserting that paragraph 5 applies, shall have the burden of establishing the validity of such assertion.

7.   Each Party shall apply the provisions of this Chapter with respect to an enterprise owned or controlled by a person of the other Party notwithstanding the incorporation or other legal constitution of such enterprise within the Party's territory.

8.   Notwithstanding that such measures may be consistent with paragraphs 1, 2 and 3 of this Article and Article 1403, neither Party shall introduce any measure, including a measure requiring the establishment or commercial presence by a person of the other Party

in its territory as a condition for the provision of a covered service, that constitutes a means of arbitrary or unjustifiable discrimination between persons of the Parties or a disguised restriction on bilateral trade in covered services.

9.   No provision of this Chapter shall be construed as imposing obligations or conferring rights upon either Party with respect to government procurement or subsidies.

Article 1403: Licensing and Certification

1.   The Parties recognize that measures governing the licensing and certification of nationals providing covered services should relate principally to competence or the ability to provide such covered services.

2.   Each Party shall ensure that such measures shall not have the purpose or effect of discriminatorily impairing or restraining the access of nationals of the other Party to such licensing or certification.

3.   The Parties shall encourage the mutual recognition of licensing and certification requirements for the provision of covered services by nationals of the other Party.

Article 1404: Sectoral Annexes

The provisions of this Chapter shall apply to the Sectoral Annexes set out in Annex 1404, except as specifically provided in the Annexes.

Article 1405:   Future Implementation

1.   The Parties shall endeavour to extend the obligations of this Chapter by negotiating and, subject to their respective legal procedures, implementing:

a) the modification or elimination of existing measures incon-
sistent with the provisions of paragraphs 1, 2 or 3 of Article 1402 and Article 1403; and

b) further Sectoral Annexes.

2.   The Parties shall periodically review and consult on the
provisions of this Chapter for the purpose of including additional
services and for identifying further opportunities for increasing access
to each other's services markets.

Article 1406: Denial of Benefits

1.   Subject to prior notification and consultation in accordance with
Articles 1803 and 1804, a Party may deny the benefits of this Chapter
to persons of the other Party providing a covered service if the Party
establishes that the covered service is indirectly provided by a person
of a third country.

2.   The Party denying benefits pursuant to paragraph 1 shall have
the burden of establishing that such action is in accordance with that
paragraph.

Article 1407:   Taxation

Subject to Article 2011, this Chapter shall not apply to any new
taxation measure, provided that such taxation measure does not
constitute a means of arbitrary or unjustifiable discrimination between
persons of the Parties or a disguised restriction on trade in covered
services between the Parties.

Article 1408:   Definitions

For purposes of this Chapter:

activity associated with the provision of a covered service
includes the organization, control, operation, maintenance and
disposition of companies, branches, agencies, offices, or other
facilities for the conduct of business; the acquisition, use, protection
and disposition of property of all kinds; and the borrowing of funds;

covered service means a service listed in the Schedule to Annex
1408 and described for purposes of reference in that Annex;

investment has the same meaning as in Article 1611; and

provision of a covered service into the territory of a Party
includes the cross-border provision of that covered service.

Annex 1408

Services Covered by this Chapter

Services covered by this Chapter shall be limited to those services corresponding to the Standard Industrial Classification (SIC) numbers included in the Schedule to this Annex, with the addition of computer services, telecommunications-network-based enhanced services and tourism services. For purposes of reference, the services covered by this Chapter are broadly identified below.

Agriculture and forestry services

Soil preparation services
Crop planting, cultivating and protection services
Crop harvesting services (primarily by machine)
Farm management services
Landscape and horticultural services
Forestry services (such as reforestation, forest firefighting)
Crop preparation services for market
Livestock and animal specialty services (except veterinary)

Mining services

Metal mining services
Coal mining services
Oil and gas field services
Non-metallic minerals (except fuels) services

Construction services

Building, developing and general contracting services
Special trade contracting services

Distributive trade services

Wholesale trade services
Vending machine services
Direct selling services

Insurance and real estate services

Insurance services
Segregated and other funds services (managed by insurance companies
      only)
Insurance agency and brokering services
Subdivision and development services
Patent ownership and leasing services
Franchising services
Real estate agency and management services
Real estate leasing services

Commercial services

Commercial cleaning services
Advertising and promotional services
Credit bureau services
Collection agency services
Stenographic, reproduction and mailing services
Telephone answering services
Commercial graphic art and photography services
Services to buildings
Equipment rental and leasing services
Personnel supply services
Security and investigation services
Security systems services
Hotel reservation services
Automotive rental and leasing services
Commercial educational correspondence services
Professional services, such as
      Engineering, architectural, and surveying services
      Accounting and auditing services
      Agrology services
      Scientific and technical services
      Management consulting services
      Librarian services
      Agriculture consulting services
Non-professional accounting and book-keeping services
Training services
Commercial physical and biological research services
Commercial economic, marketing, sociological, statistical and
      educational research services

Public relations services
Commercial testing laboratory services
Repair and maintenance services
Other business consulting services
Management services
  Hotel and motel management services
  Health care facilities management services
  Building management services
  Retail management services
Packing and crating services

Other Services

Computer services
Telecommunications-network-based enhanced services
Tourism services

Schedule

Each Party shall apply the provisions of this Chapter to the services listed under the Party's respective section below and shall extend those provisions to all subdivisions of each division, two-digit, three-digit or four-digit industrial code listed, except as specified, and shall also extend those provisions for each Party to tourism services as specifically defined in Annex 1404 (B) and to computer services and enhanced services as specifically defined in Annex 1404 (C).

For Canada

(Standard Industrial Classification (SIC) numbers as set out in Statistics Canada, *Standard Industrial Classification,* fourth edition, Department of Supply and Services, 1980)

02 (except 0211), 05, 09 (incidental to 06, 07, 08), 40, 41, 42, 44, 4599 - packing and crating only, 51, 52, 53, 54, 55, 56, 57, 59, 60 (except 602) - management services only, 61 - management services only, 62 - management services only, 63 - management services only, 635, 64 - management services only, 65 (except 651) - management services only, 69, 7211 - managed by insurance companies only, 7212 - managed by insurance companies only, 7213 - managed by insurance companies only, 7291 - managed by insurance companies only, 73 (except 732), 7499 - franchising, 75 - except mobile home and railroad property leasing, 76, 77 (except 776, 7794), 852 - commercial services only, 861 - management services only, 862 - management services only, 863 - management services only, 865 - management services only, 866 - management services only, 867 - management services only, 868 - commercial services only, 911 - management services only, 92, 9725, 99 (except 9931, 996, 9991).

For the United States of America

(Standard Industrial Classification (SIC) numbers as set out in the United States Office of Management and Budget, *Standard Industrial Classification Manual, 1987*)

071, 0721, 0722, 0723, 075, 0762, 078, 085, 108, 124, 138, 148, 15, 16, 17, 4783, 50, 51, 52 - management services only, 53 - management services only, 54 - management services only, 55 - management services only, 56 - management services only, 57 - management services only, 58 - management services only, 59 - management services only, 596, 63 (except 639), 64, 6512, 6513, 6514, 6519, 653, 6552, 6794 - franchising, 701 - management services only, 7213, 7218, 731, 732, 733, 734, 735, 736, 7381, 7382, 7389 - hotel reservation services and telephone answering services only, 751, 753, 76 - repair and maintenance services only, 80 (except 807) - management services only, 807 - commercial services only, 824 - commercial services only, 871, 872, 8731, 8732, 8734, 8741, 8742, 8743, 8748.

Annex 1404

Sectoral Annexes

A. Architecture

Article 1: Scope and Coverage

This Sectoral Annex shall apply to any measure relating to the mutual recognition of professional standards and criteria for the licensing and conduct of architects and the provision of architectural services.

Article 2: Development of Mutually Acceptable Professional Standards and Criteria

The Parties acknowledge that the Royal Architectural Institute of Canada and the American Institute of Architects, in consultation with appropriate professional and regulatory bodies, are endeavouring to develop mutually acceptable professional standards and criteria regarding the following matters for the purpose of making recommendations on mutual recognition, on or before December 31, 1989:

a) education -- accreditation of schools of architecture;

b) examination -- qualifying examinations for licensing;

c) experience -- determination of experience required in order to be licensed to practise;

d) conduct and ethics -- specification of professional conduct required of practising architects and the disciplinary action for non-conformity; and

e) professional development -- continuing education of practising architects.

Article 3: Implementation

Upon receipt of the recommendations of the professional associations, the Parties shall:

a) complete their review of the recommendations within 180 days following receipt; and

b) if such recommendations are consistent with this Chapter and acceptable to the Parties, encourage their respective state and provincial governments to adopt or amend, within the six-month period following completion of the review, those measures necessary so that:

   i) the respective state and provincial licensing authorities accept the licensing and certification requirements of the other Party on the same basis as their own; and

   ii) the treatment accorded persons of a Party providing architectural services within or into the territory of the other Party is consistent with paragraphs 1, 2, and 3 of Article 1402.

Article 4: Review

The Parties shall establish a committee for the purpose of reviewing compliance by the licensing authorities with the standards and criteria implemented pursuant to Article 3 of this Sectoral Annex.

B. Tourism

Article 1: Scope and Coverage

1.   This Sectoral Annex shall apply to any measure related to trade in tourism services.

2.   For purposes of this Sectoral Annex:

tourism services include the tourism-related activities of the following: travel agency and related travel services including tour wholesaling, travel counselling, arranging and booking; issuance of travellers insurance; all modes of international passenger transportation; hotel reservation services; terminal services for all modes of transport, including concessions; transportation catering services; airport transfer; lodging, including hotels, motels, and rooming houses; local sightseeing, regardless of mode of transportation; intercity tour operation; guide and interpreter services; automobile rental; provision of resort facilities; rental of recreational equipment; food services; retail services; organizational and support services for international conventions; marina-related services including the fueling, supply, and repair of, and provision of docking space to, pleasure boats; recreational vehicle rental; campground and trailer park services; amusement park services; commercial tourist attractions; and tourism-related services of a financial nature;

tourism-related services of a financial nature means such services provided by an entity that is not a financial institution as defined in Article 1706; and

trade in tourism services means the provision of a tourism service by a person of a Party

   a) within the territory of that Party to a visitor who is a resident of the other Party, or

   b) within the territory of the other Party to a resident of, or visitor to, the other Party, either cross-border, through a commercial presence or through an establishment in the territory of the other Party.

Article 2: Obligations

1.   This Chapter shall apply to all measures related to trade in tourism services, which measures include:

a) provision of tourism services in the territory of a Party, either individually or with members of a travel industry trade association;

b) appointment, maintenance and commission of agents or representatives in the territory of a Party to provide tourism services;

c) establishment of sales offices or designated franchises in the territory of a Party; and

d) access to basic telecommunications transport networks.

2.   Provided that such promotional activities do not include the provision of tourism services for profit, each Party may promote officially in the territory of the other Party the travel and tourism opportunities in its own territory, including engagement in joint promotions with tourism enterprises of that Party and provincial, state and local governments.

3.   The Parties recognize that the adoption or application of fees or other charges on the departure or arrival of tourists from their territories impedes the free flow of tourism services. When such fees or other charges are imposed, they shall be applied in a manner consistent with Article 1402 and limited in amount to the approximate cost of the services rendered.

4.   Neither Party shall impose, except in conformity with Article VIII of the *Articles of Agreement of the International Monetary Fund,* restrictions on the value of tourism services that its residents or visitors to its territory may purchase from persons of the other Party.

Article 3: Relationship to the Agreement

Nothing in this Sectoral Annex shall be construed as:

a) conferring rights or imposing obligations on a Party relating to computer services and enhanced services as defined in Annex

1404(C), financial services as defined in Article 1706 and transportation services that are not otherwise conferred or imposed pursuant to any other provision of this Agreement and its annexes; or

b) affecting in any way the application of measures relating to the provision of tourism-related services of a financial nature.

Article 4: Consultation

The Parties shall consult at least once a year to:

a) identify and seek to eliminate impediments to trade in tourism services; and

b) identify ways to facilitate and increase tourism between the Parties.

C. Computer Services and Telecommunications-Network-Based Enhanced Services

Article 1: Objective

The objective of this Sectoral Annex is to maintain and support the further development of an open and competitive market for the provision of enhanced services and computer services within or into the territories of the Parties. The provisions of this Sectoral Annex shall be construed in accordance with this objective.

Article 2: Scope and Coverage

This Sectoral Annex shall apply to any measure of a Party related to the provision of an enhanced or computer service by or on behalf of a person of the other Party within or into the territory of the Party.

Article 3: Rights and Obligations

1. This Chapter shall apply to all measures covered by this Sectoral Annex, which includes measures related to:

a) access to, and use of, basic telecommunications transport services, including, but not limited to, the lease of local and long-distance telephone service, full-period, flat-rate private-line services, dedicated local and intercity voice channels, public data network services, and dedicated local and intercity digital and analog data services for the movement of information, including intracorporate communications;

b) the resale and shared use of such basic telecommunications transport services;

c) the purchase and lease of customer-premises equipment or terminal equipment and the attachment of such equipment to basic telecommunications transport networks;

d) regulatory definitions of, or classifications as between, basic telecommunications transport services and enhanced services or computer services;

e) subject to Chapter Six (Technical Standards), standards, certification, testing or approval procedures; and

f) the movement of information across the borders and access to data bases or related information stored, processed or otherwise held within the territory of a Party.

2.   The establishment of a commercial presence as set out in this Chapter shall include the establishment of offices, appointment of agents, and installation of customer-premises equipment or terminal equipment for the purpose of distributing, marketing, delivering or facilitating the provision of an enhanced or computer service within or into the territory of a Party.

3.   Investment as set out in this Chapter shall include the purchase, lease, construction, or operation of equipment necessary for the provision of an enhanced or computer service.

Article 4:   Existing Access

1.   Each Party shall maintain existing access, within and across the borders of both Parties, for the provision of enhanced services through the use of the basic telecommunications transport network of the Party and for the provision of computer services.

2.   Nothing in paragraph 1 shall be construed to restrict or prevent a Party from introducing measures related to the provision of enhanced services and computer services provided that such measures are consistent with this Chapter.

Article 5:   Monopolies

1.   Where a Party maintains or designates a monopoly to provide basic telecommunications transport facilities or services, and the monopoly, directly or through an affiliate, competes in the provision of enhanced services, the Party shall ensure that the monopoly shall not engage in anticompetitive conduct in the enhanced services market, either directly or through its dealings with its affiliates, that adversely affects a person of the other Party. Such conduct may include cross-subsidization, predatory conduct, and the discriminatory provision of access to basic telecommunications transport facilities or services.

2.   Each Party shall maintain or introduce effective measures to prevent the anticompetitive conduct referred to in paragraph 1. These measures may include accounting requirements, structural separation, and disclosure.

Article 6:   Exceptions

1.   Nothing in this Agreement shall be construed:

   a) to require a Party to authorize a person of the other Party

      i) to establish, construct, acquire, lease or operate basic telecommunications transport facilities; or

      ii) to offer basic telecommunications transport services within its territory;

   b) to prevent a Party from maintaining, authorizing or designating monopolies for the provision of basic telecommunications transport facilities or services; or

   c) to prevent a Party from maintaining or introducing measures requiring basic telecommunications transport service traffic to be carried on basic telecommunications transport networks within its territory, where such traffic

      i) originates and terminates within its territory,

      ii) originates within its territory and is destined for the territory of the other Party or a third country, or

      iii) terminates in its territory, having originated in the territory of the other Party or a third country.

2.   The inclusion of intracorporate communications in this Sectoral Annex shall not be construed to indicate whether or not such communications are traded internationally. Their inclusion is to indicate that they may serve to facilitate trade in goods and services.

Article 7:   Definitions

For purposes of this Sectoral Annex:

basic telecommunications transport service means any service, as defined and classified by measures of the regulator having jurisdiction, that is limited to the offering of transmission capacity for the movement of information;

computer services means those services, whether or not conveyed over the basic telecommunications transport network, that involve generating, acquiring, storing, transforming, processing, retrieving, utilizing or making available information in a computerized form, including, but not limited to:

> computer programming,
> prepackaged software,
> computer integrated systems design,
> computer processing and data preparation,
> information retrieval services,
> computer facilities management,
> computer leasing and rental,
> computer maintenance and repair, and
> other computer-related services, including those integral to the
> > provision of other covered services;

enhanced service means any service offering over the basic telecommunications transport network that is more than a basic telecommunications transport service as defined and classified by measures of the regulator having jurisdiction; and

monopoly means any entity, including any consortium, that, in any relevant market in the territory of a Party, is the sole provider of basic telecommunications transport facilities or services.

Chapter Fifteen

Temporary Entry for Business Persons

Article 1501: General Principle

The provisions of this Chapter reflect the special trading relationship between the Parties, the desirability of facilitating temporary entry on a reciprocal basis and of establishing transparent criteria and procedures for temporary entry, and the need to ensure border security and protect indigenous labour and permanent employment.

Article 1502: Obligations

1.   The Parties shall provide, in accordance with Annex 1502.1, for the temporary entry of business persons who are otherwise qualified for entry under applicable law relating to public health and safety and national security.

2.   Each Party shall publish its laws, regulations and procedures relating to the provisions of this Chapter and provide to the other Party such explanatory materials as may be reasonably necessary to enable the other Party and its business persons to become acquainted with them.

3.   Any fees for processing applications for temporary entry of business persons shall be limited in amount to the approximate cost of services related thereto.

4.   Data collected and maintained by a Party respecting the granting of temporary entry to business persons under this Chapter shall be made available to the other Party in conformity with applicable law.

5.   The application and enforcement of measures governing the granting of temporary entry to business persons shall be accomplished expeditiously so as to avoid unduly impairing or delaying the conduct of trade in goods or services, or of investment activities, under this Agreement.

Article 1503: Consultation

The Parties shall establish a procedure, which shall involve the participation of immigration officials of both Parties, for consultation at least once a year respecting:

a) the implementation of this Chapter; and

b) the development of measures for the purpose of further facilitating temporary entry of business persons on a reciprocal basis and the development of amendments and additions to Annex 1502.1.

Article 1504: Dispute Settlement

1.   Subject to paragraph 2, a Party may invoke the provisions of Chapter Eighteen with respect to any matter governed by this Chapter.

2.   A Party may not invoke the provisions of Articles 1806 or 1807 of this Agreement with respect to the denial of a business person's request for temporary entry or a matter under paragraph 5 of Article 1502 unless:

a) the matter involves a pattern of practice; and

b) available administrative remedies have been exhausted with respect to the particular matter involving a business person's request for temporary entry, provided that such remedies shall be deemed to be exhausted if a final decision in the matter has not been issued within one year of the institution of administrative proceedings and the failure to issue a decision is not attributable to delay caused by the business person.

Article 1505: Relationship to other Chapters

No provision of any other Chapter of this Agreement shall be construed as imposing obligations upon the Parties with respect to the Parties' immigration measures.

Article 1506: Definitions

For purposes of this Chapter:

business person means a citizen of a Party who is engaged in the trade of goods or services or in investment activities; and

temporary entry means entry without the intent to establish permanent residence.

Annex 1502.1
Temporary Entry for Business Persons

<u>United States of America</u>

A.   Business Visitors

1.   A business person seeking temporary entry into the United States of America for purposes set forth in Schedule 1, who otherwise meets existing requirements under section 101(a)(15)(B) of the *Immigration and Nationality Act,* including but not limited to requirements regarding the source of remuneration, shall be granted entry upon presentation of proof of Canadian citizenship and documentation demonstrating that the business person is engaged in one of the occupations or professions set forth in Schedule 1 and describing the purpose of entry.

2.   A business person engaged in an occupation or profession other than those listed in Schedule 1 shall be granted temporary entry under section 101(a)(15)(B) of the *Immigration and Nationality Act* if the business person meets existing requirements for entry.

3.   The United States of America shall not require, as a condition for temporary entry under paragraphs 1 or 2, prior approval procedures, petitions, labour certification tests, or other procedures of similar effect.

B.   Traders and Investors

4.   A business person seeking temporary entry into the United States of America to carry on substantial trade in goods or services, in a capacity that is supervisory or executive or involves essential skills, principally between the United States of America and Canada, or solely to develop and direct the operations of an enterprise in which the business person has invested, or is actively in the process of investing, a substantial amount of capital, shall be granted entry under section 101(a)(15)(E) of the *Immigration and Nationality Act,* and be provided confirming documentation, if the business person meets existing requirements for visa issuance and for entry.

5.   The United States of America shall not require, as a condition for temporary entry under paragraph 4, labour certification tests or other procedures of similar effect.

C.   Professionals

6.   A business person seeking temporary entry into the United States of America to engage in business activities at a professional level who meets existing requirements under section 214(e) of the *Immigration and Nationality Act* shall be granted entry, and be provided confirming documentation, upon presentation of proof of Canadian citizenship and documentation demonstrating that the business person is engaged in one of the professions set forth in Schedule 2 and describing the purpose of entry.

7.   The United States of America shall not require, as a condition for temporary entry under paragraph 6, prior approval procedures, petitions, labour certification tests, or other procedures of similar effect.

D.   Intra-Company Transferees

8.   A business person seeking temporary entry into the United States of America as an intra-company transferee shall be granted entry under section 101(a)(15)(L) of the *Immigration and Nationality Act,* and be provided confirming documentation, if the business person:

a) immediately preceding the time of application for admission has been employed continuously for one year by a firm or corporation or other legal entity or an affiliate or subsidiary thereof;

b) is seeking temporary entry in order to continue to render services to the same employer or a subsidiary or affiliate thereof in a capacity that is managerial, executive, or involves specialized knowledge; and

c) meets existing requirements for entry.

9.   The United States of America shall not require, as a condition for temporary entry under paragraph 8, labour certification tests or other procedures of similar effect.

Canada

A. Business Visitors

1.   A business person seeking temporary entry into Canada for purposes set forth in Schedule 1, who otherwise meets existing requirements under the *Immigration Act, 1976,* shall be granted entry without being required to obtain an employment authorization pursuant to subsection 19(1) of the Immigration Regulations, 1978, upon presentation of proof of United States citizenship and documentation demonstrating that the business person is engaged in one of the occupations or professions set forth in Schedule 1 and describing the purpose of entry.

2.   A business person engaged in an occupation or profession other than those listed in Schedule 1 shall be granted temporary entry under the *Immigration Act, 1976,* without being required to obtain an employment authorization pursuant to subsection 19(1) of the Immigration Regulations, 1978, if the business person meets existing requirements for entry.

3.   Canada shall not require, as a condition for temporary entry under paragraphs 1 or 2, prior approval procedures, petitions, labour certification tests, or other procedures of similar effect.

B. Traders and Investors

4.   A business person seeking temporary entry into Canada to carry on substantial trade in goods or services, in a capacity that is supervisory or executive or involves essential skills, principally between Canada and the United States of America, or solely to develop and direct the operations of an enterprise in which the business person has invested, or is actively in the process of investing, a substantial amount of capital, shall be granted entry under the *Immigration Act, 1976,* and shall be issued an employment authorization pursuant to subsection 20(5) of the Immigration Regulations, 1978, if the business person meets existing requirements for entry.

5.   Canada shall not require, as a condition for temporary entry under paragraph 4, labour certification tests or other procedures of similar effect.

C.   Professionals

6.   A business person seeking temporary entry into Canada to engage in business activities at a professional level who meets existing requirements for entry under the *Immigration Act, 1976,* shall be granted entry and shall be issued an employment authorization pursuant to subsection 20(5) of the Immigration Regulations, 1978, upon presentation of proof of United States citizenship and documentation demonstrating that the business person is engaged in one of the professions set forth in Schedule 2 and describing the purpose of entry.

7.   Canada shall not require, as a condition for temporary entry under paragraph 6, prior approval procedures, petitions, labour certification tests, or other procedures of similar effect.

D.   Intra-Company Transferees

8.   A business person seeking temporary entry into Canada as an intra-company transferee shall be granted entry under the *Immigration Act, 1976,* and shall be issued an employment authorization pursuant to subsection 20(5) of the Immigration Regulations, 1978, if the business person:

a) immediately preceding the time of application for admission has been employed continuously for one year by a firm or corporation or other legal entity or an affiliate or subsidiary thereof;

b) is seeking temporary entry in order to continue to render services to the same employer or a subsidiary or affiliate thereof in a capacity that is managerial, executive, or involves specialized knowledge; and

c) meets existing requirements for entry.

9.   Canada shall not require, as a condition for temporary entry under paragraph 8, labour certification tests or other procedures of similar effect.

Schedule 1[1]
to
Annex 1502.1

Research and Design

- technical, scientific, and statistical researchers conducting independent research, or research for an enterprise located in Canada/the United States.

Growth, Manufacture and Production

- harvester owner supervising a harvesting crew admitted under applicable law.

- purchasing and production management personnel conducting commercial transactions for an enterprise located in Canada/the United States.

Marketing

- market researchers and analysts conducting independent research or analysis, or research or analysis for an enterprise located in Canada/ the United States.

- trade fair and promotional personnel attending a trade convention.

---

[1] Where Schedule 1 refers to "Canada/the United States" the applicable reference is to:
    a) Canada, if the business person is seeking temporary entry into the United States of America; or
    b) the United States of America, if the business person is seeking temporary entry into Canada.
Where Schedule 1 refers to "the United States/ Canada" the applicable reference is to:
    a) the United States of America, if the business person is seeking temporary entry into the United States of America; or
    b) Canada, if the business person is seeking temporary entry into Canada.

Sales

- sales representatives and agents taking orders or negotiating contracts for goods or services but not delivering goods or providing services.

- buyers purchasing for an enterprise located in Canada/ the United States.

Distribution

- transportation operators delivering to the United States/Canada or loading and transporting back to Canada/ the United States, with no intermediate loading or delivery within the United States/Canada.

- customs brokers performing brokerage duties associated with the export of goods from the United States/ Canada to or through Canada/ the United States.

After-Sales Service

- installers, repair and maintenance personnel, and supervisors, possessing specialized knowledge essential to the seller's contractual obligation, performing services or training workers to perform such services, pursuant to a warranty or other service contract incidental to the sale of commercial or industrial equipment or machinery, including computer software, purchased from an enterprise located outside the United States/Canada, during the life of the warranty or service agreement.

General Service

- professionals: with respect to entry into the United States of America, otherwise classifiable under section 101(a)(15)(H)(i) of the *Immigration and Nationality Act,* but receiving no salary or other remuneration from a United States source; and, with respect to entry into Canada, exempt from the requirement to obtain an employment authorization pursuant to subsection 19(1) of the Immigration Regulations, 1978, but receiving no salary or other remuneration from a Canadian source.

- management and supervisory personnel engaging in commercial transactions for an enterprise located in Canada/the United States.

- computer specialists: with respect to entry into the United States of America, otherwise classifiable under section 101(a)(15)(H)(i) of the *Immigration and Nationality Act,* but receiving no salary or other remuneration from a United States source; and, with respect to entry into Canada, exempt from the requirement to obtain an employment authorization pursuant to subsection 19(1) of the Immigration Regulations, 1978, but receiving no salary or other remuneration from a Canadian source.

- financial services personnel (insurers, bankers or investment brokers) engaging in commercial transactions for an enterprise located in Canada/ the United States.

- public relations and advertising personnel consulting with business associates, or attending or participating in conventions.

- tourism personnel (tour and travel agents, tour guides or tour operators) attending or participating in conventions or conducting a tour that has begun in Canada/ the United States.

- translators or interpreters performing services as employees of an enterprise located in Canada/ the United States.

Schedule 2
to
Annex 1502.1

- accountant
- engineer
- scientist
    ° biologist
    ° biochemist
    ° physicist
    ° geneticist
    ° zoologist
    ° entomologist
    ° geophysicist
    ° epidemiologist
    ° pharmacologist
    ° animal scientist
    ° agriculturist (agronomist)
    ° dairy scientist
    ° poultry scientist
    ° soil scientist

- research assistant
  (working in a post-secondary
  educational institution)
- medical/allied professional

    ° physician (teaching and/or
      research only)
    ° dentist
    ° registered nurse
    ° veterinarian
    ° medical technologist
    ° clinical lab technologist

- architect
- lawyer
- teacher
    ° college
    ° university
    ° seminary
- economist
- social worker
- vocational counselor
- mathematician (baccalaureate)
- hotel manager (baccalaureate
  and 3 years experience)
- librarian (MLS)
- animal breeder
- plant breeder
- horticulturist
- sylviculturist (forestry
  specialist)
- range manager (range
  conservationist)
- forester
- journalist (baccalaureate and 3
  years experience)
- nutritionist
- dietitian
- technical publications
  writer
- computer systems
  analyst

- psychologist

- scientific technician/technologist [2]
- disaster relief insurance claims adjuster [3]

- management consultant (baccalaureate, or equivalent professional experience[1])

---

[1] Standards for equivalence to be developed prior to entry into force of this Agreement.

[2] Must
   a) work in direct support of professionals in the following disciplines: chemistry, geology, geophysics, meteorology, physics, astronomy, agricultural sciences, biology, or forestry;
   b) possess theoretical knowledge of the discipline;
   c) solve practical problems in the discipline; and
   d) apply principles of the discipline to basic or applied research.

[3] Standards for qualification to be developed prior to entry into force of this Agreement.

Chapter Sixteen

Investment

Article 1601: Scope and Coverage

1.   Subject to paragraphs 2 and 3, this Chapter shall apply to any measure of a Party affecting investment within or into its territory by an investor of the other Party.

2.   This Chapter shall not apply to any measure affecting investments related to:

   a) the provision of financial services unless such measure relates to the provision of insurance services and is not dealt with under paragraph 1 of Article 1703;

   b) government procurement; or

   c) the provision of transportation services.

3.   The provisions of subparagraph 1(c) of Article 1602 shall not apply to any measure affecting investments related to the provision of services other than covered services.

Article 1602:   National Treatment

1.   Except as otherwise provided in this Chapter, each Party shall accord to investors of the other Party treatment no less favourable than that accorded in like circumstances to its investors with respect to its measures affecting:

   a) the establishment of new business enterprises located in its territory;

   b) the acquisition of business enterprises located in its territory;

   c) the conduct and operation of business enterprises located in its territory; and

   d) the sale of business enterprises located in its territory.

263

2.   Neither Party shall impose on an investor of the other Party a requirement that a minimum level of equity (other than nominal qualifying shares for directors or incorporators of corporations) be held by its nationals in a business enterprise located in its territory controlled by such investor.

3.   Neither Party shall require an investor of the other Party by reason of its nationality to sell or otherwise dispose of an investment (or any part thereof) made in its territory.

4.   The treatment accorded by a Party under paragraph 1 shall mean, with respect to a province or a state, treatment no less favourable than the most favourable treatment accorded by such province or state in like circumstances to investors of the Party of which it forms a part.

5.   Canada may introduce any new measure in respect of any business enterprise that is carried on at the date of entry into force of this Agreement by or on behalf of Canada or a province or a Crown corporation that:

a) is inconsistent with the provisions of paragraphs 1 or 2 and relates to the acquisition or sale of such business enterprise; or

b) relates to the direct or indirect ownership at any time of such business enterprise.

6.   Once Canada has introduced a new measure pursuant to paragraph 5, it shall not:

a) in the case of a new measure introduced pursuant to subparagraph 5(a), amend such new measure or introduce any subsequent measure that, as the case may be, renders such new measure more inconsistent with, or is more inconsistent with, the provisions of paragraphs 1 or 2; or

b) in the case of a new measure introduced pursuant to subparagraph 5(b), increase any ownership restrictions contained in such new measure.

7.   If, subsequent to the date of entry into force of this Agreement, a business enterprise is established or acquired by or on behalf of Canada or a province or a Crown corporation, the provisions of

paragraphs 1 and 2 shall not apply to the subsequent acquisition of such business enterprise as a result of its disposition by or on behalf of Canada or a province or a Crown corporation. Once such subsequent acquisition has been completed, the provisions of paragraphs 1 and 2 shall apply.

8.   Notwithstanding paragraph 1, the treatment a Party accords to investors of the other Party may be different from the treatment the Party accords its investors provided that:

   a) the difference in treatment is no greater than that necessary for prudential, fiduciary, health and safety, or consumer protection reasons;

   b) such different treatment is equivalent in effect to the treatment accorded by the Party to its investors for such reasons; and

   c) prior notification of the proposed treatment has been given in accordance with Article 1803.

9.   The Party proposing or according different treatment under paragraph 8 shall have the burden of establishing that such treatment is consistent with that paragraph.

Article 1603:   Performance Requirements

1.   Neither Party shall impose on an investor of the other Party, as a term or condition of permitting an investment in its territory, or in connection with the regulation of the conduct or operation of a business enterprise located in its territory, a requirement to:

   a) export a given level or percentage of goods or services;

   b) substitute goods or services from the territory of such Party for imported goods or services;

   c) purchase goods or services used by the investor in the territory of such Party or from suppliers located in such territory or accord a preference to goods or services produced in such territory; or

   d) achieve a given level or percentage of domestic content.

2.   Neither Party shall impose on an investor of a third country, as a term or condition of permitting an investment in its territory, or in connection with the regulation of the conduct or operation of a business enterprise located in its territory, a commitment to meet any of the requirements described in paragraph 1 where meeting such a requirement could have a significant impact on trade between the two Parties.

3.   For purposes of paragraphs 1 and 2 and paragraph 2 of Article 1602, a Party "imposes" a requirement or commitment on an investor when it requires particular action of an investor or when, after the date of entry into force of this Agreement, it enforces any undertaking or commitment of the type described in paragraphs 1 and 2 or in paragraph 2 of Article 1602 given to that Party after that date.

Article 1604:   Monitoring

1.   Each Party may require an investor of the other Party who makes or has made an investment in its territory to submit to it routine information respecting such investment solely for informational and statistical purposes. The Party shall protect such business information that is confidential from disclosure that would prejudice the investor's competitive position.

2.   Nothing in paragraph 1 shall preclude a Party from otherwise obtaining or disclosing information in connection with the non-discriminatory and good faith application of its laws.

Article 1605:   Expropriation

Neither Party shall directly or indirectly nationalize or expropriate an investment in its territory by an investor of the other Party or take any measure or series of measures tantamount to an expropriation of such an investment, except:

a) for a public purpose;

b) in accordance with due process of law;

c) on a non-discriminatory basis; and

d) upon payment of prompt, adequate and effective compensation at fair market value.

Article 1606: Transfers

1.   Subject to paragraph 2, neither Party shall prevent an investor of the other Party from transferring:

  a) any profits from an investment, including dividends;

  b) any royalties, fees, interest and other earnings from an investment; or

  c) any proceeds from the sale of all or any part of an investment or from the partial or complete liquidation of such investment.

2.   A Party may, through the equitable, non-discriminatory and good faith application of its laws, prevent any transfer referred to in paragraph 1 if such transfer is inconsistent with any measure of general application relating to:

  a) bankruptcy, insolvency or the protection of the rights of creditors;

  b) issuing, trading or dealing in securities;

  c) criminal or penal offences;

  d) reports of currency transfers;

  e) withholding taxes; or

  f) ensuring the satisfaction of judgments in adjudicatory proceedings.

Article 1607: Existing Legislation

1.   The provisions of Articles 1602, 1603, 1604, 1605 and 1606 of this Chapter shall not apply to:

  a)   a non-conforming provision of any existing measure;

  b)   the continuation or prompt renewal of a non-conforming provision of any existing measure; or

c) an amendment to a non-conforming provision of any existing measure to the extent that the amendment does not decrease its conformity with any of the provisions of Articles 1602, 1603, 1604, 1605 or 1606.

2.   The Party asserting that paragraph 1 applies shall have the burden of establishing the validity of such assertion.

3.   The *Investment Canada Act,* its regulations and guidelines shall be amended as provided for in Annex 1607.3.

4.   In the event that Canada requires the divestiture of a business enterprise located in Canada in a cultural industry pursuant to its review of an indirect acquisition of such business enterprise by an investor of the United States of America, Canada shall offer to purchase the business enterprise from the investor of the United States of America at fair open market value, as determined by an independent, impartial assessment.

Article 1608:   Disputes

1.   A decision by Canada following a review under the *Investment Canada Act,* with respect to whether or not to permit an acquisition that is subject to review, shall not be subject to the dispute settlement provisions of this Agreement.

2.   Each Party and investors of each Party retain their respective rights and obligations under customary international law with respect to portfolio and direct investment not covered under this Chapter or to which the provisions of this Chapter do not apply.

3.   Nothing in this Chapter shall affect the rights and obligations of either Party under the *General Agreement on Tariffs and Trade* or under any other international agreement to which both are party.

4.   In view of the special nature of investment disputes and the expertise required to resolve them, where the procedures of Chapter Eighteen (Institutional Provisions) are invoked, the Parties and the Commission shall give the fullest consideration, in any particular case, to settling any dispute regarding the interpretation or application of this Chapter by arbitration or panel procedures pursuant to Articles 1806 or 1807, and shall make every attempt to ensure that the panelists are individuals experienced and competent in the field of international

investment. When deciding a dispute pursuant to Articles 1806 or 1807, the panel shall take into consideration how such disputes before it are normally dealt with by internationally recognized rules for commercial arbitration.

Article 1609:   Taxation and Subsidies

1.   Subject to Article 2011, this Chapter shall not apply to any new taxation measure, provided that such measure does not constitute a means of arbitrary or unjustifiable discrimination between investors of the Parties or a disguised restriction on the benefits accorded to investors of the Parties under this Chapter.

2.   Subject to Article 2011, this Chapter shall not apply to any subsidy, provided that such subsidy does not constitute a means of arbitrary or unjustifiable discrimination between investors of the Parties or a disguised restriction on the benefits accorded to investors of the Parties under this Chapter.

Article 1610:   International Agreements

The Parties shall endeavour, in the Uruguay Round and in other international forums, to improve multilateral arrangements and agreements with respect to investment.

Article 1611:   Definitions

For purposes of this Chapter, not including Annex 1607.3:

acquisition with respect to:

a) a business enterprise carried on by an entity, means an acquisition, as a result of one or more transactions, of the ultimate direct or indirect control of the entity through the acquisition of the ownership of voting interests; or

b) any business enterprise, means an acquisition, as a result of one or more transactions, of the ownership of all or substantially all of the assets of the business enterprise used in carrying on the business.

business enterprise means a business that has, or in the case of an establishment thereof will have:

a) a place of business;
b) an individual or individuals employed or self-employed in connection with the business; and
c) assets used in carrying on the business.

NOTE: A part of a business enterprise that is capable of being carried on as a separate business enterprise is itself a business enterprise.

control or controlled, with respect to:

a) a business enterprise carried on by an entity, means
  i) the ownership of all or substantially all of the assets used in carrying on the business enterprise; and
  ii) includes, with respect to an entity that controls a business enterprise in the manner described in subparagraph (i), the ultimate direct or indirect control of such entity through the ownership of voting interests; and
b) a business enterprise other than a business enterprise carried on by an entity, means the ownership of all or substantially all of the assets used in carrying on the business enterprise.

Crown corporation means a Crown corporation within the meaning of the *Financial Administration Act (Canada)* or a Crown corporation within the meaning of any comparable provincial legislation or that is incorporated under other applicable provincial legislation.

cultural industry has the same meaning as in Article 2012.

entity means a corporation, partnership, trust or joint venture.

establishment means a start-up of a new business enterprise and the activities related thereto.

indirect acquisition has the same meaning as in Annex 1607. 3.

investment means:

a) the establishment of a new business enterprise, or
b) the acquisition of a business enterprise;
and includes:
c) as carried on, the new business enterprise so established or the business enterprise so acquired, and controlled by the investor who has made the investment; and

d) the share or other investment interest in such business enterprise owned by the investor provided that such business enterprise continues to be controlled by such investor.

investor of a Party means:

a) such Party or agency thereof;
b) a province or state of such Party or agency thereof;
c) a national of such Party;
d) an entity ultimately controlled directly or indirectly through the ownership of voting interests by:
   i)   such Party or one or more agencies thereof,
   ii) one or more provinces or states of such Party or one or more agencies thereof,
   iii) one or more nationals of such Party,
   iv) one or more entities described in paragraph (e), or
   v)   any combination of persons or entities described in (i), (ii), (iii) and (iv); or
e) an entity that is not ultimately controlled directly or indirectly through the ownership of voting interests where a majority of the voting interests of such entity are owned by:
   i)   persons described in subparagraphs (d) (i), (ii) and (iii),
   ii) entities incorporated or otherwise duly constituted in the territory of such Party and, in the case of entities that carry on business, carrying on a business enterprise located in the territory of such Party, other than any such entity in respect of which it is established that nationals of a third country control such entity or own a majority of the voting interests of such entity, or
   iii) any combination of persons or entities described in (i) and (ii);

that makes or has made an investment.

NOTE: For purposes of paragraph (e), in respect of individuals each of whom holds not more than one percent of the total number of the voting interests of an entity the voting interests of which are publicly traded, it shall be presumed, in the absence of evidence to the contrary, that those voting interests are owned by nationals of such Party on the basis of a statement by a duly authorized officer of the entity that, according to the records of the entity, those individuals have addresses in the territory of such Party and that the signatory to the statement has no knowledge or reason to believe that those voting interests are owned by individuals who are not nationals of such Party.

investor of a third country means an investor other than an investor of a Party, that makes or has made an investment.

investor of the United States of America for purposes of paragraph 4 of Article 1607 shall have the same meaning as in Annex 1607.3.

joint venture means an association of two or more persons or entities where the relationship among those associated persons or entities does not, under the laws in force in the territory of the Party in which the investment is made, constitute a corporation, a partnership or a trust and where all those associated persons or entities own or will own assets of a business enterprise, or directly or indirectly own or will own voting interests in an entity that carries on a business enterprise.

located in the territory of a Party means, with respect to a business enterprise, a business enterprise that is, or in the case of an establishment will be, carried on in the territory of such Party and has, or in the case of an establishment will have therein:

a) a place of business;
b) an individual or individuals employed or self-employed in connection with the business; and
c) assets used in carrying on the business.

measure shall have the same meaning as in Article 201, except that it shall also include any published policy.

ownership means beneficial ownership and with respect to assets also includes the beneficial ownership of a leasehold interest in such assets.

person means a Party or agency thereof, a province or state of a Party or agency thereof, or a national of a Party.

voting interest with respect to

a) a corporation with share capital, means a voting share;
b) a corporation without share capital, means an ownership interest in the assets thereof that entitles the owner to rights similar to those enjoyed by the owner of a voting share; and
c) a partnership, trust, joint venture or other organization means an ownership interest in the assets thereof that entitles the owner

to receive a share of the profits and to share in the assets on dissolution.

voting share means a share in the capital of a corporation to which is attached a voting right ordinarily exercisable at meetings of shareholders of the corporation and to which is ordinarily attached a right to receive a share of the profits, or to share in the assets of the corporation on dissolution, or both.

Annex 1607.3

1.   Unless otherwise expressly provided in this Annex, words and phrases used herein shall be interpreted and construed in accordance with the provisions of the *Investment Canada Act* and its regulations.

2.   The *Investment Canada Act* and its regulations shall be amended as of the date of entry into force of this Agreement in accordance with the provisions that follow:

a) Canada may continue to review the acquisition of control of a Canadian business by an investor of the United States of America, in order to determine whether or not to permit the acquisition, provided that the value of the gross assets of the Canadian business is not less than the following applicable threshold.

i) The threshold for the review of a direct acquisition of control of a Canadian business shall be:

A)   for the twelve-month period commencing on the date of entry into force of this Agreement, current Canadian $25 million;

B)   for the twelve-month period commencing on the first anniversary of the date of entry into force of this Agreement, current Canadian $50 million;

C)   for the twelve-month period commencing on the second anniversary of the date of entry into force of this Agreement, current Canadian $100 million;

D)   for the twelve-month period commencing on the third anniversary of the date of entry into force of this Agreement, current Canadian $150 million; and

E)   commencing on the fourth anniversary of the date of entry into force of this Agreement, Canadian $150 million in constant third-anniversary-year dollars.

ii) The threshold for the review of an indirect acquisition of control of a Canadian business shall be:

A) for the twelve-month period commencing on the date of entry into force of this Agreement, current Canadian $100 million;

B) for the twelve-month period commencing on the first anniversary of the date of entry into force of this Agreement, current Canadian $250 million;

C) for the twelve-month period commencing on the second anniversary of the date of entry into force of this Agreement, current Canadian $500 million; and

D) commencing on the third anniversary of the date of entry into force of this Agreement, there shall be no review of indirect acquisitions implemented on or after that date.

b) In the event that a Canadian business controlled by an investor of the United States of America is being acquired by an investor of a third country, Canada may continue to review such acquisition to determine whether or not to permit it, provided that the value of the gross assets of the business is not less than the applicable threshold referred to in this paragraph.

c) i) The Canadian $150 million in constant third-anniversary-year dollars referred to in subparagraph (a)(i)(E) shall be determined in January of each year after 1992 by use of the following formula:

$$\frac{\text{Current GDP Price Index}}{\text{Effective Date GDP Price Index}} \quad \text{times} \quad \$150\ \text{million}$$

where:

GDP Price Index means the seasonally adjusted implicit quarterly price index for Gross Domestic Product at market prices as most recently published by Statistics Canada, or any successor index thereto.

Current GDP Price Index means the arithmetic average of the GDP Price Indices for the four most recent consecutive quarters available on the date on which a calculation takes place.

Effective Date GDP Price Index means the arithmetic average of the GDP Price Indices for the four most recent consecutive quarters available as of January 1, 1992.

ii) The amounts obtained by applying the formula set out in (i) shall be rounded to the nearest million dollars.

3.   The guidelines or regulations pursuant to the *Investment Canada Act* shall be amended to provide that Canada shall comply with the provisions of paragraphs 2 and 3 of Article 1602 and the provisions of Article 1603.

4.   The amendments described in paragraphs 2 and 3 and the provisions of paragraph 2 of Article 1602 and of Article 1603 shall not apply in respect of the oil and gas and uranium-mining industries. These industries are subject to published policies that are implemented through the review process set out in the *Investment Canada Act*. The Parties shall by exchange of letters, prior to introduction of legislation to implement this Agreement by either Party in its respective legislature, set out the aforementioned policies, which policies shall be no more restrictive than those in effect on October 4, 1987.

5.   For purposes of this Annex:

American shall have the same meaning as investor of the United States of America.

controlled by an investor of the United States of America, with respect to a Canadian business, means:

a) the ultimate direct or indirect control by such investor through the ownership of voting interests; or
b) the ownership by such investor of all or substantially all of the assets used in carrying on the Canadian business.

direct acquisition of control means an acquisition of control pursuant to the provisions of the *Investment Canada Act* other than an indirect acquisition of control.

indirect acquisition of control means an acquisition of control pursuant to the provisions of the *Investment Canada Act* through the acquisition of voting interests of an entity that controls, directly or indirectly, an entity in Canada carrying on the Canadian business where:

a) there is an acquisition of control described in subparagraph 28(1)(d)(ii) of the *Investment Canada Act;* and

b) the value, calculated in the manner prescribed, of the assets of the entity carrying on the Canadian business, and of all other entities in Canada, the control of which is acquired, directly or indirectly, amounts to not more than fifty percent of the value, calculated in the manner prescribed, of the assets of all entities the control of which is acquired, directly or indirectly, in the transaction of which the acquisition of control of the Canadian business forms a part.

investor of a third country means an individual, a government or an agency thereof or an entity that is not a Canadian within the meaning of the *Investment Canada Act* and is not an investor of the United States of America.

investor of the United States of America means

a) an individual who is a "national of the United States" or an individual who is "lawfully admitted for permanent residence" as those terms are defined in the existing provisions of the United States *Immigration and Nationality Act,* other than an individual who is a Canadian within the meaning of the *Investment Canada Act;*

b) a government of the United States of America, whether federal or state, or an agency thereof; or

c) an entity that is not Canadian-controlled as determined pursuant to subsections 26(1) and (2) of the *Investment Canada Act* and is American-controlled.

NOTE: For purposes only of determining whether an entity is "American-controlled" under paragraph (c), the rules in subsections 26 (1) and (2) of the *Investment Canada Act* shall be applied as though the references therein to "Canadian", "Canadians", "non-Canadian", "non-Canadians" and "Canadian-controlled", were references to "American", "Americans", "non-American", "non-Americans" and "American-controlled".

non-American means an individual, a government or an agency thereof or an entity that is not an American and is not a Canadian within the meaning of the *Investment Canada Act.*

PART FIVE
FINANCIAL SERVICES

Chapter Seventeen

Financial Services

Article 1701: Scope and Coverage

1. This Part and Articles 1601, 2001, 2002, 2003, 2010, 2101, 2104, 2105 and 2106 shall apply to financial services and constitute the entirety of the agreement between the Parties with respect to financial services. No other provision of this Agreement confers rights or imposes obligations on the Parties with respect to financial services.

2. The provisions of this Part, with the exception of Article 1601 as referred to in paragraph 1, shall not apply to any measure of a political subdivision of either Party.

Article 1702: Commitments of the United States of America

1. To the extent that domestic and foreign banks, including bank holding companies and affiliates thereof, are permitted to engage in the dealing in, underwriting, and purchasing of debt obligations backed by the full faith and credit of the United States of America or its political subdivisions, the United States of America shall permit domestic and foreign banks, including bank holding companies and affiliates thereof, to engage in the dealing in, underwriting, and purchasing of debt obligations backed to a comparable degree by Canada or its political subdivisions, which include, but are not limited to, obligations of or guaranteed by Canada or its political subdivisions, and obligations of agents thereof where the obligations of the agents are incurred in their capacity as agents for their principals and the principals are ultimately and unconditionally liable in respect of the obligations.

2. The United States of America shall not adopt or apply any measure under federal law that would accord treatment less favourable to Canadian-controlled banks than that accorded on October 4, 1987, with respect to their ability to establish and operate, outside their home states, any state branch, state agency or bank or commercial lending company subsidiary.

3.   The United States of America shall accord Canadian-controlled financial institutions the same treatment as that accorded United States financial institutions with respect to amendments to the *Glass-Steagall Act* and associated legislation and resulting amendments to regulations and administrative practices.

4.   This Part shall not be construed as representing the mutual satisfaction of the Parties concerning the treatment of their respective financial institutions. Accordingly, the United States of America shall, subject to Canada's commitment to consult and to liberalize further the rules governing its markets and to extend the benefits of such liberalization to United States-controlled financial institutions established under the laws of Canada, continue to provide Canadian-controlled financial institutions established under the laws of the United States of America with the rights and privileges they now have in the United States market as a result of existing laws, regulations, practices and stated policies of the United States of America. The continued provision of such rights and privileges shall be subject to normal regulatory and prudential considerations.

Article 1703: Commitments of Canada

1.   United States persons ordinarily resident in the United States of America shall not be subject to restrictions that limit foreign ownership of Canadian-controlled financial institutions and, in accordance with this obligation, such United States persons shall not be subject to:

  a) subsection 110(1) of the *Bank Act;*

  b) subsections 19(1) and 20(2) of the *Canadian and British Insurance Companies Act;*

  c) subsections 11(1) and 12(2) of the *Investment Companies Act;*

  d) subsections 45(1) and 46(2) of the *Loan Companies Act (Canada);* or

  e) subsections 38(1) and 39(2) of the *Trust Companies Act (Canada).*

This paragraph shall not apply to provincially constituted financial institutions.

2.   Canada shall exempt United States-controlled Canadian bank subsidiaries, individually and collectively, from the limitations on the total domestic assets of foreign bank subsidiaries in Canada and, in accordance with this obligation, Canada shall:

a) not refuse to incorporate a United States-controlled Canadian bank subsidiary, nor refuse to increase the authorized capital of such subsidiaries solely on the ground that such incorporation or increase would contravene subsection 302(7) of the *Bank Act;*

b) not apply the provisions of subsection 174(6) of the *Bank Act* to such subsidiaries;

c) exempt such subsidiaries from the requirement to obtain approval of the Minister of Finance prior to opening additional branches within Canada; and

d) permit, subject to prudential requirements of general application, including measures regarding transactions between related parties, a United States-controlled Canadian bank subsidiary to transfer loans to its parent.

3.   Canada shall not use review powers governing the entry of United States-controlled financial institutions in a manner inconsistent with the aims of this Part.

4.   This Part shall not be construed as representing the mutual satisfaction of the Parties concerning the treatment of their respective financial institutions. Accordingly, Canada shall, subject to the United States commitment to consult and to liberalize further the rules governing its markets and to extend the benefits of such liberalization to Canadian-controlled financial institutions established under the laws of the United States of America, continue to provide United States-controlled financial institutions established under the laws of Canada with the rights and privileges they now have in the Canadian market as a result of existing laws, regulations, practices and stated policies of Canada. The continued provision of such rights and privileges is subject to normal regulatory and prudential considerations.

Article 1704: Notification and Consultation

1.   To the extent possible, each Party shall make public, and allow opportunity for comment on, legislation and proposed regulations regarding any matter covered by this Part.

2.   Either Party may request consultations at any time regarding a matter covered by this Part. Any consultations under this Part shall be between the Canadian Department of Finance and the United States Department of the Treasury.

Article 1705:   General Provisions

1.   Any reference to a specific Act or portion thereof in this Part, shall be deemed to include a reference to any successor Act or portion thereof.

2.   Each Party may deny the benefits of this Part to a company of the other Party if the Party establishes that such company is controlled by a person of a third country.

Article 1706:   Definitions

For purposes of this Part:

administrative practices means all actions, practices and procedures by any federal agency having regulatory responsibility over the activities of financial institutions, including but not limited to rules, orders, directives, and approvals;

Canadian-controlled means controlled, directly or indirectly, by one or more individuals who are ordinarily resident in Canada;

A company is **controlled** by one or more persons if

  a) shares of the company to which are attached more than 50 percent of the votes that may be cast to elect directors of the company are beneficially owned by the person or persons; and the votes attached to those shares are sufficient to elect a majority of the directors of the company, or

  b) the person or persons has or have, directly or indirectly, control in fact of the company;

company means any kind of corporation, company, association, or other organization, legally authorized to do business under the laws and regulations of a Party or a political subdivision thereof;

existing means in effect at the time of the entry into force of this Agreement;

financial institution is any company authorized to do business under laws of a Party or its political subdivisions relating to financial institutions as defined by a Party, or a holding company thereof;

financial service is a service of a financial nature offered by a financial institution excluding the underwriting and selling of insurance policies;

measure includes any law, regulation, procedure, requirement or practice;

ordinarily resident in a country generally means sojourning in that country for a period of, or periods the aggregate of which is, 183 days or more during the relevant year;

political subdivision includes a province, state, and local government;

third country means any country other than Canada or the United States of America or any territory not a part of the territory of the Parties;

United States-controlled means controlled, directly or indirectly, by one or more United States nationals;

United States national means an individual who is a United States citizen or permanent resident of the United States of America; and

United States persons ordinarily resident in the United States of America, for purposes of paragraph 1 of Article 1703, means:

a) in the case of a company, a company legally constituted or organized under the laws of the United States of America and controlled, directly or indirectly, by one or more United States individuals described in subparagraph (b), and

b) in the case of an individual, one who is ordinarily resident in the United States of America.

PART SIX
INSTITUTIONAL PROVISIONS

Chapter Eighteen

Institutional Provisions

Article 1801: Application

1.   Except for the matters covered in Chapter Seventeen (Financial Services) and Chapter Nineteen (Binational Dispute Settlement in Antidumping and Countervailing Duty Cases), the provisions of this Part shall apply with respect to the avoidance or settlement of all disputes regarding the interpretation or application of this Agreement or whenever a Party considers that an actual or proposed measure of the other Party is or would be inconsistent with the obligations of this Agreement or cause nullification or impairment in the sense of Article 2011, unless the Parties agree to use another procedure in any particular case.

2.   Disputes arising under both this Agreement and the *General Agreement on Tariffs and Trade,* and agreements negotiated thereunder (GATT), may be settled in either forum, according to the rules of that forum, at the discretion of the complaining Party.

3.   Once the dispute settlement provisions of this Agreement or the GATT have been initiated pursuant to Article 1805 or the GATT with respect to any matter, the procedure initiated shall be used to the exclusion of any other.

Article 1802: The Commission

1.   The Parties hereby establish the Canada-United States Trade Commission (the Commission) to supervise the implementation of this Agreement, to resolve disputes that may arise over its interpretation and application, to oversee its further elaboration, and to consider any other matter that may affect its operation.

2.   The Commission shall be composed of representatives of both Parties. The principal representative of each Party shall be the cabinet-level officer or Minister primarily responsible for international trade, or their designees.

3.   The Commission shall convene at least once a year in regular session to review the functioning of this Agreement. Regular sessions of the Commission shall be held alternately in the two countries.

4.   The Commission may establish, and delegate responsibilities to, ad hoc or standing committees or working groups and seek the advice of non-governmental individuals or groups.

5.   The Commission shall establish its rules and procedures. All decisions of the Commission shall be taken by consensus.

Article 1803: Notification

1.   Each Party shall provide written notice to the other Party of any proposed or actual measure that it considers might materially affect the operation of this Agreement. The notice shall include, whenever appropriate, a description of the reasons for the proposed or actual measure.

2.   The written notice shall be given as far in advance as possible of the implementation of the measure. If prior notice is not possible, the Party implementing the measure shall provide written notice to the other Party as soon as possible after implementation.

3.   Upon request of the other Party, a Party shall promptly provide information and respond to questions pertaining to any actual or proposed measure, whether or not previously notified.

4.   The provision of written notice shall be without prejudice as to whether the measure is consistent with this Agreement.

Article 1804: Consultations

1.   Either Party may request consultations regarding any actual or proposed measure or any other matter that it considers affects the operation of this Agreement, whether or not the matter has been notified in accordance with Article 1803.

2.   The Parties shall make every attempt to arrive at a mutually satisfactory resolution of any matter through consultations under this Article or other consultative provisions in this Agreement.

3.   Each Party shall treat any confidential or proprietary information exchanged in the course of consultations on the same basis as the Party providing the information.

Article 1805: Initiation of Procedures

1.   If the Parties fail to resolve a matter through consultations within 30 days of a request for consultations under Article 1804, either Party may request in writing a meeting of the Commission. The request shall state the matter complained of, and shall indicate what provisions of this Agreement are considered relevant. Unless otherwise agreed, the Commission shall convene within 10 days and shall endeavour to resolve the dispute promptly.

2.   The Commission may call on such technical advisors as it deems necessary, or on the assistance of a mediator acceptable to both Parties, in an effort to reach a mutually satisfactory resolution of the dispute.

Article 1806: Arbitration

1   If a dispute has been referred to the Commission under Article 1805 and has not been resolved within a period of 30 days after such referral, the Commission:

a) shall refer a dispute regarding actions taken pursuant to Chapter Eleven (Emergency Action); and

b) may refer any other dispute,

to binding arbitration on such terms as the Commission may adopt.

2.   Unless the Commission directs otherwise, an arbitration panel shall be established and perform its functions in a manner consistent with the provisions of paragraphs 1, 3 and 4 of Article 1807.

3.   If a Party fails to implement in a timely fashion the findings of a binding arbitration panel and the Parties are unable to agree on appropriate compensation or remedial action, then the other Party shall have the right to suspend the application of equivalent benefits of this Agreement to the non-complying Party.

Article 1807: Panel Procedures

1.   The Commission shall develop and maintain a roster of individuals who are willing and able to serve as panelists. Wherever possible, panelists shall be chosen from this roster. In all cases, panelists shall be chosen strictly on the basis of objectivity, reliability and sound judgment and, where appropriate, have expertise in the particular matter under consideration. Panelists shall not be affiliated with or take instructions from either Party.

2.   If a dispute has been referred to the Commission under Article 1805 and has not been resolved within a period of 30 days after such referral, or within such other period as the Commission has agreed upon, or has not been referred to arbitration pursuant to Article 1806, the Commission, upon request of either Party, shall establish a panel of experts to consider the matter. A panel shall be deemed to be established from the date of the request of a Party.

3.   The panel shall be composed of five members, at least two of whom shall be citizens of Canada and at least two of whom shall be citizens of the United States. Within 15 days of establishment of the panel, each Party, in consultation with the other Party, shall choose two members of the panel and the Commission shall endeavour to agree on the fifth who shall chair the panel. If a Party fails to appoint its panelists within 15 days, such panelists shall be selected by lot from among its citizens on the roster described in paragraph 1. If the Commission is unable to agree on the fifth panelist within such period, then, at the request of either Party, the four appointed panelists shall decide on the fifth panelist within 30 days of establishment of the panel. If no agreement is possible, the fifth panelist shall be selected by lot from the roster described in paragraph 1.

4.   The panel shall establish its rules of procedure, unless the Commission has agreed otherwise. The procedures shall assure a right to at least one hearing before the panel as well as the opportunity to provide written submissions and rebuttal arguments. The proceedings of the panel shall be confidential. Unless otherwise agreed by the Parties, the panel shall base its decision on the arguments and submissions of the Parties.

5.   Unless the Parties otherwise agree, the panel shall, within three months after its chairman is appointed, present to the Parties an initial report containing findings of fact, its determination as to whether the

measure at issue is or would be inconsistent with the obligations of this Agreement or cause nullification and impairment in the sense of Article 2011, and its recommendations, if any, for resolution of the dispute. Where feasible, the panel shall afford the Parties opportunity to comment on its preliminary findings of fact prior to completion of its report. If requested by either Party at the time of establishment of the panel, the panel shall also present findings as to the degree of adverse trade effect on the other Party of any measure found not to conform with the obligations of the Agreement. Panelists may furnish separate opinions on matters not unanimously agreed.

6.   Within 14 days of issuance of the initial report of the panel, a Party disagreeing in whole or in part shall present a written statement of its objections and the reasons for those objections to the Commission and the panel. In such an event, the panel on its own motion or at the request of the Commission or either Party may request the views of both Parties, reconsider its report, make any further examination that it deems appropriate and issue a final report, together with any separate opinions, within 30 days of issuance of the initial report.

7.   Unless the Commission agrees otherwise, the final report of the panel shall be published along with any separate opinions, and any written views that either Party desires to be published.

8.   Upon receipt of the final report of the panel, the Commission shall agree on the resolution of the dispute, which normally shall conform with the recommendation of the panel. Whenever possible, the resolution shall be non-implementation or removal of a measure not conforming with this Agreement or causing nullification or impairment in the sense of Article 2011 or, failing such a resolution, compensation.

9.   If the Commission has not reached agreement on a mutually satisfactory resolution under paragraph 8 within 30 days of receiving the final report of the panel (or such other date as the Commission may decide), and a Party considers that its fundamental rights (under this Agreement) or benefits (anticipated under this Agreement) are or would be impaired by the implementation or maintenance of the measure at issue, the Party shall be free to suspend the application to the other Party of benefits of equivalent effect until such time as the Parties have reached agreement on a resolution of the dispute.

Article 1808:   Referrals of Matters from Judicial or Administrative Proceedings

1.   In the event an issue of interpretation of this Agreement arises in any domestic judicial or administrative proceeding of a Party which either Party considers would merit its intervention, or if a court or administrative body solicits the views of a Party, the Parties shall endeavour to agree on the interpretation of the applicable provisions of this Agreement.

2.   The Party in whose territory the court or administrative body is located shall submit any agreed interpretation to the court or administrative body in accordance with the rules of that forum. If the Parties are unable to reach agreement on the interpretation of the provision of this Agreement at issue, either Party may submit its own views to the court or administrative body in accordance with the rules of that forum.

Chapter Nineteen

Binational Panel Dispute Settlement in Antidumping and Countervailing Duty Cases

Article 1901: General Provisions

1. The provisions of Article 1904 shall apply only with respect to goods that the competent investigating authority of the importing Party, applying the importing Party's antidumping or countervailing duty law to the facts of a specific case, determines are goods of the other Party.

2. For the purposes of Articles 1903 and 1904, panels shall be established in accordance with the provisions of Annex 1901.2.

Article 1902: Retention of Domestic Antidumping Law and Countervailing Duty Law

1. Each Party reserves the right to apply its antidumping law and countervailing duty law to goods imported from the territory of the other Party. Antidumping law and countervailing duty law include, as appropriate for each Party, relevant statutes, legislative history, regulations, administrative practice, and judicial precedents.

2. Each Party reserves the right to change or modify its antidumping law or countervailing duty law, provided that in the case of an amendment to a Party's antidumping or countervailing duty statute:

   a) such amendment shall apply to goods from the other Party only if such application is specified in the amending statute;

   b) the amending Party notifies the other Party in writing of the amending statute as far in advance as possible of the date of enactment of such statute;

   c) following notification, the amending Party, upon request of the other Party, consults with the other Party prior to the enactment of the amending statute; and

d) such amendment, as applicable to the other Party, is not inconsistent with

    i) the *General Agreement on Tariffs and Trade* (GATT), *the Agreement on Implementation of Article VI of the General Agreement on Tariffs and Trade* (the Antidumping Code), or the *Agreement on the Interpretation and Application of Articles VI, XVI and XXIII of the General Agreement on Tariffs and Trade* (the Subsidies Code), or

    ii) the object and purpose of this Agreement and this Chapter, which is to establish fair and predictable conditions for the progressive liberalization of trade between the two countries while maintaining effective disciplines on unfair trade practices, such object and purpose to be ascertained from the provisions of this Agreement, its preamble and objectives, and the practices of the Parties.

Article 1903: Review of Statutory Amendments

1.   A Party may request in writing that an amendment to the other Party's antidumping statute or countervailing duty statute be referred to a panel for a declaratory opinion as to whether:

a) the amendment does not conform to the provisions of subparagraph (d)(i) or (d)(ii) of paragraph 2 of Article 1902; or

b) such amendment has the function and effect of overturning a prior decision of a panel made pursuant to Article 1904 and does not conform to the provisions of subparagraph (d)(i) or (d)(ii) of paragraph 2 of Article 1902.

Such declaratory opinion shall have force or effect only as provided in this Article.

2.   The panel shall conduct its review in accordance with the procedures of Annex 1903.2.

3.   In the event that the panel recommends modifications to the amending statute to remedy a non-conformity that it has identified in its opinion:

a) the Parties shall immediately begin consultations and shall seek to achieve a mutually satisfactory solution to the matter within 90 days of the issuance of the panel's final declaratory opinion. Such solution may include seeking remedial legislation with respect to the statute of the amending Party;

b) if remedial legislation is not enacted within nine months from the end of the 90-day consultation period referred to in subparagraph (a) and no other agreement has been reached, the Party that requested the panel may

    i) take comparable legislative or equivalent executive action, or

    ii) terminate the Agreement upon 60-day written notice to the other Party.

Article 1904:   Review of Final Antidumping and Countervailing Duty Determinations

1.   As provided in this Article, the Parties shall replace judicial review of final antidumping and countervailing duty determinations with binational panel review.

2.   Either Party may request that a panel review, based upon the administrative record, a final antidumping or countervailing duty determination of a competent investigating authority of either Party to determine whether such determination was in accordance with the antidumping or countervailing duty law of the importing Party. For this purpose, the antidumping or countervailing duty law consists of the relevant statutes, legislative history, regulations, administrative practice, and judicial precedents to the extent that a court of the importing Party would rely on such materials in reviewing a final determination of the competent investigating authority. Solely for purposes of the panel review provided for in this Article, the antidumping and countervailing duty statutes of the Parties, as those statutes may be amended from time to time, are incorporated into this Agreement.

3.   The panel shall apply the standard of review described in Article 1911 and the general legal principles that a court of the importing Party otherwise would apply to a review of a determination of the competent investigating authority.

4.   A request for a panel shall be made in writing to the other Party within 30 days following the date of publication of the final determination in question in the *Federal Register* or the *Canada Gazette*.   In the case of final determinations that are not published in the *Federal Register* or the *Canada Gazette*, the importing Party shall immediately notify the other Party of such final determination where it involves a good from the other Party, and the other Party may request a panel within 30 days of receipt of such notice. Where the competent investigating authority of the importing Party has imposed provisional measures in an investigation, the other Party may provide notice of its intention to request a panel under this Article, and the Parties shall begin to establish a panel at that time. Failure to request a panel within the time specified in this paragraph shall preclude review by a panel.

5.   Either Party on its own initiative may request review of a final determination by a panel and shall, upon request of a person who would otherwise be entitled under the law of the importing Party to commence domestic procedures for judicial review of a final determination, request such review.

6.   The panel shall conduct its review in accordance with the procedures established by the Parties pursuant to paragraph 14. Where both Parties request a panel to review a final determination, a single panel shall review that determination.

7.   The competent investigating authority that issued the final determination in question shall have the right to appear and be represented by counsel before the panel. Each Party shall provide that other persons who, pursuant to the law of the importing Party, otherwise would have had standing to appear and be represented in a domestic judicial review proceeding concerning the determination of the competent investigating authority, shall have the right to appear and be represented by counsel before the panel.

8.   The panel may uphold a final determination, or remand it for action not inconsistent with the panel's decision. Where the panel remands a final determination, the panel shall establish as brief a time as is reasonable for compliance with the remand, taking into account the complexity of the facts and legal issues involved and the nature of the panel's decision. In no event shall the time permitted for compliance with a remand exceed an amount of time equal to the maximum amount of time (counted from the date of the filing of a

petition, complaint or application) permitted by statute for the competent investigating authority in question to make a final determination in an investigation. If review of the action taken by the competent investigating authority on remand is needed, such review shall be before the same panel, which shall issue a final decision within 90 days of the date on which such remand action is submitted to it.

9.   The decision of a panel under this Article shall be binding on the Parties with respect to the particular matter between the Parties that is before the panel.

10.   This Agreement shall not affect:

   a) the judicial review procedures of either Party, or

   b) cases appealed under those procedures,

with respect to determinations other than final determinations.

11.   A final determination shall not be reviewed under any judicial review procedures of the importing Party if either Party requests a panel with respect to that determination within the time limits set forth in this Article. Neither Party shall provide in its domestic legislation for an appeal from a panel decision to its domestic courts.

12.   The provisions of this Article shall not apply where:

   a) neither Party seeks panel review of a final determination;

   b) a revised final determination is issued as a direct result of judicial review of the original final determination by a court of the importing Party in cases where neither Party sought panel review of that original final determination; or

   c) a final determination is issued as a direct result of judicial review that was commenced in a court of the importing Party before the entry into force of this Agreement.

13.   Where, within a reasonable time after the panel decision is issued, a Party alleges that:

a) i)   a member of the panel was guilty of gross misconduct, bias, or a serious conflict of interest, or otherwise materially violated the rules of conduct,

   ii)   the panel seriously departed from a fundamental rule of procedure, or

   iii) the panel manifestly exceeded its powers, authority or jurisdiction set forth in this Article, and

b) any of the actions set out in subparagraph (a) has materially affected the panel's decision and threatens the integrity of the binational panel review process,

that Party may avail itself of the extraordinary challenge procedure set out in Annex 1904.13.

14.   To implement the provisions of this Article, the Parties shall adopt rules of procedure by January 1, 1989.   Such rules shall be based, where appropriate, upon judicial rules of appellate procedure, and shall include rules concerning the content and service of requests for panels, a requirement that the competent investigating authority transmit to the panel the administrative record of the proceeding, the protection of business proprietary and other privileged information (including sanctions against persons participating before panels for improper release of such information), participation by private persons, limits on panel review to errors alleged by the Parties or private persons, filing and service, computation and extensions of time, the form and content of briefs and other papers, pre- and post-hearing conferences, oral argument, requests for rehearing, and voluntary terminations of panel reviews.   The rules shall be designed to result in final decisions within 315 days of the date on which a request for a panel is made, and shall allow:

a) 30 days for the filing of the complaint;

b) 30 days for designation or certification of the administrative record and its filing with the panel;

c) 60 days for the complainant to file its brief;

d) 60 days for the respondent to file its brief;

e) 15 days for the filing of reply briefs;

f) 15 to 30 days for the panel to convene and hear oral argument; and

g) 90 days for the panel to issue its written decision.

15.   The Parties shall, in order to achieve the objectives of this Article, amend their statutes and regulations, as necessary, with respect to antidumping or countervailing duty proceedings involving goods of the other Party. In particular, without limiting the generality of the foregoing:

a) Canada shall amend sections 56 and 58 of the *Special Import Measures Act,* as amended, to allow the United States of America or a United States manufacturer, producer, or exporter, without regard to payment of duties, to make a written request for a re-determination; and section 59 to require the Deputy Minister to make a ruling on a request for a re-determination within one year of a request to a designated officer or other customs officer;

b) Canada shall amend section 28(4) of the *Federal Court Act* to render that section inapplicable; and shall provide in its statutes or regulations that persons (including producers of goods subject to an investigation) have standing to ask Canada to request a panel review where such persons would be entitled to commence domestic procedures for judicial review if the final determination were reviewable by the Federal Court pursuant to section 28;

c) the United States of America shall amend section 301 of the *Customs Courts Act of 1980,* as amended, and any other relevant provisions of law, to eliminate the authority to issue declaratory judgments;

d) each Party shall amend its statutes or regulations to ensure that existing procedures concerning the refund, with interest, of antidumping or countervailing duties operate to give effect to a final panel decision that a refund is due;

e) each Party shall amend its statutes or regulations to ensure that its courts shall give full force and effect, with respect to any person within its jurisdiction, to all sanctions imposed pursuant to the laws of the other Party to enforce provisions of any protective order or undertaking that such other Party has promulgated or accepted in order to permit access for purposes of panel review or of the extraordinary challenge procedure to confidential, personal, business proprietary or other privileged information;

f) Canada shall amend the *Special Import Measures Act,* and any other relevant provisions of law, to provide that the following actions of the Deputy Minister shall be deemed for the purposes of this Article to be final determinations subject to judicial review:

   i) a determination by the Deputy Minister pursuant to section 41,

   ii) a re-determination by the Deputy Minister pursuant to section 59, and

   iii) a review by the Deputy Minister of an undertaking pursuant to section 53(1); and

g) each Party shall amend its statutes or regulations to ensure that:

   i) domestic procedures for judicial review of a final determination may not be commenced until the time for requesting a panel under paragraph 4 has expired, and

   ii) as a prerequisite to commencing domestic judicial review procedures to review a final determination, a Party or other person intending to commence such procedures shall provide notice of such intent to the Parties and to other persons entitled to commence such review procedures of the same final determination no later than ten days prior to the latest date on which a panel may be requested.

Article 1905: Prospective Application

The provisions of this Chapter shall apply only prospectively to:

a) final determinations of a competent investigating authority made after the entry into force of this Agreement; and

b) with respect to declaratory opinions under Article 1903, amendments to antidumping or countervailing duty statutes enacted after the entry into force of this Agreement.

Article 1906: Duration

The provisions of this Chapter shall be in effect for five years pending the development of a substitute system of rules in both countries for antidumping and countervailing duties as applied to their bilateral trade. If no such system of rules is agreed and implemented at the end of five years, the provisions of this Chapter shall be extended for a further two years. Failure to agree to implement a new regime at the end of the two-year extension shall allow either Party to terminate the Agreement on six-month notice.

Article 1907: Working Group

1.   The Parties shall establish a Working Group that shall:

   a) seek to develop more effective rules and disciplines concerning the use of government subsidies;

   b) seek to develop a substitute system of rules for dealing with unfair pricing and government subsidization; and

   c) consider any problems that may arise with respect to the implementation of this Chapter and recommend solutions, where appropriate.

2.   The Working Group shall report to the Parties as soon as possible. The Parties shall use their best efforts to develop and implement the substitute system of rules within the time limits established in Article 1906.

Article 1908: Consultations

The Parties shall each designate one or more officials to be responsible for ensuring that consultations take place, where required, so that the provisions of this Chapter are carried out expeditiously.

Article 1909:   Establishment of Secretariat

1.   The Parties shall establish permanent Secretariat offices to facilitate the operation of this Chapter and the work of panels or committees that may be convened pursuant to this Chapter.

2.   The permanent offices of the Secretariat shall be in Washington, District of Columbia, and in the National Capital Region of Canada.

3.   Each Party shall be responsible for the operating cost of its Secretariat office.

4.   The United States of America shall appoint an individual to serve as secretary of the United States section of the Secretariat who shall be responsible for all administrative matters involving the Secretariat in the United States of America.

5.   Canada shall appoint an individual to serve as secretary of the Canadian section of the Secretariat who shall be responsible for all administrative matters involving the Secretariat in Canada.

6.   The secretaries of the United States and Canadian sections of the Secretariat shall manage their respective Secretariat offices.

7.   The Secretariat may provide support for the Commission established pursuant to Article 1802 if so directed by the Commission.

8.   The secretaries shall act jointly to service all meetings of panels or committees established pursuant to this Chapter. The secretary of the country in which a panel or committee proceeding is held shall prepare a record thereof and each secretary shall preserve an authentic copy of the same in the permanent offices.

9.   Each secretary shall receive and file all requests, briefs and other papers properly presented to a panel or committee in any proceeding before it that is instituted pursuant to this Chapter and shall number in numerical order all requests for a panel or committee. The number given to a request shall be the primary file number for briefs and other papers relating to such request.

10.   Each secretary shall forward to the other copies of all official letters, documents, records or other papers received or filed with the Secretariat office pertaining to any proceeding before a panel or

committee, so that there shall be on file in each office of the Secretariat either the original or a copy of all official letters and other papers relating to the proceeding.

Article 1910: Code of Conduct

The Parties shall, by the date of the entry into force of this Agreement, exchange letters establishing a code of conduct for panelists and members of committees established pursuant to Articles 1903 and 1904.

Article 1911: Definitions

For purposes of this Chapter,

administrative record means, unless otherwise agreed by the Parties and the other persons appearing before a panel:

a) all documentary or other information presented to or obtained by the competent investigating authority in the course of the administrative proceeding, including any governmental memoranda pertaining to the case, and including any record of ex parte meetings as may be required to be kept;
b) a copy of the final determination of the competent investigating authority, including reasons for the determination;
c) all transcripts or records of conferences or hearings before the competent investigating authority; and
d) all notices published in the *Canada Gazette* or the *Federal Register* in connection with the administrative proceeding.

antidumping statute as referred to in Articles 1902 and 1903 means:

a) in the case of Canada, the relevant provisions of the *Special Import Measures Act,* as amended, and any successor statutes;
b) in the case of the United States of America, the relevant provisions of Title VII of the *Tariff Act of 1930,* as amended, and any successor statutes; and
c) the provisions of any other statute that provides for judicial review of final determinations under subparagraph (a) or (b) or indicates the standard of review to be applied.

competent investigating authority means:

a) in the case of Canada,
   i)   the Canadian Import Tribunal, or its successor, or
   ii)   the Deputy Minister of National Revenue for Customs and Excise as defined in the *Special Import Measures Act*, or his successor; and
b) in the case of the United States of America,
   i)   the International Trade Administration of the United States Department of Commerce, or its successor, or
   ii)   the United States International Trade Commission, or its successor.

countervailing duty statute as referred to in Articles 1902 and 1903 means:

a) in the case of Canada, the relevant provisions of the *Special Import Measures Act*, as amended, and any successor statutes;
b) in the case of the United States of America, section 303 and the relevant provisions of Title VII of the *Tariff Act of 1930*, as amended, and any successor statutes; and
c) the provisions of any other statute that provides for judicial review of final determinations under subparagraph (a) or (b) or indicates the standard of review to be applied.

final determination means:

a) in the case of Canada,
   i)   an order or finding of the Canadian Import Tribunal under subsection 43(1) of the *Special Import Measures Act,*
   ii)   an order by the Canadian Import Tribunal under subsection 76(4) of the *Special Import Measures Act,* continuing an order or finding made under subsection 43(1) of the Act with or without amendment,
   iii) a determination by the Deputy Minister of National Revenue for Customs and Excise pursuant to section 41 of the *Special Import Measures Act,*
   iv) a re-determination by the Deputy Minister pursuant to section 59 of the *Special Import Measures Act,*
   v)   a decision by the Canadian Import Tribunal pursuant to subsection 76(3) of the *Special Import Measures Act* not to initiate a review,

    vi) a reconsideration by the Canadian Import Tribunal pursuant to subsection 91(3) of the *Special Import Measures Act,* and

    vii) a review by the Deputy Minister of an undertaking pursuant to section 53(1) of the *Special Import Measures Act;* and

b) in the case of the United States of America,

    i)   a final affirmative determination by the International Trade Administration of the United States Department of Commerce or by the United States International Trade Commission under section 705 or 735 of the *Tariff Act of 1930,* as amended, including any negative part of such a determination,

    ii)   a final negative determination by the International Trade Administration of the United States Department of Commerce or by the United States International Trade Commission under section 705 or 735 of the *Tariff Act of 1930,* as amended, including any affirmative part of such a determination,

    iii) a final determination, other than a determination in (iv), under section 751 of the *Tariff Act of 1930,* as amended,

    iv) a determination by the United States International Trade Commission under section 751(b) of the *Tariff Act of 1930,* as amended, not to review a determination based upon changed circumstances, and

    v)   a determination by the International Trade Administration of the United States Department of Commerce as to whether a particular type of merchandise is within the class or kind of merchandise described in an existing finding of dumping or antidumping or countervailing duty order.

general legal principles includes principles such as standing, due process, rules of statutory construction, mootness, and exhaustion of administrative remedies.

remand means a referral back for a determination not inconsistent with the panel or committee decision.

standard of review means the following standards, as may be amended from time to time by a Party:

a) in the case of Canada, the grounds set forth in section 28(1) of the *Federal Court Act* with respect to all final determinations; and

b) in the case of the United States of America,
   i) the standard set forth in section 516A (b)(1)(B) of the *Tariff Act of 1930,* as amended, with the exception of a determination referred to in (ii), and
   ii) the standard set forth in section 516A (b)(1)(A) of the *Tariff Act of 1930,* as amended, with respect to a determination by the United States International Trade Commission not to initiate a review pursuant to section 751(b) of the *Tariff Act of 1930,* as amended.

Annex 1901.2

Establishment of Binational Panels

1.   Prior to the entry into force of the Agreement, the Parties shall develop a roster of individuals to serve as panelists in disputes under this Chapter. The Parties shall consult in developing the roster, which shall include 50 candidates. Each Party shall select 25 candidates, and all candidates shall be citizens of Canada or the United States of America. Candidates shall be of good character, high standing and repute, and shall be chosen strictly on the basis of objectivity, reliability, sound judgment, and general familiarity with international trade law. Candidates shall not be affiliated with either Party, and in no event shall a candidate take instructions from either Party. Judges shall not be considered to be affiliated with either Party. The Parties shall maintain the roster, and may amend it, when necessary, after consultations.

2.   A majority of the panelists on each panel shall be lawyers in good standing. Within 30 days of a request for a panel, each Party shall appoint two panelists, in consultation with the other Party. The Parties normally shall appoint panelists from the roster. If a panelist is not selected from the roster, the panelist shall be chosen in accordance with and be subject to the criteria of paragraph 1. Each Party shall have the right to exercise four peremptory challenges, to be exercised simultaneously and in confidence, disqualifying from appointment to the panel up to four candidates proposed by the other Party.   Peremptory challenges and the selection of alternative panelists shall occur within 45 days of the request for the panel. If a Party fails to appoint its members to a panel within 30 days or if a panelist is struck and no alternative panelist is selected within 45 days, such panelist shall be selected by lot on the 31st or 46th day, as the case may be, from that Party's candidates on the roster.

3.   Within 55 days of the request for a panel, the Parties shall agree on the selection of a fifth panelist. If the Parties are unable to agree, the four appointed panelists shall select, by agreement, from the roster the fifth panelist within 60 days of the request for a panel. If there is no agreement among the four appointed panelists, the fifth panelist shall be selected by lot on the 61st day from the roster, excluding candidates eliminated by peremptory challenges.

4.   Upon appointment of the fifth panelist, the panelists shall promptly appoint a chairman from among the lawyers on the panel by majority vote of the panelists. If there is no majority vote, the chairman shall be appointed by lot from among the lawyers on the panel.

5.   Decisions of the panel shall be by majority vote and be based upon the votes of all members of the panel. The panel shall issue a written decision with reasons, together with any dissenting or concurring opinions of panelists.

6.   Panelists shall be subject to the code of conduct established pursuant to Article 1910. If a Party believes that a panelist is in violation of the code of conduct, the Parties shall consult and if the Parties agree, the panelist shall be removed and a new panelist shall be selected in accordance with the procedures of this Annex.

7.   When a panel is convened pursuant to Article 1904, each panelist shall be required to sign:

a) a protective order for information supplied by the United States of America or its persons covering business proprietary and other privileged information; and

b) an undertaking for information supplied by Canada or its persons covering confidential, personal, business proprietary and other privileged information.

8.   The United States of America shall establish appropriate sanctions for violations of protective orders issued by it and of undertakings given to Canada.   Canada shall establish appropriate sanctions for violations of undertakings given to it and protective orders issued by the United States of America. Each Party shall enforce such sanctions with respect to any person within its jurisdiction.   Failure by a panelist to sign a protective order or undertaking shall result in disqualification of the panelist.

9.   If a panelist becomes unable to fulfill panel duties or is disqualified, proceedings of the panel shall be suspended pending the selection of a substitute panelist in accordance with the procedures of this Annex.

10.   Subject to the code of conduct established by the Parties, and provided that it does not interfere with the performance of the duties of such panelist, a panelist may engage in other business during the term of the panel.

11.   While acting as a panelist, a panelist may not appear as counsel before another panel.

12.   With the exception of violations of protective orders or undertakings signed pursuant to paragraph 7, panelists shall be immune from suit and legal process relating to acts performed by them in their official capacity.

13.   The remuneration of panelists, their travel and lodging expenses, and all general expenses of the panel shall be borne equally by the Parties. Each panelist shall keep a record and render a final account of his time and expenses, and the panel shall keep a record and render a final account of all general expenses. The Commission shall establish amounts of remuneration and expenses that will be paid to the panelists.

Annex 1903.2

Panel Procedures Under Article 1903

1.　The panel shall establish its own rules of procedure unless the Parties otherwise agree prior to the establishment of that panel. The procedures shall ensure a right to at least one hearing before the panel, as well as the opportunity to provide written submissions and rebuttal arguments. The proceedings of the panel shall be confidential, unless the Parties otherwise agree. The panel shall base its decisions solely upon the arguments and submissions of the Parties.

2.　Unless the Parties otherwise agree, the panel shall, within 90 days after its chairman is appointed, present to the Parties an initial written declaratory opinion containing findings of fact and its determination pursuant to Article 1903.

3.　If the findings of the panel are affirmative, the panel may include in its report its recommendations as to the means by which the amending statute could be brought into conformity with the provisions of subparagraph 2(d) of Article 1902. In determining what, if any, recommendations are appropriate, the panel shall consider the extent to which the amending statute affects interests under this Agreement. Individual panelists may provide separate opinions on matters not unanimously agreed. The initial opinion of the panel shall become the final declaratory opinion, unless a Party requests a reconsideration of the initial opinion pursuant to paragraph 4.

4.　Within 14 days of the issuance of the initial declaratory opinion, a Party disagreeing in whole or in part with the opinion may present a written statement of its objections and the reasons for those objections to the panel. In such event, the panel shall request the views of both Parties and shall reconsider its initial opinion. The panel shall conduct any further examination that it deems appropriate, and shall issue a final written opinion, together with dissenting or concurring views of individual panelists, within 30 days of the request for reconsideration.

5.　Unless the Parties otherwise agree, the final declaratory opinion of the panel shall be published, along with any separate opinions of individual panelists and any written views that either Party may wish to be published.

6.   Unless the Parties otherwise agree, meetings and hearings of the panel shall take place at the office of the amending Party's section of the Secretariat.

Annex 1904.13

Extraordinary Challenge Procedure

1.   The Parties shall establish an extraordinary challenge committee, comprised of three members, within fifteen days of a request pursuant to paragraph 13 of Article 1904. The members shall be selected from a ten-person roster comprised of judges or former judges of a federal court of the United States of America or a court of superior jurisdiction of Canada. Each Party shall name five persons to this roster. Each Party shall select one member from this roster and the third shall be selected from the roster by the two members chosen by the Parties or, if necessary, by lot from the roster.

2.   The Parties shall establish by January 1, 1989 rules of procedure for committees. The rules shall provide for a decision of a committee typically within 30 days of its establishment.

3.   Committee decisions shall be binding on the Parties with respect to the particular matter between the Parties that was before the panel. Upon finding that one of the grounds set out in paragraph 13 of Article 1904 has been established, the committee shall vacate the original panel decision or remand it to the original panel for action not inconsistent with the committee's decision; if the grounds are not established, it shall affirm the original panel decision. If the original decision is vacated, a new panel shall be established pursuant to Annex 1901.2.

PART SEVEN
OTHER PROVISIONS

Chapter Twenty

Other Provisions

Article 2001: Tax Convention

Nothing in this Agreement shall affect the rights and obligations of the Parties under the *1980 Convention between Canada and the United States of America with respect to Taxes on Income and on Capital (with Exchange of Notes)*, including any amendments or any successor convention. Articles XXV and XXVI of the Convention shall govern exclusively issues or matters involving the *Income Tax Act* of Canada or the *Internal Revenue Code* of the United States of America.

Article 2002: Balance of Payments

Notwithstanding any other provision of this Agreement, either Party may:

a) apply trade restrictions in accordance with Article XII of the *General Agreement on Tariffs and Trade,* including the Declaration on Trade Measures for Balance-of-Payments Purposes adopted by the GATT Contracting Parties 28 November 1979; or

b) apply restrictions to persons of the other Party on:

   i) the making of payments and transfers for current international transactions in conformity with Article VIII of the *Articles of Agreement of the International Monetary Fund,* or

   ii) international capital movements in accordance with Article 7, paragraphs (c) through (e), of the *1961 OECD Code of Liberalization of Capital Movements,*

provided that such restrictions do not constitute a means of arbitrary or unjustifiable discrimination between persons of the

Parties or a disguised restriction on the benefits accorded to persons or goods under this Agreement.

Article 2003: National Security

Subject to Articles 907 and 1308, nothing in this Agreement shall be construed:

a) to require any Party to furnish or allow access to any information the disclosure of which it considers contrary to its essential security interests;

b) to prevent any Party from taking any action which it considers necessary for the protection of its essential security interests,

    i)   relating to the traffic in arms, ammunition and implements of war and to such traffic in other goods, materials and services as is carried on directly or indirectly for the purpose of supplying a military establishment,

    ii) taken in time of war or other emergency in international relations, or

    iii) relating to the implementation of national policies or international agreements relating to the non-proliferation of nuclear weapons or other nuclear explosive devices; or

c) to prevent any Party from taking action in pursuance of its obligations under the United Nations Charter for the maintenance of international peace and security.

Article 2004: Intellectual Property

The Parties shall cooperate in the Uruguay Round of multilateral trade negotiations and in other international forums to improve protection of intellectual property.

Article 2005: Cultural Industries

1.   Cultural industries are exempt from the provisions of this Agreement, except as specifically provided in Article 401 (Tariff Elimination), paragraph 4 of Article 1607 (divestiture of an indirect acquisition) and Articles 2006 and 2007 of this Chapter.

2.   Notwithstanding any other provision of this Agreement, a Party may take measures of equivalent commercial effect in response to actions that would have been inconsistent with this Agreement but for paragraph 1.

Article 2006: Retransmission Rights

1.   Each Party's copyright law shall provide a copyright holder of the other Party with a right of equitable and non-discriminatory remuneration for any retransmission to the public of the copyright holder's program where the original transmission of the program is carried in distant signals intended for free, over-the-air reception by the general public. Each Party may determine the conditions under which the right shall be exercised. For Canada, the date on which a remuneration system shall be in place, and from which remuneration shall accrue, shall be twelve months after the amendment of Canada's *Copyright Act* implementing Canada's obligations under this paragraph, and in any case no later than January 1, 1990.

2.   Each Party's copyright law shall provide that:

a) retransmission to the public of program signals not intended in the original transmission for free, over-the-air reception by the general public shall be permitted only with the authorization of the holder of copyright in the program; and

b) where the original transmission of the program is carried in signals intended for free, over-the-air reception by the general public, willful retransmission in altered form or non-simultaneous retransmission of signals carrying a copyright holder's program shall be permitted only with the authorization of the holder of copyright in the program.

3.   Nothing in paragraph 2(b) shall be construed to prevent a Party from:

a) maintaining those measures in effect on October 4, 1987 that

i) require cable systems to substitute a higher priority or non-distant signal broadcast by a television station for a simultaneous lower priority or distant signal when the lower priority or distant signal carries programming substantially identical to the higher priority or non-distant signal,

ii) prohibit the retransmission of a distant signal by a cable system where

  A) broadcast of the program is blacked out in the local market, or

  B) the cable system distributes a network-carried program broadcast by a local network-affiliated television station,

iii) prohibit the retransmission of certain programming content, such as abusive and obscene material, alcoholic beverages or other prohibited products, provided that these measures are applied on a non-discriminatory basis and that the program or advertisement in which the programming content appears is deleted in its entirety,

iv) prohibit the retransmission of certain programs, advertisements or announcements during an election or referendum,

v) authorize the preemption of programs at the request of a Party for urgent and important non-commercial communications,

vi) require a cable system, whose licence as of October 4, 1987 contained an invocable condition requiring the system to delete commercial materials and substitute therefore non-commercial materials, to implement such a condition; provided that with respect to those cable systems that were not implementing such licensing conditions as of that date, such conditions of licence shall be eliminated upon licence renewal, or

vii) permit non-simultaneous retransmissions in remotely-located areas where simultaneous reception and retransmission are impractical; or

b) introducing measures, including measures such as those specified in subparagraphs (a)(i) and (a)(ii)(B), to enable the local licensee of the copyrighted program to exploit fully the commercial value of its licence.

4.   Immediately following implementation of the obligations in paragraph 1, the Parties shall establish a joint advisory committee comprised of government and private sector experts to review outstanding issues related to retransmission rights in both countries to make recommendations to the Parties within twelve months.

Article 2007: Print-in-Canada Requirement

Canada shall repeal section 19(5)(a)(i)(A) and (B) and section 19(5)(a)(ii)(A) and (B) of the *Income Tax Act,* which define a Canadian issue of a newspaper or a periodical for purposes of deduction from income of expenses of a taxpayer for advertising space, as one that is printed or typeset in Canada.

Article 2008: Plywood Standards

If the panel of experts referred to in the exchange of letters between the Parties of January 2, 1988 does not agree with the findings or evaluation of the Canada Mortgage and Housing Corporation (CMHC) or any successor regarding the use of C-D grade plywood in housing financed by CMHC, or if the panel has not completed its review by the date of entry into force of this Agreement, the United States may delay its tariff concessions on softwood plywood (4412.19.40 and 4412.99.40 in its Schedule in Annex 401.2) and waferboard, oriented strand board and particle-board of all species (4410.10.00), pending agreement by the Parties that the issues have been resolved satisfactorily. Should the United States of America delay implementation of these tariff concessions, Canada may delay implementation of its concessions on tariff items 4412.19.90, 4410.10.10 and 4410.10.91 in its Schedule in Annex 401.2.

Article 2009: Softwood Lumber

The Parties agree that this Agreement does not impair or prejudice the exercise of any rights or enforcement measures arising out of the Memorandum of Understanding on Softwood Lumber of December 30, 1986.

Article 2010: Monopolies

1.   Subject to Article 2011, nothing in this Agreement shall prevent a Party from maintaining or designating a monopoly.

2.   Prior to designating a monopoly, and where the designation may affect interests of persons of the other Party, a Party shall:

a) i) notify the other Party, and

    ii) at the request of the other Party, engage in consultations prior to the designation; and

b) endeavour to introduce such conditions on the operation of the monopoly as will minimize or eliminate any nullification or impairment of benefits under this Agreement.

3.   Where a Party designates a monopoly, that Party shall ensure, whether through regulatory supervision, administrative control, or the application of other measures, that the monopoly shall not:

a) in the monopolized market, engage in discrimination in its sales against persons or goods of the other Party, contrary to the principles of this Agreement; or

b) in any other market, either directly or through its dealings with an affiliated enterprise, use its monopoly position to engage in anticompetitive practices that adversely affect a person of the other Party, whether through the discriminatory provision of the monopoly good or covered service, through cross-subsidization, or through predatory conduct.

Article 2011: Nullification and Impairment

1.   If a Party considers that the application of any measure, whether or not such measure conflicts with the provisions of this Agreement, causes nullification or impairment of any benefit reasonably expected to accrue to that Party, directly or indirectly under the provisions of this Agreement, that Party may, with a view to the satisfactory resolution of the matter, invoke the consultation provisions of Article 1804 and, if it considers it appropriate, proceed to dispute settlement pursuant to Articles 1805 and 1807 or, with the consent of the Party, proceed to arbitration pursuant to Article 1806.

2.   The provisions of paragraph 1 shall not apply to Chapter Nineteen and Article 2005.

Article 2012:   Definitions

For purposes of this Chapter:

cultural industry means an enterprise engaged in any of the following activities:

   a) the publication, distribution, or sale of books, magazines, periodicals, or newspapers in print or machine readable form but not including the sole activity of printing or typesetting any of the foregoing,
   b) the production, distribution, sale or exhibition of film or video recordings,
   c) the production, distribution, sale or exhibition of audio or video music recordings,
   d) the publication, distribution, or sale of music in print or machine readable form, or
   e) radio communication in which the transmissions are intended for direct reception by the general public, and all radio, television and cable television broadcasting undertakings and all satellite programming and broadcast network services;

C-D grade plywood means C-D grade plywood with exterior glue as described in U.S. Product Standard PS-1 for Construction and Industrial Plywood that is marked by a grading organization such as the American Plywood Association;

designate means to establish, designate, or authorize, or to expand the scope of a monopoly franchise to cover an additional good or covered service;

monopoly means any entity, including any consortium, that, in any relevant market in the territory of a Party, is the sole provider of a good or a covered service; and

sale includes offer for sale or distribution.

PART EIGHT
FINAL PROVISIONS

Chapter Twenty-One

Final Provisions

Article 2101: Statistical Requirements

All statistical requirements for the administration and enforcement of this Agreement should generally be met from data issued by Statistics Canada and the United States Department of Commerce and other United States Government agencies. The Parties shall, whenever necessary, depend upon Statistics Canada and the Department of Commerce to ensure jointly that data necessary to administer and enforce the provisions of the Agreement:

a) are collected, tabulated, analyzed and disseminated and, where appropriate, exchanged on a comparable basis; and

b) are protected according to the standards established in the laws and regulations of the supplying Party regarding confidentiality.

2. Subject to the provisions of paragraph 1, the Parties shall exchange data of a more detailed, specific or additional nature promptly upon the request of either Party.

Article 2102: Publication

1. All laws, regulations, procedures and administrative rulings of general application respecting matters covered by this Agreement shall be published promptly.

2. Each Party shall, to the extent possible, publish in advance, and allow opportunity for comment on, any law, regulation, procedure or administrative ruling of general application that it proposes to adopt respecting the matters covered by this Agreement.

317

Article 2103: Annexes

The Annexes to this Agreement constitute an integral part of this Agreement.

Article 2104: Amendments

1.   The Parties may agree upon any modification of or addition to this Agreement.

2.   When so agreed and approved in accordance with the applicable domestic legal procedures of each Party, such modifications or additions shall constitute an integral part of this Agreement.

Article 2105: Entry into Force

This Agreement shall enter into force on January 1, 1989 upon an exchange of diplomatic notes certifying the completion of necessary legal procedures by each Party.

Article 2106: Duration and Termination

This Agreement shall remain in force unless terminated by either Party upon six-month notice to the other Party.

IN WITNESS WHEREOF the undersigned, being duly authorized thereto by their respective Governments, have signed this Agreement.

DONE in duplicate, in the English and French languages, each language version being equally authentic, at _____, this _____ day of _____, 198_.

EN FOI DE QUOI les soussignés, dûment autorisés par leurs gouvernements respectifs, ont signé le présent accord.

FAIT en double exemplaire, dans les langues anglaise et française, les deux textes faisant également foi, à _____, ce _____ jour de _____, 198_.

_____   _____

FOR THE GOVERNMENT OF   FOR THE GOVERNMENT OF
CANADA   THE UNITED STATES OF AMERICA
POUR LE GOUVERNEMENT   POUR LE GOUVERNEMENT
DU CANADA   DES ÉTATS-UNIS D'AMERIQUE

Ottawa, Ontario
January 2, 1988

The Honourable Clayton Yeutter
United States Trade Representative
Washington, D.C.

Dear Mr. Yeutter:

I have the honour to reconfirm the following understanding reached
between the delegations of Canada and of the United States of America
in the course of negotiating the Free-Trade Agreement between our
two Governments signed on this day:

> "The Parties recognize that this Agreement is subject to
> domestic approval procedures. Accordingly, both Parties
> understand the need to exercise their discretion in the
> period prior to entry into force so as not to jeopardize the
> approval process or undermine the spirit and mutual
> benefits of the Free Trade Agreement."

I would be grateful if you would confirm that this understanding is
shared by your Government.

Yours sincerely,

Pat Carney

The Honorable Pat Carney
Minister of International Trade
Ottawa, Ontario

Dear Mrs. Carney:

I am pleased to receive your letter of today's date, which reads as follows:

"I have the honour to reconfirm the following understanding reached between the delegations of Canada and of the United States of America in the course of negotiating the Free-Trade Agreement between our two Governments signed this day:

The Parties recognize that this Agreement is subject to domestic approval procedures. Accordingly, both Parties understand the need to exercise their discretion in the period prior to entry into force so as not to jeopardize the approval process or undermine the spirit and mutual benefits of the Free Trade Agreement."

"I would be grateful if you would confirm that this understanding is shared by your Government."

I have the honor to reconfirm that the understanding referred to in your letter is shared by my Government.

Yours sincerely,

Clayton Yeutter

Washington, D.C.
January 2, 1988

The Honorable Pat Carney
Minister for International Trade
Ottawa, Ontario

Dear Mrs. Carney

I have the honor to confirm the following understanding reached between the delegations of the United States of America and of Canada in the course of negotiations regarding Article 301 (Rules of Origin) and Article 401 (Tariff Elimination) of the Free-Trade Agreement between our two Governments that was signed on this day:

> In the event it appears that either Party is unable to complete the conversion of its Tariff Schedule to the Harmonized System prior to the entry into force of the Agreement, the Parties shall enter into consultations with a view to implementing the provisions of the Agreement, subject to domestic approval, under existing Tariff Schedules on a basis that would preserve the rights and obligations set out in the Agreement.

I have the honor to propose that this understanding be treated as an integral part of the Agreement.

I further have the honor to propose that this letter and your letter of confirmation in reply constitute an agreement between our two Governments, to enter into force on this day.

Yours sincerely,

Clayton Yeutter

The Honourable Clayton Yeutter
United States Trade Representative
Washington, D.C.

Dear Mr. Yeutter,

I am pleased to receive your letter of today's date, which reads as
follows:

"I have the honor to confirm the following understanding
reached between the delegations of the United States of America
and of Canada in the course of negotiations regarding Article
301 (Rules of Origin) and Article 401 (Tariff Elimination) of
the Free-Trade Agreement between our two Governments that
was signed on this day:

In the event it appears that either Party is unable to
complete the conversion of its Tariff Schedule to the
Harmonized System prior to the entry into force of the
Agreement, the Parties shall enter into consultations with
a view to implementing the provisions of the Agreement,
subject to domestic approval, under existing Tariff
Schedules on a basis that would preserve the rights and
obligations set out in the Agreement.

"I have the honor to propose that this understanding be treated
as an integral part of the Agreement.

"I further have the honor to propose that this letter and your
letter of confirmation in reply constitute an agreement between
our two Governments, to enter into force on this day."

I have the honour to confirm that the understanding referred to in your letter is shared by my Government, and that your letter and this reply shall constitute an agreement between our respective Governments, to enter into force on this day.

Yours sincerely,

Pat Carney

The Honourable Clayton Yeutter
United States Trade Representative
Washington, D.C.

Dear Mr. Yeutter,

I have the honour to confirm the following understanding reached between the delegations of Canada and of the United States of America in the course of negotiations regarding Article 2008 of the Free-Trade Agreement between our two governments signed this day:

1. No later than March 15, 1988, the Canada Mortgage and Housing Corporation (CMHC), or its successor, shall evaluate C-D grade plywood and decide whether to approve its use in housing financed by CMHC.

2. If the CMHC grants approval for the use of C-D grade plywood in CMHC-financed housing, the Parties shall begin tariff reductions on January 1, 1989 for plywood tariff linkage categories.

3. If the CMHC does not grant approval for the use of C-D grade plywood in CMHC-financed housing, or grants approval only in part, the Parties shall not begin tariff reduction for plywood tariff linkage categories until completion of a review of the CMHC evaluation by an impartial panel of experts acceptable to both Parties.

    a. The review shall examine whether the findings in the CMHC report and its evaluation of the American Plywood Association's application for CMHC approval of C-D grade plywood are unbiased and technically accurate.

b.   If the panel agrees that the CMHC findings and evaluation are unbiased and technically accurate, the Parties shall begin tariff reductions on January 1, 1989 for plywood tariff linkage categories.

c.   If the panel does not complete its review by January 1, 1989 or does not agree with the CMHC findings and evaluation, the provisions of Article 2008 shall apply.

4.   For the purpose of this letter: "C-D grade plywood" shall mean C-D grade plywood with exterior glue as described in U.S. Product Standard PS-1 for Construction and Industrial Plywood, which is marked by a grading organization such as the American Plywood Association.

I have the honour to propose that this understanding be treated as an integral part of the Free-Trade Agreement.

I further have the honour to propose that this letter and your letter of confirmation in reply constitute an agreement between our two Governments, to enter into force on this day.

Yours sincerely,

Pat Carney

Washington, D.C.
January 2, 1988

The Honorable Pat Carney
Minister of International Trade
Ottawa, Ontario

Dear Mrs. Carney,

I am pleased to receive your letter of today's date, which reads as
follows:

"I have the honour to confirm the following understanding
reached between the delegations of Canada and of the United
States of America in the course of negotiations regarding
Article 2008 of the Free-Trade Agreement between our two
governments signed this day:

"1. No later than March 15, 1988, the Canada Mortgage and
Housing Corporation (CMHC), or its successor, shall
evaluate C-D grade plywood and decide whether to
approve its use in housing financed by CMHC.

"2. If the CMHC grants approval for the use of C-D grade
plywood in CMHC-financed housing, the Parties shall
begin tariff reductions on January 1, 1989 for plywood
tariff linkage categories.

"3. If the CMHC does not grant approval for the use of C-D
grade plywood in CMHC-financed housing, or grants
approval only in part, the Parties shall not begin tariff
reduction for plywood tariff linkage categories until
completion of a review of the CMHC evaluation by an
impartial panel of experts acceptable to both Parties.

"a. The review shall examine whether the findings in the
CMHC report and its evaluation of the American
Plywood Association's application for CMHC approval
of C-D grade plywood are unbiased and technically
accurate.

327

"b. If the panel agrees that the CMHC findings and evaluation are unbiased and technically accurate, the Parties shall begin tariff reductions on January 1, 1989 for plywood tariff linkage categories.

"c. If the panel does not complete its review by January 1, 1989 or does not agree with the CMHC findings and evaluation, the provisions of Article 2008 shall apply.

"4.   For the purpose of this letter: "C-D grade plywood" shall mean C-D grade plywood with exterior glue as described in U.S. Product Standard PS-1 for Construction and Industrial Plywood, which is marked by a grading organization such as the American Plywood Association.

"I have the honour to propose that this understanding be treated as an integral part of the Free-Trade Agreement.

"I further have the honour to propose that this letter and your letter of confirmation in reply constitute an agreement between our two Governments to enter into force on this day."

I have the honor to confirm that the understandings expressed in your letter are shared by my Government, and that your letter and this reply shall constitute an agreement between our respective Governments, to enter into force on this day.

Yours sincerely,

Clayton Yeutter

T H E   C A N A D A - U. S.

FREE TRADE AGREEMENT

S Y N O P S I S

Table of Contents

Trade: Securing Canada's Future

Introduction

On December 11, the Government tabled the Canada-United States Trade Agreement in the House of Commons. The Canada-United States Trade Agreement is the biggest trade agreement ever concluded between two countries. It covers trade and trade-related issues, and breaks important new ground which will be of lasting value to the Canadian and U.S. economies.

The Agreement sets a new standard for trade Agreements concluded under the *General Agreement on Tariffs and Trade* (GATT). It builds upon a patchwork of GATT commitments, bilateral arrangements and ad hoc understandings and expands them into a treaty between Canada and the United States which should govern the trade and economic relationship for the foreseeable future. The Agreement meets the tests of fairness and mutual advantage. It is an Agreement that sets the stage for greater prosperity in Canada and the United States.

The accord provides a powerful signal against protectionism and for trade liberalization. It reflects the commitment of both governments to liberalize trade on a global basis through multilateral trade negotiations under the GATT.

Once in force, the Agreement will chart a new course for the largest and most important trading relationship in the world. As a result, the economies of both countries will grow and prosper. It will add significantly to economic growth, incomes and employment in Canada. Canadian business will become more competitive in the Canadian market and world markets. Canada will become a stronger, more confident country in the world trading community. It will mean a richer Canada, a Canada which can afford to maintain and enhance the quality of life through, and for, Canadian cultural endeavours. A richer Canada will allow governments to continue to stimulate economic development in Canada's poorer regions and strengthen social programs for all Canadians.

The Road to the Agreement

The Agreement represents the culmination of efforts over the past century by Canadians and Americans to establish a better and more secure basis for managing their trade and economic relationship. Even before Canada became a nation, the United States and Britain sought to ensure that the 49th parallel did not become an unnecessary and artificial barrier to commerce between Canadians and Americans. The first free-trade agreement was signed in 1854. Unfortunately, it did not survive the hostilities created between the United States and Britain during the American Civil War and was abrogated by the United States in 1866. There followed various efforts in the 1870s, 1880s and 1890s to return to the free-trade conditions established by the 1854 treaty. Each foundered because either one government or the other was not ready to enter into an agreement.

In 1911, the Liberal government of Sir Wilfrid Laurier concluded a comprehensive agreement. It too, however, proved premature. Business people in both countries were lukewarm and, following the defeat of the Laurier government later that year, the accord became a dead letter. In the following two decades, the two countries learned to their regret what could happen without free trade. Passion and protectionism ruled supreme and the two nations built ever higher barriers to commerce between them.

The spiral of ever-increasing protectionism was finally broken in 1935 when the two countries negotiated a modest but historic most-favoured-nation agreement between them. It was one of a series of agreements concluded under the U.S. Reciprocal Trade Agreements Program, the Roosevelt Administration's answer to the infamous Smoot-Hawley Tariff Act of 1930, which had raised trade barriers to their highest level ever.

The 1935 accord marked the beginning of a bipartisan effort in Canada to expand trading opportunities for Canadian entrepreneurs. Started by the Conservative government of R.B. Bennett, it was concluded by the Liberals under Mackenzie King. Three years later, the Agreement was enlarged and improved. It confirmed the commitment of both governments to more liberal trading conditions, a commitment they pursued throughout the next 50 years.

At the conclusion of the Second World War, Canada and the United States co-operated in an ambitious effort to translate the gains made under the Reciprocal Trade Agreements Program into a general exchange of benefits among all participating countries. Originally confined to 23 countries, the General Agreement on Tariffs and Trade, signed at Geneva in October, 1947, became the foundation for the largest expansion of world trade in history. The GATT now boasts 95 members, with a further 30 countries applying its rules on a de facto basis.

Throughout seven rounds of GATT negotiations held between 1947 and 1979, Canada and the United States gradually lowered barriers between them and established better and more certain rules to govern trade. Concurrently, they also explored whether a basis existed for an even better regime. As early as 1947, a comprehensive free-trade agreement was being negotiated between the two countries. Before the pact could be ratified, however, Prime Minister Mackenzie King concluded that the country was not ready for such an agreement and satisfied himself that the GATT would serve for the time being. Prime Minister Louis St. Laurent came to a similar conclusion in 1953 when President Eisenhower suggested that the two countries go further.

Bilateral accords, however, were pursued in the defence sector, building on the experience gained in the allied war effort. The Defence Production Sharing Arrangements, based on the 1941 Hyde Park Agreement between President Roosevelt and Prime Minister Mackenzie King, ensured virtual free trade in defence materiel and equipment. These arrangements provided Canadian industry with the opportunity to participate in North American defence efforts. In 1965, the two governments concluded the Auto Pact, providing for duty-free trade in cars, trucks, buses and parts. That accord allowed Canadian industry to rationalize and prosper. Today, the Canadian automotive industry is the mainstay of the Ontario economy, employing over 130,000 Canadians and exporting 90 percent of its production.

Early in this decade, however, Canadians began to question whether enough was being done to enhance and secure access to our principal market. They looked south with wary eyes as one congressional bill after another threatened their access and as action after action closed or narrowed their export opportunities. In 1983, the government of Prime Minister Trudeau concluded that something more than reliance on GATT was required and initiated efforts to conclude more bilateral accords modelled on the Auto Pact. The U.S. government welcomed the initiative and officials on both sides of the border tackled the challenge of identifying the right sectors. A year later, the two governments concluded that, while the goal was right, the chosen method was not. Finding the right sectoral fit was proving too difficult. Other means had to be found.

March 17-18, 1985, in Quebec City marked the first bilateral summit between Prime Minister Mulroney and President Reagan and the beginning of a co-operative effort to conclude a new trade agreement. The Prime Minister and the President agreed that they "would give the highest priority to finding mutually acceptable means to reduce and eliminate existing barriers to trade in order to secure and facilitate trade and investment flows". They charged their trade ministers to explore all possible ways to reduce and eliminate existing barriers to trade.

Six months later, the two leaders exchanged letters pledging their two governments to an effort to negotiate "a new trade agreement involving the broadest possible package of mutually beneficial reductions in barriers to trade in goods and services." That effort culminated in the historic accord signed on October 4, 1987. U.S. Treasury Secretary James Baker, Trade Representative Clayton Yeutter and Deputy Treasury Secretary Peter McPherson, working closely with Ambassador Peter Murphy on the American side, and Finance Minister Michael Wilson, International Trade Minister Pat Carney, the Prime Minister's Chief of Staff, Derek Burney, and Trade Ambassador Simon Reisman for Canada, agreed on the elements of a new bilateral trade Agreement.

During the next seven weeks the negotiators, supported by their teams of lawyers worked to put the final touches to the Agreement which was tabled in the House of Commons on December 11 .

Benefits for All Canadians

This is the most important trade agreement Canada has ever concluded. It is the culmination of almost 100 years of Canadian efforts to secure open and stable markets.

Canadians earn their living through trade. Over 30 percent of the national income comes from trade; more than three million Canadian jobs depend on trade; farmers, fishermen, manufacturers and service companies in many sectors depend on trade. The trading rules which determine whether markets are open or closed, whether there are customs duties, quotas, restrictions of every sort, are critically important to Canadian prosperity.

Canadians know how important trade is to the country and the living standards it provides to its hard-working citizens. Canadians understand that in a competitive world, where the traditional basis of our wealth -- our fisheries, our farms, our natural resources, our manufacturing is changing; they need to change too. They know how important it is that the trading rules be fair to small countries as well as large countries. They know that small countries need to have a say in what the rules are and how they are enforced.

In Western Canada, the Agreement builds on the work already begun with the creation of the Western Diversification Agency. The gains will be solid, especially in the expansion of the petrochemical industry, more open markets for oil, gas, uranium, potash, forest products, fish, cattle exports, and better access to U.S. manufactured goods. After all, the U.S. is the West's largest trading partner. According to research done for the Canada West Foundation, nearly 60 percent of the region's exports, worth over $12 billion in 1986, go to sixteen states. Nearly half of those exports are from the oil and gas sector where entry is now secure.

For British Columbians, it will mean that their forest products, which account for 45 percent of exports, will now have more secure access to the United States. Over time, the penalties imposed by the U.S. on shakes and shingles will disappear. To ensure that manufacturing of forest products continues to take place in Canada, the export controls on logs currently in place will be retained. The future of hydro-electric exports is more secure. Earlier this year, the provincial government announced the removal of membership restrictions on its provincially-regulated securities firms. The

Agreement is entirely consistent with this direction and will help Vancouver to build on its international orientation towards the Pacific Rim.

For British Columbia's fisheries, the Agreement will end the abuse of U.S. technical standards and the removal of the tariff will improve British Columbia's competitive edge in U.S. markets. The right to control the export of unprocessed fish will be pursued under the GATT. In recognition of the seasonal nature of horticultural production in the province, the Agreement keeps the right to restore temporary tariffs on fresh fruits and vegetables for the next two decades.

With over 75 percent of its exports headed south, the Agreement provides prodigious opportunity to Alberta. The oilpatch will soon find that its entry into the U.S. market is more secure as tariffs, as well as customs user and import fees, are removed. The removal of tariffs and non-tariff barriers on petrochemicals will secure the industry's future. Canada is a world leader in the exploration and development of energy resources -- now we will have free access to a market to match our expertise.

Cattle ranchers will find the market for their beef and veal wide open without the threat of quotas under the U.S. meat import law, nuisance border inspections or compliance with health standards. By the end of the next decade, Alberta's meat and livestock, grains and oilseeds will be able to compete in the U.S. market on an equal footing with Americans without fear of barrier.

Saskatchewan thrives on its exports and the Agreement has benefits for all industries. The uranium industry, which exports over $300 million worth of its product to the U.S., will benefit from the removal of threat of import restrictions. Firms like Eldorado Nuclear have already indicated that millions of dollars in new investment will result from the security of access to U.S. markets guaranteed by the Agreement. For potash producers, who send 60 percent of their ore to the U.S., the dispute settlement mechanisms created by the Agreement will ensure that future actions are subject to accountability with better enforcement of rules. As Canada's second largest oil producer, Saskatchewan will gain more secure access for future exports. The Agreement also marks the first tangible effort to address the current agricultural subsidy war being waged worldwide. Saskatchewan beef producers will benefit from their exemption under the U.S. Meat

Import Law. Direct export subsidies will be prohibited from use in bilateral trade. By agreeing to the elimination of costly export subsidies on bilateral trade, Canada and the U.S. take a pioneering step forward.

In addition to opening up the U.S. market to manufacturing, Manitobans have been anticipating the economic activities and export dollars that the Limestone II hydro-electric project will create when it comes on stream at the end of the decade. Access to the U.S. market for electricity is now more secure. Possessing the most diversified economy of the Prairie Provinces and with over half of its exports directed towards the U.S., Manitoba industry, especially manufacturers, will find new opportunities. The urban and intercity bus sector and the aerospace industry will benefit from more open access to U.S. procurement.

Clothing manufacturers, particularly those making parkas and winter outerwear, will find their coats more competitive in the U.S. The tariff-free entry of unlimited amounts of garments made with Canadian or U.S. fabrics will ensure many new jobs, not only for Manitoban apparel makers but for textile makers. Health and technical standards will no longer be permitted to inhibit agricultural exports. Insurance companies will have secure access to the larger U. S. market.

No part of Canada has more to gain from the Agreement than Ontario. Ontario's economy was built largely on its trade with the U.S. Today, over 90 percent of its exports go to the U.S. With over two- thirds of these exports in the automotive sector, the government had two objectives in the negotiations: to preserve the benefits of the Auto Pact and to expand the opportunity for future growth in this industry. This was achieved. In recognition of the importance of the auto industry in both countries, a select panel will be struck to recommend public policy measures and private initiatives to improve competitiveness.

The phase-out of tariffs over the next decade will benefit manufacturing in Ontario. Ontario's exports of electricity will be more secure. Ontario will continue to have assured access to U.S. coal for its steel mills and electricity plants. The Agreement secures the U.S. market for uranium. Ontario farmers, whose output is the largest of all provinces, will benefit from better access to the U.S. market, while the interests of the dairy, poultry and egg producers are safeguarded. The present marketing boards and the capacity to implement new supply management programs and import controls, where necessary, remains. Existing Canadian beer practices are untouched by the Agreement, while the wine industry is provided with a seven-year adjustment period before it will compete on an equal footing with U.S. vintners.

New opportunities have also been provided for the financial service industry. Canada's service industries, which account for 70 percent of the labour force and are concentrated in Ontario, will be major beneficiaries from easier access to the U.S. market for their services and their personnel.

Quebecers have a major stake in rolling back protectionism and gaining easier access to the U.S. market. The electricity generated by the hydro plants from James Bay to the St. Lawrence are assured secure entry to the American market. More importantly, in securing access, Quebec has achieved the market access that is essential for further expansion of hydro power. Tariff elimination on forest products, metals like aluminium and copper, and finished goods like ceramics will enhance trade opportunities. For example, two-thirds of Quebec's pulp and paper exports go to the U.S.

U.S. technical regulations and inspection procedures, such as those that handicapped Quebec pork producers, will no longer be used. There is scope for further exports by veal producers, as well as food processors. The deal on agriculture is a good one for Quebecers. By eliminating tariffs as well as ending the threat of red-meat quotas, it will open new markets for farmers. Recognizing the special situation of the horticulture industry, safeguards remain in place to ensure a period of adjustment. The negotiations have also safeguarded the special interests of the sensitive agricultural sector such as marketing boards and supply management. The Agreement explicitly provides for recourse to supply-management trade restrictions permitted by virtue of Article 11 of the GATT.

Quebec's service industries, such as life insurance and tourism will benefit from the new code governing trade in services and the improved access for business travellers. There will also be new opportunities for Quebec industry to sell to U.S. federal government agencies as a result of the improved procurement rules. The Auto Pact will remain in place for current participants like GM and production-based duty waivers for offshore suppliers like Hyundai will be honoured. For shipbuilders, Canada has reserved the right to apply quantitative restrictions on U.S. vessels as long as the U.S. maintains the Jones Act provisions which apply to Canadian vessels.

In the Atlantic, the Government has created the Atlantic Opportunities Agency as a step in the direction of new growth. The federal government's commitment to increase the levels of procurement and industrial benefits by $600 million over the period 1986-1990 is unequivocal. The government's capacity to pursue such regional development initiatives remains undiminished. The Atlantic Provinces Economic Council has concluded that the fishery and resource-based industries of the Maritimes would gain considerably from free trade. By gaining more secure and enhanced access to the largest market in the world, Atlantic Canadians will be able to realize their potential.

New Brunswick's exports of forestry products will gain more secure entry to the U.S. market. There will be new scope for New Brunswick to further process its resources, turning fish to fillets, forest products to waferboard and paper and its ores into zinc and lead. The elimination of the 50 percent U.S. tariff on ship repairs will be welcomed by the marine industry. At the same time the government has reserved the right to apply quantitative restrictions on U.S. vessels so long as the U. S. maintains the prohibitions which apply to Canadian vessels because of the Jones Act. In the future, the application of American laws which handicapped exports like lumber and processed potatoes will be subject to a bi-national panel that will ensure fair application of the law.

Electricity exports, valued at over $275 million in 1986, will benefit from secure access to the U.S. market. New Brunswick refiners will profit from the removal of U.S. import tariffs on petroleum products, like gasoline and heating oil, customs user fees and the discriminatory application of the "superfund" levy.

Jobs and development go hand in hand with trade expansion in Nova Scotia, an historic trader with the Americas. A fair and equitable dispute settlement mechanism will go some distance toward providing more security of access for traditional exports like fish and lumber and manufactured goods like tires, all of which have been subject to U.S. trade-remedy laws. Michelin Tires, the largest Canadian manufacturer of tires and the biggest private employer in the province, will benefit from improved access for automotive exports. Tariff elimination will offer scope for the fishing industry which already sends 75 percent of its exports to the U.S., to expand its processing capacity. National Sea, the largest fish company in Canada, has already stated that this opportunity could lead to 400 new jobs.

For forest products, the elimination of the tariff will encourage the creation of more jobs at paper mills. Shipyards will benefit from the elimination of the 50 percent tariff on U.S. ship repairs. The Offshore Energy Accord is unaffected by the Agreement. Exports of energy through the development of offshore gas fields or the construction of coal-fired generators will benefit from secure and free access to the U. S. market.

The ground-breaking accomplishments of the Agreement in providing a set of disciplines covering a large number of service sectors will create new opportunities for Nova Scotians who work in insurance, computers and construction. Industrial benefits arising from federal purchasing are not affected by the chapter on procurement. Haligonians can rest assured that the offset advantages from programs like the Aurora/Litton Repair and Overhaul facility are untouched.

Prince Edward Island's potato farmers have been hard hit by U.S. harassment of its potato exports. The dispute settlement procedures outlined in the Agreement will provide greater fairness and curb the unilateral application of unfair trade actions. Elimination of tariffs will encourage producers to export potatoes in baker-count boxes and other specialty products for the restaurant and convenience food markets. Manufacturers of fish processing equipment and eyeglass frames will also find new opportunity with the gradual elimination of tariffs.

Newfoundland's ocean wealth will be augmented in the future by oil and gas from the huge reserves discovered in the province's coastal waters. The incentives for new investment contained in the Agreement will create the right climate for exploration and development. The abolition of all barriers to energy trade will give Newfoundlanders assured access to the American market. The Come-by-Chance petroleum refinery will have the assured free entry it requires for long-term success. Removal of tariffs on specialty papers and processed minerals will add to the potential for growth. The procurement chapter leaves untouched provincial purchasing practices as well as the ability of the Departments of Defence, Transport and Fisheries and Oceans to direct their repair work and purchase of vessels to Canadian yards. The investment chapter does not limit the industrial benefits provisions of the Atlantic Accord.

Equally important are the advantages for growth the Agreement will provide to Newfoundland's fishermen. For example, the removal of the tariff (10-20% on fishsticks, 10-17.5% on prepared meals and 7.5% on crab) will provide Newfoundlanders with opportunities for manufacturing. Secure and open access to the U.S. will encourage investment and more permanent jobs in further processing of Newfoundland's abundant supply of fish, lumber and iron ore. The provincial controls on the amount of fish that can be exported in unprocessed form remains. The trade-remedy provisions will limit harassment from U.S. countervail complaints that have plagued the fishery.

EXPLANATORY NOTES TO THE AGREEMENT

The text of the Agreement translates the Elements of Agreement reached on October 4, 1987 into binding legal language. To aid in the interpretation of this text, the annotations put in clear language the meaning of each of the principal sections and provide examples of the implications of the Agreement for Canadian business. The tariff annexes setting out the detailed schedules for tariff elimination, product by product, are printed separately.

The Agreement has a Preamble and is divided into eight parts as follows:

Preamble: recording the political commitment of the two governments in entering into this Agreement;

Part One: establishing the objectives and scope of the Agreement;

Part Two: setting out the rules for trade in goods;

Part Three: dealing with government procurement;

Part Four: contains the three ground-breaking chapters in the Agreement: services, business travel and investment;

Part Five: contains the general dispute settlement provisions and the special arrangements for dealing with antidumping and countervailing duty procedures;

Part Six: collects in one chapter a series of provisions which did not fit readily into any of the other chapters;

Part Seven: contains provisions dealing with financial services;

Part Eight: contains the final provisions dealing with annexes, entry into force and duration.

Each Part is divided into chapters. Chapters are further divided into Articles which are subdivided into paragraphs and sub-paragraphs. For ease of reference in this initialled version of the Agreement, the Articles are numbered according to the chapter in which they are found. Article 301, for example, is the first Article in chapter Three dealing with rules of origin.

Various Articles call up annexes located at the end of each chapter. In terms of drafting style, where matters of great detail need to be covered, the Article establishes the basic obligation, whereas the annex develops how it will be implemented. Again, for ease of reference, the annex numbers correspond to the paragraph and Article establishing the annex. For example, paragraph 2 of Article 301 establishes the basic rule of origin for the Agreement; Annex 301.2 provides the detailed provisions specifying how that rule is to be applied.

Throughout the text, words that have a meaning that is critical to interpreting the text or that may vary from its plain, generic meaning, are defined. The definitions are found in the final Article of each chapter for words used in that chapter (e.g., Article 304 for rules of origin). Words that have a special or critical meaning and that are used the same way throughout the text are defined in Article 201.

Preamble

The Preamble states the political commitment of Canada and the United States in entering into the Agreement. It records the shared aspirations of the two countries in concluding the Agreement and summarizes their aims and objectives. In other words, it is an agreed statement of intent which will guide the two countries in implementing the provisions of the Agreement and in resolving disputes. This may be particularly important in the context of Chapter Seventeen which specifically provides that any review of new antidumping or countervailing duty legislation for consistency with the Agreement will be based on the object and purpose of the Agreement which can be found, inter alia, in the Preamble.

The Preamble establishes from the outset that this is a trade Agreement. Its purpose is to improve the economies of both countries, to strive for full employment and improved living standards, and to strengthen both countries as competitors in the international marketplace. Both countries' ability to take measures to safeguard public welfare is fully preserved.

Canada remains committed to the multilateral trading system and the growth of world trade and this commitment is clearly established in the Preamble.

Part One: Objectives and Scope

Chapter One: Objectives and Scope

This Chapter sets the tone for the Agreement as a whole. The objectives make clear the extent to which the Canada-United States Trade Agreement moves beyond other free-trade agreements negotiated under the GATT. Four previous agreements are particularly relevant: the 1960 European Free-Trade Area; the 1965 UK-Ireland Free-Trade Agreement; the 1983 Australia-New Zealand Closer Economic Relations Agreement; and the 1985 United States-Israel Agreement.

The new Canada-United States Agreement is broader in scope as it provides for liberalization in all sectors of the economy, including agriculture. No other trade agreement includes binding commitments on trade in services, business travel or investment. No other agreement provides a basis for developing new rules to deal with subsidies, dumping and countervailing measures.

The Chapter begins with a declaration that the Agreement is consistent with Article XXIV of the GATT, the Article which provides the framework in international law for negotiating free-trade agreements. It sets out a legal statement of the basic principle underlying the Agreement as a whole: Canada and the United States will treat each other's goods, services, investment, suppliers and investors as they treat their own insofar as the matters covered by this Agreement are concerned. Individual parts and chapters work out this principle in detail. Chapter Five in Part Two, for example, establishes national treatment for trade in goods and chapters Six, Seven, and Eight all contain important amplifications of this principle. Similarly, the services and investment chapters begin with a statement of this principle and then develop how it will be applied.

The Agreement recognizes that it is based on the precedents and commitments between Canada and the United States established in other bilateral and multilateral agreements. For purposes of interpretation, it indicates that the provisions of this Agreement take precedence over all other agreements unless there is a specific provision to the contrary. For example, Article 908 states that the undertakings of the two governments under the *Agreement on an International Energy Program* take precedence over the provisions of this Agreement.

The wide scope of the Agreement is indicated from the outset in the agreed objectives. The Agreement will:

- eliminate barriers to trade in goods and services between the two countries;

- facilitate conditions of fair competition within the free-trade area;

- significantly expand liberalization of conditions for cross-border investment;

- establish effective procedures for the joint administration of the Agreement and the resolution of disputes; and

- lay the foundation for further bilateral and multilateral co-operation to expand and enhance the benefits of the Agreement.

The Agreement will specifically involve federal, state, and provincial measures. While the two federal governments are the Parties to the Agreement, the important role of the states and provinces is recognized, for instance, in the commitments on wine and spirits.

Chapter Two: Definitions

In this chapter, words critical to the application of the agreement as a whole are defined. For example, the word "measure" is frequently used in the Agreement. It is defined as any governmental law, regulation, procedure, requirement or practice. In effect, the rights and obligations of the two governments basically involve what measures they can and cannot take and how they can take them.

Part Two:
Trade in Goods

Part Two contains chapters three through twelve dealing with trade in goods. It builds on the GATT, its ancillary agreements as well as other existing arrangements involving the two governments such as the Harmonized Commodity Description and Coding System (the so-called Harmonized System by which imports are classified for purposes of assessing customs duties), the *Canada-United States Automotive Products Trade Agreement* and the *Agreement on an International Energy Program*.. Where both governments were satisfied with existing arrangements, they are incorporated by reference into the Agreement. For example, the *GATT Code on Technical Barriers to Trade* is the basis of Chapter Six and the provisions of GATT Article XX (General Exceptions) form the basis of chapter Twelve. In most instances, however, such as chapter Three dealing with rules of origin, Canada and the United States have entered into new obligations unique to the Free-Trade Agreement.

Chapters Three through Six and Eleven and Twelve contain provisions applicable to all trade in goods. The four sectoral chapters, Seven for Agriculture, Eight for Wine and Distilled Spirits, Nine for Energy and Ten for Automotive Products, address issues of particular concern to those sectors.

Chapter Three: Rules of Origin for Goods

The Agreement will eliminate all tariffs on trade between Canada and the United States over a ten-year period. However, both countries will continue to apply their existing tariffs to imports from other countries. Rules of origin are, therefore, needed to define those goods which are entitled to duty-free, or "free-trade area" treatment when exported from one country to the other.

Since the Agreement is intended to benefit the producers of both countries and generate employment and income for Canadians and Americans, origin rules require that goods traded under the

Agreement be produced in either country or both. The origin rules establish the general principle that goods that are wholly produced or obtained in either Canada or the United States or both will qualify for area treatment. Goods incorporating offshore raw materials or components will also qualify for area treatment if they have been sufficiently changed either in Canada or the United States, or both, to be classified differently from the raw materials or components from which they are made. In certain cases, goods, in addition to being classified differently, will also need to incur a certain percentage of manufacturing cost in either or both countries, in most cases 50 percent. This is particularly important for assembly operations.

In practical terms, goods other than those which originate wholly in either Canada and/or the United States, will have to incorporate some significant Canadian or US content. For example, goods imported in bulk from offshore and repackaged and labelled in the United States would not qualify for area treatment, while a product incorporating only some imported components in most instances would. A bicycle, for example, using Canadian steel for its frame and assembled in Canada using imported wheels and gears would qualify as a product of Canadian origin, if 50 percent of its manufacturing cost is accounted for in Canada and/or the United States.

Apparel made from fabrics woven in Canada or the United States will qualify for duty-free treatment whereas apparel made from offshore fabrics will qualify for duty-free treatment only up to the following levels:

	Non-Woolen Apparel	Woolen Apparel
	(in million square yard equivalent)	
Imports from Canada	50	6
Imports from the United States	10.5	1.1

Above these levels, apparel made from offshore fabrics will be considered, for tariff purposes, as products of the country from which the fabrics were obtained. The levels established for imports from Canada are well above current trade levels. Canadian clothing manufacturers, including manufacturers of fine suits, coats, snowsuits and parkas, can, for all practical purposes, continue to buy their fabric from the most competitive suppliers around the world and still benefit from duty-free access to the United States. In addition, should their exports to the United States consume more than 56 million square yards of imported fabric, they will pay the US tariff but be able to benefit from the drawback of Canadian duties paid on such fabric (see chapter Four).

There is a similar quantitative limit governing duty-free exports to the United States of non-woolen fabrics or textile articles woven or knitted in Canada from yarn imported from a third country. Such exports, otherwise meeting the origin rules, will benefit from area treatment up to a maximum annual quantity. The level has initially been set at 30 million square yards for the first four years. The two governments will revisit this issue in 1990-1991 to work out a mutually satisfactory revision of this arrangement.

Definitions in Article 304 set out the terms which will be used by customs officials in deciding whether a good is entitled to duty-free treatment while Annex 301.2 sets out general rules of interpretation as well as detailed rules for each of the 21 individual product or commodity sections of the Harmonized System. By consulting the definitions and the annex, producers can determine whether the goods they export to the other country will be entitled to area treatment.

The rules of interpretation in Annex 301 make clear that goods that are further processed in a third country before being shipped to their final destination would not qualify for area treatment even if they meet the rule of origin. For example, cloth woven from U.S. fibres, cut in the United States but sewn into a shirt in Mexico, would qualify for duty-free re-entry into the United States under its outward-processing program, but would not qualify for duty-free entry into Canada under the Agreement.

The chapter contains safeguards to prevent circumvention of the rules as well as a process for consultation and revision to ensure that the rules of origin evolve to take account of changes in production processes.

Chapter Four: Border Measures

Key to any free-trade agreement, and required by the provisions of the GATT, is the elimination of duties and other restrictions on substantially all the trade between the parties. Implementation of the provisions of Chapter Four will achieve this requirement by providing for the removal of the tariff, tariff-related measures, quantitative restrictions and other restrictive measures applied at the border by January 1, 1998. This ten-year period is consistent with similar transition periods established in previous agreements. For example, the European Community initially provided a twelve-year period. The Tokyo Round tariff cuts were phased in over eight years.

Tariffs

The tariff has been an important but waning import policy instrument in Canada for many decades. More than 75 percent of Canada-United States trade now moves free of duty. This figure, however, fails to take account of the trade which could take place but for tariffs. High U.S. tariffs -- 15 percent and more on petro-chemicals, metal alloys, clothing and many other products -- continue to pose serious barriers to the U.S. market and prevent Canadian firms from achieving the economies of scale on which increased competitiveness and employment in Canadian industry depend. In addition to high tariffs, escalating tariffs on resource-based products discourage the development of more sophisticated manufacturing in Canada. While a 1.7 cent per kilo tariff on zinc ore may not impose a significant barrier, a 19 percent tariff on zinc alloy has effectively retarded the establishment of a zinc metal fabricating industry in Canada. Additionally, the existence of Canadian tariffs on imports from the United States is often costly to Canadian consumers and producers.

This chapter eliminates all remaining tariffs over a ten-year period in order to allow companies to adjust to the new competitive circumstances. The cuts will begin January 1, 1989 and after that date, no existing tariff may be increased unless specifically provided elsewhere in the Agreement (for example, in chapter Eleven providing for temporary emergency safeguards). Tariffs will be eliminated by January 1, 1998 on the basis of three formulas:

- for those sectors ready to compete now, tariffs will be eliminated on the Agreement entering into force on January 1, 1989, for example:

computers and equipment	some pork
some unprocessed fish	fur & fur garments
leather	whiskey
unwrought aluminum	ferro alloys
yeast	animal feeds

vending machines and parts	needles
airbrakes for railroad cars	skis
skates	warranty repairs
some paper-making machinery	motorcycles

- for other sectors, tariffs will be eliminated in five equal steps, starting on January 1, 1989, for example:

subway cars	chemicals including resins
printed matter	(excluding drugs and
paper and paper products	cosmetics)
paints	furniture
explosives	hardwood plywood
aftermarket auto parts	most machinery

- all other tariffs will be eliminated in ten steps, most starting on January 1, 1989, for example:

most agricultural products	steel
textiles and apparel	appliances
softwood plywood	pleasure craft
railcars	tires

Annex 401 (published separately) sets out the schedule of tariff cuts for each product according to its classification in the Harmonized System. If both countries agree, the staging can be accelerated. Both the European Community and the European Free-Trade Association concluded after a few years that they would benefit from accelerated tariff elimination. Australia and New Zealand are currently discussing speeding up their tariff reductions.

In the case of certain specialty steel items currently subject to temporary emergency safeguards by the United States, tariff cuts will not begin until October 1, 1989, as required by U.S. law. Large telephone switching equipment will be phased out in three annual steps ending January 1, 1991.

Canada has also undertaken to continue providing relief from customs duties on some machinery and equipment and repair and replacement parts for such machinery and equipment not available from Canadian suppliers. Between now and January 1, 1989, Canada will examine this list of machinery and equipment with a view to adding to it. This will ensure that Canadian manufacturers seeking to modernize to take advantage of other provisions of the Agreement will be able to purchase new machinery and equipment at competitive prices.

Canadian and United States tariffs applied to products from other countries will be unchanged as a result of this Agreement. Both governments are participating in the Uruguay Round of Multilateral Trade Negotiations which could result in reductions or elimination of many of these tariffs. These reductions would, of course, form part of a larger package which would involve improved market access to the European Community, Japan and other developed, as well as developing, countries. These reductions will be addressed on their own merits and wholly separately from the bilateral Agreement.

The combined effect of eliminating both Canadian and U.S. tariffs will be to allow Canada's manufacturing industry to rationalize and modernize and become more competitive. Canadian companies will be able to increase their penetration of the U.S. market and of world markets in general. The result should be more and better jobs for Canadians.

Customs Matters

Whatever the level of tariffs, the way in which they are applied, including provisions for granting duty remissions to importers, can affect trade flows. To ensure that the objectives of tariff elimination are achieved, Canada and the United States have also agreed to eliminate or regulate tariff-related programs which influence the flow of trade. The gradual elimination of most of these programs will ensure that by the end of the transition period, when all tariffs will have been eliminated, Canadian and U.S. companies will operate according to similar customs rules on bilateral trade. Both governments, however, will retain separate customs and tariff regimes for trade with third countries.

Specifically, the Agreement addresses customs user fees, duty drawbacks, and duty remissions.

The United States applies a customs user fee calculated as a percentage of the value of each import transaction (currently 0.17 percent). Even if the tariff is zero, the exporter must pay this amount when goods cross from Canada into the United States. This fee constitutes an additional tariff and increases the cost of exporting.

Article 403 provides that the customs user fee applied by the United States will be phased out on imports from Canada by January 1, 1994 and prevents either country from establishing a new customs user fee on imports of goods which meet the origin rules. Canadian exporters will save tens of millions of dollars with the elimination of this fee.

Both countries refund the customs duty levied on imported materials and components when these are incorporated into exported goods. This is called duty drawback. In the U.S., for example, foreign trade zones are often used as a means for U.S. exporters to avoid having to pay U.S. duties on imported components. Some of the advantages of the free-trade area, however, would be eroded if a U.S. producer could source some components from a third country, manufacture a final product in a U.S. foreign trade zone without paying any duty on these components and compete in Canada with a manufacturer who has paid Canadian duties on the same components. Accordingly, the Agreement provides for duty drawbacks on third-country materials and similar programs to be eliminated for bilateral trade after January 1, 1994.

There are two exceptions to the general drawback obligation. Drawbacks will continue to be permitted on citrus products. As well, duties paid on fabric imported and made up into apparel and subsequently exported to the other country can be recovered if the apparel does not qualify for duty-free treatment. Chapter Three establishes quotas for duty-free treatment for apparel made up from imported fabrics. Should trade rise above these levels, Canadian manufacturers using imported fabric will be able to apply for drawback of Canadian duties paid on fabric incorporated into apparel exported to the United States.

Canadian customs law permits duties on imports to be refunded to specific companies if these companies meet commitments (performance requirements) related to production, exports or employment. This practice is called duty waivers or remissions. The Agreement provides for the elimination of duty waivers wherever such waivers are tied to specific performance requirements such as production in one country or exports to the other except for automotive waivers as listed in Chapter Ten. No new customs duty waivers incorporating performance requirements can be introduced as of June, 1988, or whenever the U.S. Congress approves the Agreement, and all such customs duty waivers will be eliminated by January 1, 1998.

Given the size of our existing bilateral trade, there is already extensive cooperation between Canadian and U.S. customs authorities. Article 406 and its annex provides for further cooperation by specifying a number of matters where it is not only desirable but necessary for the two customs authorities to work closely together. These matters include declarations of origin on imported and exported goods, administration and enforcement, the uniform application of rules of origin, the facilitation of trade in the areas of statistics collection and documentation, as well as the operations of customs offices.

Import and Export Restrictions

Import or export quotas can be severely damaging to international trade by limiting the quantity which may be traded. In Article 407, Canada and the United States affirm their GATT obligations not to prohibit or restrict imports or exports of goods in bilateral trade except under strictly defined circumstances. Nothing in the Agreement, for example, in any way prevents Canada from prohibiting the import of pornographic materials (see chapter Twelve). Outside of such special circumstances, these obligations provide a guarantee that the benefits of tariff elimination will not be eroded by quotas or other restrictions. Unless specifically allowed by the Agreement, e.g., "grandfathered" or permitted under the GATT, existing quantitative restrictions will be eliminated, either immediately or according to a timetable.

Among those restrictions eliminated are the Canadian embargoes on used aircraft and used automobiles (provided in chapter Ten) and the U.S. embargo on lottery materials. Canada and the United States will retain their right to control log exports while the United States will retain marine transportation restrictions under the *Jones Act* (provided for in chapter Twelve). For shipbuilders, Canada has reserved the right to apply quantitative restrictions on U.S. vessels until such time as the United States removes the prohibitions under the *Jones Act* on Canadian vessels. Provincial laws governing the export of unprocessed fish caught off the East Coast have been safeguarded (also provided for in chapter Twelve). Both countries will continue to be able to apply import restrictions to agricultural goods where these are necessary to ensure the operation of a domestic supply management or support program.

Where either Canada or the United States applies restrictions on trade with other countries, it may limit or prohibit the pass-through of imports from those other countries into its own territory. It may also require that its exports to the other be consumed within the other's territory. Controls on exports to third countries for strategic reasons will thus continue to be enforced.

Export Taxes

Neither country applies export taxes as a matter of general policy. These render exporters less competitive and are highly disruptive of production and investment. Article 408 confirms existing practice by specifically prohibiting export taxes or duties on bilateral trade unless the same tax is applied on the same goods consumed domestically.

The 1986 Softwood Lumber Understanding, which requires Canada to collect an export tax on Canadian softwood exports to the United States until such time as the provincial governments have adjusted certain stumpage practices, is specifically grandfathered by Article 1910.

Other Export Measures

GATT obligations recognize that circumstances may arise where export restrictions are necessary. These circumstances include situations of short supply, conservation of natural resources where domestic production or consumption is also restrained and restrictions imposed in conjunction with domestic price stabilization schemes.

Article 409 requires that export restrictions for such purposes do not reduce the proportion of the good exported to the other Party relative to the total supply of the good compared to the proportion exported prior to the imposition of the restriction. Any such restriction must not be designed to disrupt normal channels of supply or proportions among specific goods being restricted. It prohibits the use of licenses, fees or other measures to charge higher prices for exports than for domestic sales (see also chapter Nine on energy).

Chapter Five: National Treatment

This chapter incorporates the fundamental national treatment obligation of the GATT into the Free-Trade Agreement. This means that once goods, have been imported into either country, they will not be the object of discrimination. Such an obligation is an essential part of any Agreement eliminating trade barriers since it prevents their replacement by internal measures favouring domestic goods over imports. If such a provision were not part of the Agreement, exporters in either country would have no guarantee of equal treatment.

The practical effect of this chapter is to require that internal taxes, such as sales or excise taxes, cannot be higher on imported goods than on domestic goods and health and safety standards cannot be more rigorous for imported goods than for domestic goods. In other words, the obligation prevents either country from imposing internal taxes such as excise or sales taxes, regulations respecting matters such as, health and safety standards, laws respecting sale, purchase and use in a manner to discriminate against imported products. It is thus a guarantee that goods will be free of discrimination and will allow producers, traders, investors, farmers and fishermen to plan and invest with confidence.

National treatment does not mean that imported goods have to be treated in the same way in the foreign market as they are in their country of origin. For example, Canada can prohibit or restrict the sale of imported firearms so long as the sale of domestically produced firearms is also prohibited or restricted. Moreover, all goods, imported or domestic, must continue to meet Canadian requirements for bilingual labelling and metric measurement.

This chapter makes more explicit the GATT national treatment obligation to measures adopted by provinces or states. This means that a province or state cannot discriminate in respect of measures falling within its jurisdiction against imported products.

Chapter Six: Technical Barriers

The right to maintain regulations to protect human, animal and plant life, the environment or for a variety of other purposes is a sovereign issue for each country to decide. Such regulations for health, safety, environmental, national security and consumer protection reasons can, however, constitute severe barriers to trade unless there are rules to prevent their explicit use to impede trade, technical regulations can be highly protectionist trade measures.

In the Tokyo Round of Multilateral Trade Negotiations, an *Agreement on Technical Barriers to Trade* was reached which provides that technical regulations and standards including packaging and labelling requirements and methods for certifying conformity should not create unnecessary barriers to trade. No country is prevented from taking measures to ensure protection of human, animal or plant life or other measures so long as they are not applied to cause arbitrary or unjustifiable discrimination between imported or domestic goods.

In this chapter, Canada and the United States affirm their obligations under the GATT Agreement respecting federal government measures affecting industrial products (agricultural and fish standards are covered in chapter Seven).

This means that the two federal governments have agreed to avoid the use of standards-related measures as unnecessary obstacles to trade. Standards-related measures are defined to include specifications and regulations, standards and rules for certification systems that apply to goods, and processes and production methods. For example, the federal government can require that children's pyjamas be manufactured from fire-proof material, but it must impose this requirement on both imported and domestically produced pyjamas. Nothing in the Agreement prevents Canada from requiring bilingual labelling of goods, as long as both domestic and imported goods meet the same requirement.

The two governments will endeavour to make their respective standards-related measures more compatible to reduce the obstacles to trade and the costs of exporting which arise from having to meet different standards. A particular problem with plywood standards is addressed in chapter Twenty. Many standards-related measures are developed by private organizations in both Canada and the United States (such as the Canadian Standards Association or the Underwriters Laboratory) and the two governments will encourage these organizations to continue to work toward achieving greater compatibility in the standards they establish.

The methods by which products are tested for conformity with standards can, in themselves, constitute a barrier to trade. Hence, the two countries have agreed to recognize each others' laboratory accreditation systems and will not require that testing and inspection agencies and certification bodies be located, or make decisions within its territory in order to gain accreditation.

The chapter requires that, except in urgent cases, full texts of proposed federal standards-related measures be provided to the other country and that at least 60 days be allowed for those who would be affected to comment on any proposed federal measure before the measure takes effect.

Article 608 provides for further negotiations respecting the compatibility of standards-related measures, accreditation and the acceptance of test data.

Chapter Seven: Agriculture

Canadian farmers export almost $3 billion in agricultural products to the United States and sought conditions which would make their access to the U.S. market both more open and more secure. At the same time, they did not want to impair either existing marketing systems for dairy and poultry products or the right to implement new supply management programs and import controls in accordance with our international obligations.

The government thus had three objectives in the agricultural area: to improve access for farm products; to make that access more secure; and to preserve Canada's agricultural policy instruments. The Agreement meets all three objectives: there is an important package of trade liberalizing measures; agricultural products will benefit from the increased security of access flowing from the arrangements on dispute settlement; and nothing in the Agreement will in any way affect the right of the federal government and the provinces to introduce and maintain programs to protect and stabilize farm incomes.

The principal trade liberalizing elements agreed in agriculture are:

- Article 701: prohibition of export subsidies on bilateral trade. This marks the first time that any two governments have agreed to prohibitions on export subsidies in the agricultural sector and marks an important signal to others around the world;

- Article 701: elimination of Canadian Western Grain Transportation rail subsidies on exports to the United States shipped through Canadian west coast ports; the provision does not affect shipments through Thunder Bay or exports to third countries through west coast ports;

- Articles 401 and 702: the phased elimination of all tariffs over a period of ten years (Canada is allowed to restore temporarily tariffs on fresh fruits and vegetables for a 20-year period under depressed price conditions in order to give Canada's horticultural industry an opportunity to adjust to more open trading conditions). This snapback provision applies only if the average acreage under cultivation for that product is constant or declining. Acreage converted from wine-grape cultivation is not included in this cultivation;

- Article 704: mutual exemption from restrictions under meat import laws, thus ensuring free trade in beef and veal. Canadian beef and veal producers have in the past found their exports limited as the U.S. triggered its meat import restrictions or sought voluntary export restraints. Both countries have agreed to consult and take measures to avoid diversion should either country apply its meat import law against third countries;

- Article 705: elimination of Canadian import licenses for wheat, barley and oats and their products when U.S. grain support levels become equal to Canadian grain support levels. Both countries retain the right to impose or re-impose restrictions on grains and grain products if imports increase significantly as a result of substantial change in grain support programs. Annex 705.4 sets out the method for calculating support levels;

- Article 706: the Canadian global import quotas on chicken, turkey and eggs have been set at average levels of actual imports over the past five years;

- Article 707: an exemption for Canada from any future quantitative import restrictions on products containing ten percent or less sugar. The U.S. enjoys a waiver under the GATT to impose restrictions if imports are interfering with U.S. price support programs. Without this exemption, further products could be included;

- Article 708: regulatory barriers resulting from technical regulations, the kind which in the past have frustrated the export of Canadian pork products, have been reduced. Over the next few years, both countries will seek to harmonize such technical regulations. As part of this Agreement, the U.S. will maintain an "open border policy" for meat inspection which will now be limited to occasional spot checks to ensure compliance with inspection requirements. Additionally, the United States has agreed to recognize the term canola oil as a trade name for rapeseed; and

• Article 710: GATT rights and obligations (including Article XI) are retained for all agricultural trade not specifically dealt with in the Agreement. For example, Canadian dairy farmers will continue to benefit from supply management programs since these are not affected by the Agreement and are consistent with Canada's GATT obligations.

Finally, the two governments agreed that some of the most pressing problems in the agricultural area go beyond Canada and the United States and will need the co-operation of all countries. For example, the stiff competition for grain export markets leading to ruinous export subsidies cannot be resolved solely on a bilateral basis. The two governments have, therefore, agreed to consult more closely with each other; to take account of each other's export interests when using export subsidies on sales to third markets; and to work together in the GATT to further improve and enhance trade in agriculture (Articles 701 and 709).

Canada's farmers will make real gains. By the end of the next decade, those agricultural and food products such as meat and livestock, grains and oilseeds, and potatoes, which we produce in abundance and which form the heart of our farm exports, will be able to compete on an equal footing in the huge American market without the burden of tariffs and other barriers at the border. At the same time, marketing systems, farm income stabilization and price support programs remain unimpaired by the Agreement.

Chapter Eight: Wine and Distilled Spirits

Chapter Eight provides for the reduction of barriers to trade in wine and distilled spirits which arise from measures related to their internal sale and distribution. It constitutes a partial derogation from the national treatment provisions of chapter Five. The specific measures covered concern listing, pricing, distribution practices, blending requirements and the standards and labelling requirements affecting distinctive products. The objective of the chapter is to provide over time equal treatment for Canadian and U.S. wine and distilled products in each other's market. Canadians will, as a result, enjoy greater access to a wide variety of California wines at competitive prices. The brewing industry is not covered by this chapter (but see chapter Twelve).

The chapter specifies that measures concerning listing for sale of wine and distilled spirits are to be transparent, treat Canadian and U.S. products in the same way and be based on normal commercial considerations. Any distiller or wine producer applying for a listing is to be informed promptly of listing decisions, given the reasons for any refusal and the right to appeal such a decision. Estate wineries in British Columbia which existed on Oct. 4, 1987 and which produce less than 30,000 gallons annually may be automatically listed in that province.

On pricing, the chapter allows a provincial liquor board or any other public body distributing wine and distilled spirits to charge the additional cost of selling the imported product. Differential charges on wine which exceed this amount are to be reduced over a seven-year period from 1989 through 1995. The method for calculating this differential is specified. Differential charges on distilled spirits which exceed this amount are to be eliminated immediately when the Agreement comes into force. All other discriminatory pricing measures are to be eliminated immediately.

On distribution, measures can be maintained which allow wineries or distilleries to limit sales on their premises to wines and spirits produced on those premises. Similarly, Ontario and British Columbia are not prevented from allowing private wine outlets existing on Oct. 4, 1987 to favour their own wine. The Quebec provision relating to in-province bottling of wine for sale in grocery stores is grandfathered.

Canada has agreed to eliminate any measure requiring that distilled spirits imported in bulk from the United States be blended with Canadian spirits.

The chapter provides for mutual recognition of Canadian Whiskey and U.S. Bourbon Whiskey as distinct products. This means that the U.S. will not allow the sale of any product as Canadian

Whiskey unless it has been manufactured in Canada in accordance with Canadian laws. Canada will not permit the sale of any product as Bourbon Whiskey unless it has been manufactured in the United States in accordance with U.S. laws.

Chapter Nine: Trade in Energy

Over the past decade, bilateral trade in energy has assumed increasing importance to Canadians. Canada exports more than $10 billion in energy products annually, including oil, gas, electricity and uranium. Billions more are exported in the form of downstream products such as various oil and gas derivatives. That trade provides a livelihood for thousands of Canadians. Some of these exports, however, are limited or threatened by U.S. restrictions and regulatory actions, including restrictions on exports of upgraded Canadian uranium, discriminatory price actions on natural gas, tariffs and threatened import fees on crude oil and products, and threatened restrictions on electricity.

This chapter, which reproduces some of the provisions of chapter Four as they relate to energy goods, will secure Canada's access to the United States market for energy goods. The two countries have recognized that they have a common interest in ensuring access to each other's market and enhancing their mutual security of supply. They have, therefore, built on their existing GATT rights and obligations and agreed that, as each other's best customers, they should get fair treatment should there be any controls on energy commodities. Both remain free to determine whether and when to allow exports and may continue to monitor and license exports.

Article 902 affirms Canadian and U.S. rights and obligations under the GATT on trade restrictions in energy products. This includes a prohibition on minimum export or import price commitments. More particularly, the United States has agreed to eliminate all U.S. restrictions on the enrichment of Canadian uranium and Canada will eliminate the requirement for uranium to be processed before it is exported to the U.S. The United States has also agreed to end its total embargo on exports of Alaskan crude oil and allow Canadians to import up to 50,000 barrels a day. These commitments are described in Annex 902.5.

Where either Canada or the U.S. applies import or export restrictions to energy trade with other countries, it may limit or prohibit the pass-through of imports from those other countries into its own territory. It may also require, in such instances, that its exports to the other be consumed within the other's territory.

Article 903 on export taxes restates the obligation of chapter Four not to impose taxes or charges on exports unless the same tax is applied to energy consumed domestically. Article 904 on other export measures restates the obligations of chapter Four that export restrictions may not reduce the proportion of the good exported to the other Party relative to the total supply of the good, compared to the proportion exported prior to the imposition of the restriction. It also prevents the use of licences, fees or other measures to charge higher prices for exports when such restrictions are used for short supply, conservation or domestic price stabilization reasons.

This Article also provides that export restrictions not be designed to disrupt normal channels of supply or alter the product mix as between various types of specific energy goods exported to the other country. For example, if Canada in future decides to implement measures to limit the consumption of oil, it can reduce exports to the United States proportional to the total supply of oil available in Canada. Any such restrictions must not be designed to disrupt normal trade patterns.

The two countries have also agreed to allow existing or future incentives for oil and gas exploration and development in order to maintain the reserve base for these energy resources.

The chapter recognizes the important role played by the National Energy Board in Canada and the Federal Energy Regulatory Commission and the Economic Regulatory Administration in the United States. If discrimination inconsistent with this Agreement results from a regulatory decision, direct consultations can be held with a view to ending any discriminatory action, such as the decisions earlier this year by the Federal Regulatory Commission prohibiting Canadian suppliers of natural gas from passing all their shipment costs on to their customers.

In Annex 905.2, Canada undertakes to eliminate one of three price tests which the National Energy Board (NEB) applies to exports. Through these tests, the NEB assesses whether all costs have been recovered, whether the offered price would not be less than the cost to Canadians for equivalent service, and whether the offered price would be materially less than the least cost alternative for the buying entity. It is this "least cost alternative test" only which is being eliminated.

The United States will require the Bonneville Power Administration to treat British Columbia Hydro no less favourably with respect to access to power transmission lines than utilities located outside the U.S. Pacific Northwest. The two governments state their expectation that Bonneville Power and British Columbia Hydro will continue to negotiate mutually beneficial arrangements on the use of power transmission lines.

Article 907 provides a tighter national security exception than is contained in the GATT and for the Agreement as a whole, while Article 908 indicates that the provisions of the *Agreement on an International Energy Program,* which governs trade in oil during tight supply conditions, take precedence over the provisions of this chapter.

Chapter Ten: Trade in Automotive Products

The automotive industry is the linchpin of Canadian manufacturing and the trade flow between Canada and the United States in autos is enormous. Autoworkers on both sides of the border have been beneficiaries of what has been our most important bilateral free-trade deal to date -- the Auto Pact. Throughout the negotiations, the Canadian government indicated that it was satisfied with the Auto Pact but was not averse to considering changes that would increase production, investment and employment in Canada. The Agreement meets these objectives.

The free and secure access to the U.S. market provided by the Auto Pact remains intact. The Auto Pact safeguards and the Canadian value-added commitments remain in place for the Big Three auto manufacturers.

Section XVII of Annex 301.2 provides that all vehicles traded under the Free-Trade Agreement will be subject to a special rule of origin. Under the Auto Pact, qualified producers, as long as they meet the safeguards, can import vehicles and parts duty-free into Canada from anywhere in the world. Fifty percent of the direct production costs of any vehicle traded under the Free-Trade Agreement, however, will have to be incurred in Canada and the United States to qualify for duty-free treatment. Under the current rule governing exports to the U.S. under the Auto Pact, overhead and other indirect costs are included in the requirement that 50 percent of the invoice price be incurred in Canada or the U.S. The new rule is the equivalent of a 70 percent requirement on the old basis. To meet this test, assemblers will have to source more parts in North America, giving Canadian parts manufacturers increased opportunities.

The United States will accord vehicles and original equipment parts exported from Canada duty-free access if they meet the new rule of origin. Such goods now enjoy duty-free access under the Auto Pact. For northbound trade, Canadian manufacturers with Auto Pact status can import duty free under the Auto Pact (by satisfying the safeguards). Goods imported by all others under the FTA must meet the FTA rule if they wish to benefit from the declining bilateral tariff.

Chapter Ten addresses issues which are unique to the auto sector. It provides that each country will endeavour to administer the Auto Pact in the best interests of production and employment in Canada and the United States. It specifies that Canada shall not add to those Canadian manufacturers operating under the Auto Pact and comparable arrangements as of the entry into force of the Agreement.

There are separate provisions respecting other automotive duty waivers or remissions. Existing remissions cannot be extended to additional recipients, nor expanded, nor extended where such remissions apply to goods imported from other countries and are tied to performance requirements on automotive or other goods. Duty remissions earned through exports will be terminated by 1998, with exports to the United States ruled out upon entry into force of the Agreement. The current recipients of these waivers are listed in an annex, as are manufacturers who qualify under the Auto Pact.

Waivers or remissions committed prior to the Agreement's entry into force and tied to the value added contained in production in Canada other than for manufacturers qualifying under the Auto Pact are to be terminated by 1996.

Article 1003 provides for the phased elimination of the used car embargo. By 1993, there will be free trade in used automobiles.

These provisions taken together mean that:

- The Big Three and other qualified auto makers will be able to continue to benefit from their privileges under the Auto Pact and comparable arrangements to bring in vehicles and parts duty-free from all over the world as long as they continue to meet the Auto Pact production safeguards. They currently save $300 million annually in duties on their imports from third countries.

- Manufacturers listed in Annex 1002.1 Part 1 who can qualify for Auto Pact status in the 1989 model year will enjoy similar benefits.

- The Canadian government will continue to honour its commitments to provide duty waivers to companies with new production facilities in Canada to encourage them to source parts in Canada. This program and the rule of origin provisions in chapter Three will provide a strong incentive for offshore producers to purchase parts in Canada.

The two governments also agreed that some of the challenges facing the North American auto industry were more than a matter of negotiating a Free-Trade Agreement. They have, therefore, agreed to establish a select panel to advise the two governments on automotive issues (Article 1004).

Chapter Eleven: Emergency Action

A traditional feature of most trade Agreements is the ability of the Parties temporarily to impose restrictions (such as quotas or surcharges) otherwise inconsistent with the Agreement to deal with surges in imports causing serious injury to domestic producers. The ability to impose such emergency restrictions is often the key to gaining acceptance for the liberalizing provisions of an Agreement. The challenge is to circumscribe the right to take emergency action in such a manner as to prevent abuse. In a free-trade Agreement, once investors have taken steps to take advantage of the new opportunities, their expectations should not be frustrated by others who have not adjusted.

In chapter Eleven, the two governments have agreed to stringent standards for the application of emergency safeguards to bilateral trade. For the transition period only (i.e., until the end of 1998), either country may respond to serious injury to domestic producers resulting from the reduction of tariff barriers under the Agreement with a suspension of the duty reductions for a limited period of time or a return to the most-favoured-nation tariff level (i.e., the current tariff which may in future be reduced through multilateral negotiations). No measure can last more than three years or extend beyond December 31, 1998. Any such action will also be subject to compensation by the other country, for example, through accelerated duty elimination on another product.

After the transition period, no measure may be taken to counteract a surge resulting from the operation of the Agreement except by mutual consent.

Additionally, Canada and the United States have agreed to exempt each other from global actions under GATT Article XIX except where the other's producers are important contributors to the injury caused by a surge of imports from all countries. This will mean that Canadian companies will no longer need to fear being sideswiped by an emergency action aimed largely at other suppliers, such as has happened in the case of specialty steel. Should either government take global emergency action, however, companies in the other country will not be allowed to rush in and take advantage of the situation. Any surge in exports in those circumstances may lead to their inclusion in the global action. Should the other Party be included in a global action either initially or subsequently, its exports will be protected against reductions below the trend line of previous bilateral trade with allowance for growth. Again, any emergency measures applied between the two countries will be subject to compensation.

For greater certainty and in order to help guide any determination by domestic tribunals as to whether or not the other country is contributing importantly to any injury justifying a global measure, Article 1102 contains specific thresholds. Imports below five percent of total imports will not generally be considered to be substantial and will be excluded from any action. Imports above ten percent would be considered substantial and would be examined further to see whether they were an important cause of the serious injury from imports.

Any dispute as to whether the conditions for imposing a bilateral measure, for including the other Party in a global action or for the adequacy of compensation will be subject to binding arbitration after the action has been taken.   Failure to meet the requirements would result in removal of the measure and, if appropriate, compensation.

The provisions of this Chapter are important in establishing a more predictable climate for investors in both countries to take advantage of the Agreement, secure in the knowledge that their access to the other market will not be impaired by capricious action stemming from domestic complaints.   They will be able to benefit from clear rules backed up by binding arbitration.

Chapter Twelve: Exceptions for Trade in Goods

As with the Chapter on emergency action, most trade agreements contain general exceptions.   Such exceptions recognize that governments must retain some freedom of action to protect their legitimate national interests.   In effect, they constitute a buffer zone without which binding international agreements could not be concluded between sovereign nations. For the part of the Agreement dealing with trade in goods, the two governments have agreed to incorporate the provisions of GATT Article XX and the grandfather provisions of the GATT's Protocol of Provisional Application. Most free-trade agreements have followed a similar practice.

GATT Article XX can justify import and export control measures, otherwise prohibited by the Agreement, for the following reasons:

- necessary to protect public morals (such as prohibitions on trade in pornographic material);

- necessary to protect human, animal or plant life or health (such as measures to protect the environment or endangered species);

- relating to trade in gold or silver;

- necessary to ensure compliance with domestic laws and regulations not otherwise inconsistent with the GATT (such as product standards);

- relating to the products of prison labour (producers should not have to compete with goods produced with prison labour);

- necessary to protect national treasures of artistic, historic or archaeological value; and

- undertaken in pursuance of an international commodity agreement (such as an international wheat or tin agreement).

Article XX also includes provisions relating to the preservation of commodities in short supply. These have been modernized and addressed in chapter Four (Border Measures) in the context of obligations relating to export measures and in chapter Nine for energy goods.

Finally, the provisions of Article XX are not absolute. They are subject to the requirement that they not be applied so as to constitute an arbitrary, unjustifiable or disguised restriction on trade. By virtue of their incorporation in the bilateral Agreement, any future dispute about the application of any measure on bilateral trade justified under this Article would be subject to the much better dispute resolution mechanism of this Agreement.

GATT's Protocol of Provisional Application was the instrument used by the original twenty-three signatories to bring the GATT into force. The signatories agreed that they would fully accept certain obligations insofar as they were not inconsistent with existing legislation on January 1, 1948. The most important policy swept up in the Protocol is the grandfathering of the United States *Jones Act* providing protection for the United States marine industry.

Chapter Twelve also includes a number of miscellaneous exceptions to the trade in goods chapters. The two governments have agreed to grandfather existing controls on the export of logs. In addition, East Coast provinces will be able to maintain existing provincial controls on the export of unprocessed fish. Both provisions will allow Canada to maintain policies aimed at upgrading these resources before export. With respect to restraints on the export of unprocessed fish caught off British Colombia, the two governments are pursuing, outside the Agreement, their rights and obligations under the GATT in light of the recent panel finding. Finally, Article 1204 grandfathers, subject to each Party's GATT rights, existing practices respecting the internal sale and distribution of beer.

Part Three
Government Procurement

The provisions on government procurement are contained in a separate part because a number of the general obligations respecting trade in goods do not apply, such as the national treatment obligations of chapter Five or the rules of origin of chapter Three. The coverage, however is limited to goods, or services incidental to the delivery of goods.

Chapter Thirteen: Government Procurement

Chapter Thirteen marks important new progress in expanding the market opportunities for suppliers of goods to government markets. Canadians have proven themselves competitive suppliers of many commercial and industrial products to the United States. These include vehicles, scientific apparatus, aircraft equipment, mineral products, industrial machinery, plastic, rubber and leather products, electrical machinery, chemical products, power generation machinery, and heating and lighting equipment. The potential for increased sales by Canadian suppliers should thus be distributed widely across all regions of Canada.

The chapter broadens and deepens the obligations both countries have undertaken in the GATT Code, commits each country to work toward the multilateral liberalization of government procurement and to negotiate further improvements in the bilateral Agreement once multilateral negotiations are concluded.

The chapter increases the amount of procurement open for competition between Canadian and U.S. suppliers in each other's market. It lowers the threshold from U.S.$171,000 (about CDN $238,000), in the GATT Code, for purchases by Code-covered entities of covered goods to U.S.$25,000 (about CDN$33,000). All government purchases above this new threshold will be open to competition unless they are reserved for small business or excluded for reasons of national security.

In addition, the chapter makes substantial improvements upon the GATT Code in transparency procedures. It establishes jointly agreed principles, contained in Annex 1305.3, governing bid-challenge procedures to ensure equitable and effective treatment for potential suppliers. An impartial reviewing authority will investigate situations where suppliers believe they have been unfairly treated and will ensure a timely decision. The reviewing authority will also be able to recommend changes in procurement procedures in accordance with the Agreement.

There are detailed provisions for the regular exchange of government procurement information. This will enable careful monitoring of the implementation of the chapter on an annual basis and will assist in resolving problems and providing the foundation for further negotiations in the GATT and bilaterally.

Annex 1304.3 reproduces the GATT Annex setting out for each country the purchasing entities whose purchases above the threshold are covered by both the GATT and this Agreement.

For the United States, 11 out of 13 government departments are covered by the GATT Code, with the only exceptions being the Departments of Energy and Transport. A total of 40 governmental agencies and commissions, as well as NASA and the General Services Administration (the common government purchasing agency) are included. Department of Defense purchases are covered within certain defined product categories such as vehicles, engines, industrial equipment and components, computer software and equipment, and commercial supplies.

For Canada, 22 government departments and 10 agencies are covered. Department of National Defence purchases of certain defined products, mainly non-military, are also covered. The Departments of Transport, Communications, and Fisheries and Oceans are not included.

Canada's access to U.S. defence procurement of military goods under the Defence Production Sharing Arrangements is not affected by this chapter.

Part Four
Services, Investment and Temporary Entry

Part Four contains the three ground-breaking chapters: services, business travel and investment.

Chapter Fourteen: Services

Trade in services represents the frontier of international commercial policy in the 1980s. Dynamic economies are increasingly dependent on the wealth generated by service transactions. International trade in services, of course, does not take place in a vacuum without rules and regulations. What it has lacked is a general framework of rules incorporating principles of general application such as those embodied in the GATT for trade in goods. Chapter Fourteen provides, for the first time, a set of disciplines covering a large number of service sectors.

The issue is also more than a matter of opening up service markets. It is no longer possible to talk about free trade in goods without talking about free trade in services because trade in services is increasingly mingled with the production, sale, distribution and service of goods. Companies today rely on advanced communications systems to co-ordinate planning, production, and distribution of products. Computer software helps to design new products. Some firms engage in-house, accountants, and engineers, some have 'captive' subsidiaries to handle their insurance and finance needs. In other words, services are both inputs for the production of manufactured goods (from engineering design to data processing) and necessary complements in organizing trade (from financing and insuring the transaction to providing installation and after-sales maintenance, especially critical for large capital goods).

The basic economic efficiency and competitiveness gains expected from the removal of barriers to trade in goods between Canada and the United States also apply to the service sectors. To achieve the same economic gains in services it was necessary to focus the negotiations on the nature of regulations that constitute trade barriers. In some cases, the focus was the right of establishment where such a right is an economic pre-condition to supplying the service, for example, travel agencies. In other cases, the opportunities to foreigners to meet the professional licensing standards imposed by countries as a condition to offering the service, for example, architecture, was the focus.

In Article 1402, the two governments agree to extend the principle of national treatment to the providers of a list of commercial services established in Annex 1408. With the exception of transportation, basic telecommunications (such as telephone service) doctors, dentists, lawyers, childcare and government provided services (health, education and social services) most commercial services are covered. This means that Canada and the United States have agreed not to discriminate between Canadian and American providers of these services. Each will be treated the same. But this is not an obligation to harmonize. If Canada chooses to treat providers of one service differently than does the United States, it is free to do so, as long as it does not discriminate between Americans and Canadians. Each government also remains free to choose whether or not to regulate and how to regulate.

The obligation to extend national treatment also does not mean the treatment has to be the same in all respects. For example, a Party may accord different treatment for legitimate purposes such as consumer protection or safety, so long as the treatment is equivalent in effect. Additionally, regulations cannot be used as a disguised restriction on trade. Article 1403, for example, specifies that either government remains free to license and certify providers of specific services, but must ensure that such licensing requirements do not act as a discriminatory barrier for persons of the other Party to meet.

The obligations are prospective, i.e., they do not require either government to change any existing laws and practices. Rather, the Parties agree that in changing existing regulations for covered services, they will be guided by the obligation not to make such regulations any more discriminatory than they are already. However, any new regulations for covered services will have to conform fully to the national treatment obligation.

While there are no rules of origin for the services chapter, as there are for trade in goods, the obligations are meant to extend benefits to Canadians and Americans. Article 1406, therefore, provides that either Party remains free to deny the benefits of this chapter if it can demonstrate that a service is in fact being provided by a provider who is a national of a third country. At the same time, neither government is obliged to discriminate against providers of services from a third country.

Sectoral annexes clarify these general obligations for three service sectors: architecture, tourism and enhanced telecommunications and computer services. Article 1405 provides scope for the two governments to negotiate more sectoral annexes in the future.

Transportation services (marine, air, trucking, rail and bus modes) are not covered by the Agreement. In effect, existing arrangements, such as ICAO and the various air bilateral agreements, will continue to govern bilateral relationships.

The new, general rules adopted for trade in services are a trail blazing effort and could lay the foundation for further work multilaterally. Applying these rules prospectively will ensure that new discrimination will not be introduced. This constitutes a major step toward ensuring that open and competitive trade in services continues between the two countries.

Chapter Fifteen: Temporary Entry for Business Persons

In this chapter, the two Parties establish a unique set of obligations to deal with an increasingly vexing problem in international trade. Export sales today require more than a good product at a good price. They also require a good sales network and, most of all, reliable after-sales service. Free and open trade conditions, therefore, require not only that goods, services and investments be treated without discrimination, but that the people required to make sales and manage investments or provide before and after service of those sales and investments should be able to move freely across the border. Furthermore, trade in professional and commercial services cannot take place unless people can move freely across the border. The challenge, therefore, was to ensure that immigration regulations would complement the rules governing the movement of goods, services and investments, but would not compromise the ability of either government to determine who may gain entry.

The government's objectives in this area were informed by the increasing frustration experienced by Canadian entrepreneurs in making and servicing sales to their U.S. customers. Many were experiencing delays and even outright denial of entry for what most considered normal business travel. Some resorted to setting up U.S. subsidiaries, dealing through third parties, or conducting their business electronically. The result was lost sales, higher costs, lower efficiency and foreclosed opportunities. In the absence of eased restrictions on border crossings, such frustrations were likely to increase as barriers to trade in goods and services and investment are reduced and eliminated as a result of other chapters of the Agreement.

To solve this problem, the two governments adapted immigration regulations to facilitate business travel. In chapter Fifteen, the two governments take the necessary steps to ensure that business persons and enterprises will have the necessary access to each other's market in order to sell their goods and services and supply after sales service to their customers.

The agreed rules are based on reciprocal access for Canadian and American business travellers to the other market. National laws and regulations governing their entry will be liberalized and entry procedures will be quick and simple. In order to limit the application of this general rule to genuine business travellers, the two governments have divided business travel into four categories and covered seven specific types of activities. These are set out in detail in the annexes to the chapter.

In order to gain temporary entry under the terms of the Agreement to the United States, therefore, Canadian business travellers must qualify for entry generally (i.e., meet normal health and safety requirements) and indicate the nature of their business (i.e., whether entering as a Business Visitor, as a Professional, as a Trader or Investor, or as an Intra-Company Transferee);

In addition, a Professional must be on the list of professions set out in Schedule 2 of the Annex . A Business Visitor must also state the specific purpose of the visit and seven general types of activities are set out in Schedule 1 of the Annex:

- ° Research and Design
- ° Growth, Manufacture and Production
- ° Marketing
- ° Sales
- ° Distribution
- ° After Sales Service
- ° General Services

For other categories of business travellers, current restrictions, such as the need to gain prior approval or to meet a labour certification test, would no longer apply to Canadians.

As they gain experience with the Agreement as a whole and with the specific provisions of this chapter, the two governments will consider ways to improve the coverage and operation of these new procedures. The dispute settlement provisions of the Agreement can be invoked if there is a clear pattern of discrimination in the administration of the entry procedures.

Chapter Sixteen: Investment

A hospitable and secure investment climate is indispensable if the two countries are to achieve the full benefits of reducing barriers to trade in goods and services. Chapter Sixteen establishes a mutually beneficial framework of principles sensitive to the national interests of both countries with the objective that investment flow more freely between Canada and the United States and that investors be treated in a fair and predictable manner.

The basic obligation is to ensure that future regulation of Canadian investors in the United States and of American investors in Canada results in treatment no different than that extended to domestic investors within each country. This basic principle is qualified on the basis of existing practice and is translated into the following specific undertakings:

- Article 1602: national treatment on the establishment of new businesses. Canadian investors in the United States and U.S. investors in Canada will be subject to the same rules as domestic investors when it comes to establishing a new business.

- Article 1602 and Article 1607: more liberal rules on the acquisition of existing businesses. Canada retains the right to review the acquisition of firms in Canada by U.S. investors, but has agreed to phase in higher threshold levels for direct acquisitions. Article 1607 provides that the review threshold for direct acquisitions will be raised in four steps to $150 million by 1992. At that time, about three-quarters of total non-financial assets in Canada now reviewable will still be reviewable. For indirect acquisitions, which involve the transfer of control of one foreign-controlled firm to another, the review process will be phased out over the same period. These changes to the Investment Canada review process will not apply to the oil and gas and uranium sectors.

- Article 1602: national treatment once established, i.e., the conduct, operation and sale of U.S.-owned firms in Canada or Canadian-owned firms in the United States will be subject to the same rules as firms owned by domestic investors. Both governments are completely free to regulate the ongoing operation of business enterprises in their respective juris-dictions under, for example, competition law, provided that they do not discriminate.

- Article 1603: limits on certain performance requirements. Both countries have agreed to prohibit investment-related performance requirements (such as local content and import substitution requirements) which significantly distort bilateral trade flows. The negotiation of product mandate, research and development, and technology transfer requirements with investors, however, will not be precluded. Moreover, this Article does not preclude the negotiation of performance requirements attached to subsidies or government procurement.

- Article 1605: due process on expropriation. If either government chooses to nationalize an industry to achieve some public policy goal, it is obligated to acquire foreign-controlled firms on the basis of due process and based on the payment of fair and adequate compensation.

- Article 1606: no restrictions on the patriation of profits or the proceeds of a sale other than those necessary to implement domestic laws of general application, such as bankruptcy laws, the regulation of securities or balance-of-payment measures.

These undertakings are prospective (i.e., applied to future changes in laws and regulations only). Existing laws, policies and practices are grandfathered, except where specific changes are required (Article 1607). The practical effect of these obligations, therefore, is to exempt the oil and gas and uranium sectors from changes to the *Investment Canada Act* (Annex 1607.3) and to freeze the various exceptions to national treatment provided in Canadian and U.S. law (such as the restrictions on foreign ownership in the communications and transportation industries). Additionally, both governments remain free to tax foreign-owned firms on a different basis than domestic firms provided this does not result in arbitrary or unjustifiable discrimination (Article 1609) and to exempt the sale of Crown-owned firms from any national treatment obligations (Article 1602). Finally, the two governments retain some flexibility in the application of the national treatment obligations (Article 1602). They need not extend identical treatment as long as the treatment is equivalent (Article 1602).

The definitions are critical to understanding the operation of this chapter. While they are complicated, they make it clear to investors exactly who benefits or is affected by the operational Articles.

To make the chapter work, the two governments have agreed to allow monitoring of foreign investment and to resolve any disputes under the dispute settlement provisions of the Agreement, with the exception that any review decisions by Investment Canada will not be subject to dispute settlement. They have also agreed to work together in the Uruguay Round of Multilateral Trade Negotiations on trade-related investment rules.

The freer flow of investment across the border will allow for the creation of new jobs and wealth in both Canada and the United States. The hospitable investment environment in Canada enhanced through the investment provisions, as well as by the operation of the Agreement as a whole, will ensure that adjustment and economic growth proceed in an efficient manner but one which is sensitive to the needs of individuals, regions and sectors.

Part Five
Financial Services

Chapter Seventeen: Financial Services

Trade is very important to Canada's financial services industry and, through its financial institutions, Canada is well represented in international financial markets. Among the larger groups of major financial services firms, the Canadian banks probably generate the largest share of foreign income and a considerable amount of that income is related to their U.S. operations and activities.

Canadian banks have been active in the U.S. for a long time while U.S. banks have only been able to provide a full range of banking services in Canada since 1980. Chapter Seventeen preserves the access that our respective financial institutions have to each other's market. Also, both Canada and the United States have agreed to continue liberalizing the rules governing their respective financial markets and to extend the benefits of such liberalization to institutions controlled by the other Party.

Prior to 1978, Canadian and other foreign banks were generally permitted to operate in more than one state. Indeed, Canadian banks had, and still have, retail and other banking operations in a number of states, unlike many of their U.S. competitors. These privileges, however, were subject to review after ten years. These privileges have been "grandfathered" indefinitely in Article 1702.

In the area of securities, Canadian banks in the United States will be able to underwrite and deal in securities of Canadian governments and their agents. Up until now, because of the 50-year old *Glass-Steagall Act* which separates commercial banking from the securities business, only dealers unaffiliated with a bank could underwrite these securities in the United States. Accordingly, a new business opportunity for Canadian banks has been created. At the same time, an important commitment from the United States will help bridge the gap between the pace of regulatory change in financial markets that has opened up between Canada and the United States. For the future, Canadian financial institutions are guaranteed, by Article 1702, that they will receive the same treatment as that accorded United States financial institutions with respect to amendments to the *Glass-Steagall Act*.

Article 1703 exempts U.S. firms and investors from some aspects of the federal "10/25" rule such that they will be treated the same as Canadians. The rule prevents any single non-resident from acquiring more than 10 percent of the shares, and all non-residents from acquiring more than 25 percent of the shares of a federally-regulated Canadian-controlled financial institution. The 10 percent limitation on any individual shareholder resident or non-resident will continue to be applied to the larger banks and thereby control of our financial system will be maintained in Canadian hands.

Additionally, U.S. bank subsidiaries in Canada will be exempted from the current 16 percent ceiling on the size of the foreign bank

sector. Finally, all U.S. applications to establish operations in Canada
have been subject to review. No changes to this review process are
required. U.S. applications will continue to be reviewed on a case-by-
case basis to ensure the suitability of the applicant, that it can make a
positive contribution to Canada's financial markets, and that prudential
concerns are met.

Financial institutions, other than insurance, are not covered by
the dispute settlement procedures of the Agreement. Rather, both
Parties have agreed to consult and these consultations will take place
between the Canadian Department of Finance and the United States
Department of the Treasury.

The financial services chapter builds on the federal government's commitment to provide more competition among financial
institutions with the resultant benefits to consumers. At the same time,
control of our financial system will remain in Canadian hands while a
new business opportunity has been opened up for our banks in the U.S.

Part Six
Institutional Provisions

Part Six contains both the general dispute settlement provisions
and the special arrangements for dealing with antidumping and
countervailing duties. In addition, this Part creates the institutional
framework for managing and implementing the trade Agreement.

Chapter Eighteen: Institutional Provisions

This chapter establishes the necessary institutional provisions to
provide for the joint management of the Agreement and to avoid and
settle any disputes between the Parties respecting the interpretation or
application of any element of the Agreement. Its essential features are
economy, joint decision-making and effective dispute resolution. Its
basic objective is to promote fairness, predictability and security by
giving each Partner an equal voice in resolving problems through
ready access to objective panels to resolve disputes and authoritative
interpretations of the Agreement.

To ensure that the Agreement is effectively implemented and
enforced, chapter Eighteen provides for:

- mandatory notification of any measure (Article 1803);

- mandatory provision of information to the other party on any measure, whether or not it has been notified(Article 1803);

- consultations at the request of either party concerning any measure or any other matter which affects the operation of the Agreement, with a view to arriving at a mutually satisfactory resolution (Article 1804);

- referral to a Canada-United States Trade Commission, should resolution through consultations fail (Article 1805); and

- use of dispute settlement procedures should the Commission fail to arrive at a mutually satisfactory resolution. Procedures are:

  ° compulsory arbitration, binding on both parties, for disputes arising from the interpretation and application of the safeguards provision (Article 1103);

  ° binding arbitration in all other disputes (Article 1806) where both parties agree; and

  ° panel recommendations to the Commission, which, in turn, is mandated to agree on a resolution of the dispute (Article 1807).

These provisions are in addition to the special dispute settlement mechanism established in Chapter Nineteen to deal with antidumping and countervailing duty issues.

The Commission is composed of equal representatives of both parties. The principal representative of each party is the ministerial rank official responsible for international trade matters, or his or her designee. Regular Commission meetings are held once a year, alternating between the two countries. As a practical matter, the day-to-day work of the Commission will be by officials of the two governments responsible for individual issues acting as working groups mandated by the Commission.

Arbitrators are selected by the Commission on such terms and in accordance with such procedures as it may adopt. Panels are composed of five members: two Canadians, two Americans, and a fifth member chosen jointly. Panelists are normally chosen from a roster developed by the Commission. Each Party chooses its national members, while the Commission chooses the fifth member. If the Commission is unable to agree on a choice, the other four members choose; should that fail, the fifth member is selected by lot.

Panels are allowed to establish their own rules of procedure, unless the Commission decides otherwise. There will be a right for at least one hearing before the panel, and the opportunity to provide written submissions and rebuttal arguments. Panel proceedings are confidential. All consultations and panel proceedings are subject to time limits, to ensure prompt resolution of disputes.

In the case of arbitral awards, the aggrieved Party has the right to suspend the application of equivalent benefits under the Agreement to the non-complying Party. In cases where the Commission does not reach agreement after receiving a Panel recommendation, and the dispute involves a measure that the aggrieved Party believes impairs its fundamental rights or anticipated benefits under the Agreement, it can suspend the application of equivalent benefits until the issue is resolved.

The combined effect of the institutional provisions and the three forms of dispute settlement (binding settlement of disputes over trade remedy actions, mutually agreed binding arbitration, and recommendatory panel procedures), will make Canada an equal partner in the resolution of disputes and provide for fair and effective solutions to difficult problems. Canadians will know what the rules are and can be confident that they will have a voice in how they will be applied.

Chapter Nineteen: Binational Dispute Settlement in Antidumping and Countervailing Duty Cases

In negotiating a better and more balanced framework for the conduct of trade between Canada and the United States, Canada sought to increase predictability and security for Canadian exporters to the United States. Without this predictability, Canadian companies cannot be sufficiently confident to take advantage of other provisions of the Agreement, such as the elimination of tariffs or improved access to government procurement.

Trade remedy procedures, such as antidumping and countervailing duty petitions, can pose a serious threat to predictability and security of access. In recent years, actions taken under U.S. trade remedy laws against Canadian exports have had a detrimental impact on investment and employment in Canada, and have become a major irritant in Canada-U.S. relations.

In this chapter, the two governments agree that in order for both sides to take equal advantage of the benefits of the Agreement, there will be need for conditions of fair competition to ensure that economic actors on both sides of the border have equal access to the whole free-trade area established by the Agreement. This will be achieved as a result of a three-track set of obligations:

- the development over a five- to seven-year period of mutually advantageous rules governing government subsidies and private anti-competitive pricing practices such as dumping, which are now controlled through the unilateral application of counter-vailing and antidumping duties;

- bilateral review of any changes in existing countervailing or antidumping laws and regulations for consistency with the GATT and the object and purpose of the Agreement; and

- the replacement of judicial review by domestic courts of countervailing and antidumping final orders by a bilateral panel.

Article 1907 provides that the two governments will work towards establishing a new regime to address problems of dumping and subsidization to come into effect no later than at the end of the seventh year. During the course of the current negotiations, the two sides recognized that developing a new regime was a complex task and would require more time. The goal of any new regime, however, will be to obviate the need for border remedies, as are now sanctioned by the GATT Antidumping and Subsidies Codes, for example, by developing new rules on subsidy practices and relying on domestic competition law. Thus the goal of the two governments remains the establishment of a new regime to replace current trade remedy law well before the end of the transition period.

In the meantime, chapter Nineteen includes provisions to prevent abuse of the current system, thus allowing Canadian exporters to compete in the U.S. market on a more secure, predictable and equitable footing. In Article 1904, the two governments have agreed to a unique dispute settlement mechanism that guarantees the impartial application of their respective antidumping and countervailing duty laws. Either government may seek a review of an antidumping or countervailing duty determination by a bilateral panel with binding powers. This will mean that producers in both countries will continue to have the right to seek redress from dumped or subsidized imports, but any relief granted will be subject to challenge and review by a binational panel which will determine whether existing laws were applied correctly and fairly. Canadian producers who have in the past complained that political pressures in the United States have disposed U.S. officials to side with complainants will now be able to appeal to a bilateral tribunal.

Findings by a panel will be binding on both governments. Should the panel determine that the law was properly applied, the matter is closed. If it finds that the administering authority (the Department of Commerce or the International Trade Commission in the United States or the Department of National Revenue or the Canadian Import Tribunal in Canada) erred on the basis of the same standards as would be applied by a domestic court, it can send the issue back to the administering authority to correct the error and make a new determination.

In order to provide symmetry in the application of panel reviews, both governments will amend their law to allow all final decisions to be subject to bilateral review.

Panelists who will review antidumping and countervailing duty decisions will be chosen from a roster of individuals who have previously agreed to act as panelists. Because of the judicial nature of the review, the majority of panelists will be lawyers. Nevertheless, the procedures allow for at least two non-lawyers who can bring other expertise to bear on any panel decision, such as business experience.

Panels must be acceptable to both sides. Each government will choose two panelists and jointly choose the fifth; if they cannot agree, the four chosen panelists will pick a fifth from the roster; if they cannot agree, the fifth panelist will be chosen by lot. Each government will be able to exercise two peremptory challenges of panelists chosen by the other side, for example, by indicating that a proposed panelist is not suitable to act on a particular issue.

Decisions will be rendered quickly based on strict time limits built into the procedures. These limits are sufficiently generous to allow the Parties opportunity to develop arguments and to challenge the arguments of the other side. While only the two governments can seek the establishment of a panel, as a practical matter, many of the issues will involve private parties and these will be allowed to make representations before the panel. In addition, both governments are obligated to invoke the panel procedure if petitioned by private parties.

To ensure fairness and the integrity of the process, procedures have been developed to address any potential for the appearance of unfairness or corruption. In the unlikely event that a panelist has a conflict of interest or there has been a serious miscarriage of justice, either government can invoke an extraordinary challenge procedure involving a panel of three former judges who will determine whether or not the allegations are valid and whether or not a new panel will be required to review the issues.

The two governments will establish a small secretariat to administer these review procedures and to give aggrieved Parties ready access to information. Additionally, they will work out detailed rules of procedures for panels and a code of conduct for panelists.

The two governments agreed in Article 1903 that changes to existing antidumping and countervailing duty legislation apply to each other only following consultation and if specifically provided for in the new legislation. Moreover, either government may ask a bilateral panel to review such changes in light of the object and purpose of the Agreement, their rights and obligations under the GATT Antidumping and Subsidies Codes and previous panel decisions. Should a panel recommend modifications, the Parties will consult to agree on such modifications. Failure to reach agreement gives the other Party the right to take comparable legislative or equivalent executive action or terminate the Agreement.

The combined effect of bilateral review of existing law and the development of a new set of rules will be to ensure that by the time all tariffs are removed and other aspects of the Agreement phased in, Canadian firms will have not only more open access, but also more secure and more predictable access. At the same time, Canada's capacity to pursue regional development and social welfare programs remains unimpaired. Indeed, it has been strengthened.

Part Seven
Other Provisions

Chapter Twenty: Other Provisions

This chapter contains a range of miscellaneous provisions. Some deal with specific issues (such as intellectual property or cultural industries) or address an existing irritant in bilateral relations (such as cable retransmission rights) while others establish a general rule which affects the application of other chapters in the Agreement (such as balance-of-payment measures or the treatment of monopolies).

In Article 104 of chapter One, the Parties agreed on a general rule of interpretation that, where there is a conflict, the trade Agreement takes precedence over all other agreements unless provided otherwise in a particular chapter. In Article 2001, the Parties agree that the provisions of the 1980 tax convention between them takes precedence over the trade Agreement.

In Article 2002, the two governments affirm their rights and obligations under the GATT, the International Monetary Fund and the OECD Code of Liberalization of Capital Movements with respect to balance-of-payments measures. In effect, the two governments agree that should either find it necessary to apply exchange controls or take trade actions (such as a surcharge or quota) to counteract a serious deterioration in its balance-of-payments position, it will do so in manner consistent with these multilateral agreements. Additionally, they agree that they will not use balance-of-payments measures as a disguised restriction on trade, thus reiterating their multilateral commitments.

Article 2003 reproduces the standard national security clause of the GATT which applies to the rights and obligations provided in all but two chapters: energy, and government procurement. In the case of energy, the two governments have agreed on a more limited national security provision and the procurement chapter relies on the national security provision of the GATT Code on Government Procurement.

All international trade and economic agreements contain a national security provision giving the Parties sufficient flexibility to deal with national emergencies, to ensure that no provision of the Agreement can be interpreted to require a government to compromise classified material, to limit trade in military goods or not to meet its commitments under the United Nations Charter.

During the course of the negotiations, the two governments worked on an overall framework covering the protection of intellectual property rights (trademarks, copyright, patents, industrial design and trade secrets). In the end, a substantive chapter was dropped. Nevertheless, in Article 2004, the two governments agree to continue to cooperate and work toward better international intellectual property rules, particularly in the Uruguay Round of Multilateral Trade Negotiations where a working group on trade-related intellectual property issues has been established.

From the beginning of the negotiations, Canadians expressed concern that an agreement might erode the government's capacity to encourage and help Canada's cultural industries (film and video, music and sound recording, publishing, cable transmission and broadcasting) and thus to contribute to the development of Canada's unique cultural identity. In order to remove any ambiguity that Canada's unique cultural identity remains untouched by the Agreement, the two governments agreed in Article 2005 on a specific provision indicating that, with four very limited exceptions, nothing in this Agreement affects the ability of either Party to pursue cultural policies. The specific exceptions are:

- the elimination of tariffs on any inputs to, and products of, the cultural industries, such as musical instruments, cassettes, film, recording tape, records and cameras (Article 401);

- any requirement to sell a foreign-owned enterprise engaged in a cultural activity acquired indirectly through the purchase of its parent will be balanced by an offer to purchase the enterprise at fair open market value (paragraph 4 of Article 1607);

- both Parties will provide copyright protection to owners of programs broadcast by distant stations and re-transmitted by cable companies; this undertaking will be on a non-discrimina-tory basis; after Canadian legislation is implemented there will be an opportunity for further review of outstanding issues in both countries (Article 2006);

- the requirement that a magazine or newspaper must be typeset and printed in Canada in order for advertisers to be able to deduct their expenses for advertising space in that magazine will be eliminated (Article 2007).

In Article 2008 and an agreed exchange of letters, the two governments address a long-standing irritant involving plywood standards. The Canada Mortgage and Housing Corporation will decide by March 15, 1988 whether to allow the use of C-D grade plywood (a U.S. standard) for use in housing it finances. If it agrees, a series of tariff concessions will begin to be implemented on January 1, 1989. If not, the issue will be placed before a panel of experts. Once the panel has completed its work, the two governments will determine how to implement the tariff concessions specified in Article 2008.

In Article 2009, the two governments agree to grandfather the 1986 Memorandum of Understanding on Softwood Lumber. That Memorandum provided that Canada would apply a tax on the export of softwood lumber to the United States until such time as the producing provinces had adjusted certain stumpage practices.

Most trade agreements contain provisions to deal with policy measures which either government may adopt which, while technically not inconsistent with the obligations of the Agreement, have the effect of nullifying or impairing benefits that could have been reasonably expected under the Agreement. The most obvious such measure is the establishment of a monopoly or state enterprise. A government can, for example, instead of regulating an industry, establish a state enterprise and give it monopoly powers. If the sole purpose of the establishment of such an enterprise is to evade an obligation under the Agreement, the other Party can legitimately cry foul. Article 2010 establishes rules governing the establishment of monopolies (based on similar provisions in Article XVII of the GATT) while Article 2011 (based on Article XXIII of the GATT) provides a framework to address any claim of nullification and impairment.

Part Eight
Final Provisions

Chapter Twenty-One: Final Provisions

In Articles 2101 and 2102, the two governments agree to exchange the necessary statistical information and to publish all necessary information to facilitate implementation and administration of the Agreement. This chapter provides for annexes and amendments and the duration and entry into force of the Agreement. The Agreement will remain in effect indeterminately. Due to a provision in the U.S. fast-track approval procedures, any agreement brought forward under its provisions must contain a six-month termination clause.

Agreed Letters

The three letters set out understandings reached between the governments during the course of the negotiations on matters that require attention before the Agreement enters into force. The first letter reconfirms the understanding on a standstill between October 4, 1987 and the entry into force of the Agreement on actions not in keeping with the spirit of the Agreement. The second ensures that in case either government fails to implement the Harmonized System (the system by which goods are classified and upon which the tariff cuts are based) before the entry force of the Agreement, that the tariff reductions would still occur under the existing classification system. The third deals with the evaluation of American plywood standards for use in housing financed by Canada Mortgage and Housing Corporation. It links tariff reductions for plywood to the outcome of the CMHC assessment.

THE TIMETABLE

October 3, 1987

President Reagan sends notice of intent to sign a trade agreement with Canada to the Congress triggering the fast track approval process

October 4, 1987

Elements of Agreement signed by Canadian and U.S. negotiators.

December 10, 1987

Chief negotiators initial legal text of trade Agreement.

December 11, 1987

Tabling of legal text of trade Agreement in the House of Commons.

January 2, 1988

Signature of the Agreement.

Spring 1988

Drafting of implementing legislation in Canada and the United States and introduction of legislation in House of Commons. The Agreement and implementing legislation are formally tabled in the U.S. Congress which begins up to 90 "sitting days" for Congress to vote yes or no to the Agreement and implementing legislation. (House of Representatives up to 45 days in committee and 15 in the House; Senate up to 15 days in committee and 15 in the full chamber).

January 1, 1989

The Trade Agreement and its rules covering such issues as procurement, services and investment and border measures come into effect after both countries exchange Instruments of Ratification. The first round of tariff reductions will begin. For those sectors ready to compete now, tariffs will be eliminated; other goods will begin phasing out their tariffs over a five-year or 10-year period.. The first tranche will cover about 15 per cent of all goods traded between the two countries including:

Computer and related-equipment	Some pork
Some unprocessed fish	Fur & fur garments
Leather	Whiskey
Yeast	Animal feeds
Unwrought aluminum	Ferro alloys
Vending machines and parts	Needles
Airbrakes for railroad cars	Skis
Skates	Warranty repairs
Some paper-making machinery	Motorcycles

Both nations will end any direct export subsidies to agricultural products going to the other partner. The embargo on used vehicles imports (those less than 15 years old) from the U.S. will be lifted in stages. Cars more than eight years old will be allowed entry to Canada duty-free immediately. The age limit will drop about two years every 12 months, until 1994.The embargo on used aircraft imports will be lifted. Buy-Canadian and buy-American government procurement policies will be eased.

The Canadian markup difference beyond normal commercial considerations on U.S. wine will begin to be phased out. The differential markups on imports of U. S. distilled liquor will be eliminated entirely. The federal government will only review direct U.S. takeovers of Canadian companies worth more than $25 million, up from the current $5 million. For indirect takeovers, review will be set at assets of $100 million, up from $50 million. Improved temporary entry for business people is implemented by both countries. U. S. uranium enrichment restrictions are ended.

October 1, 1989

Tariffs on exports to the U.S. of specialty steel products will be lifted in stages.

January 1, 1990

Tariffs will drop another fifth or tenth depending on the schedule.

January 1, 1991

Foreign investment review for direct takeovers rises to $100 million; for indirect takeovers, $500 million. Tariffs will continue to drop; the 35 percent U.S. duty on Canadian shakes and shingles is scheduled to come off.

January 1, 1992

The trigger for investment review rises to $150 million; indirect takeovers will no longer be scrutinized. Tariff cuts continue.

January 1, 1993

Tariffs will have been lifted on another 35 per cent of dutiable goods, including:

Subway cars
Printed matter
Paper and paper products
Paints
Explosives
Telecommunications equipment
Most machinery

Chemicals including resins (excluding drugs and cosmetics)
Furniture
Hardwood plywood
Aftermarket auto parts
Some meats (including lamb)

The embargo on the import of used cars ends, as does the U.S. curb on lottery materials.

January 1, 1994

U.S. customs user fees and duty drawbacks in other countries will end. U.S. foreign trade zone provisions will change to Canada's benefit. New regimes on countervail and antidumping should come into effect.

January 1, 1995

Tariffs take another drop.

January 1, 1996

There will be another tariff cut. This is the final deadline for Canada and the U.S. to agree on new trade remedy rules. Production-based duty waivers for production in the auto industry will end.

January 1, 1997

Another tariff reduction.

January 1, 1998

Tariffs will have ended on remaining goods:

Most agricultural products	Steel
Textiles and apparel	Appliances
Softwood plywood	Beef
Pleasure craft	Railcars
	Tires

The snapback provisions on vegetables and fresh fruits will remain for another decade.

CANADA-U.S. FREE TRADE AGREEMENT

SUMMARY

ELABORATIONS AND CLARIFICATIONS

TO THE

ELEMENTS OF THE AGREEMENT

AS REFLECTED IN THE LEGAL TEXT

OF THE

FREE TRADE AGREEMENT

BETWEEN CANADA

AND THE

UNITED STATES OF AMERICA

TRADE:
Securing
Canada's
Future

Canadä

INTRODUCTION:

Over the past two months, officials from Canada and the United States have translated the October 4th framework agreement into legal language. Officials have clarified the precise legal meaning of The Elements of the Agreement and elaborated on the details, ensuring that the balance of benefits is maintained.

PART ONE: OBJECTIVES AND SCOPE
Chapter 1:   Objectives and Scope

Article 105:   National Treatment
This article provides that to the extent provided in
the trade agreement, each Party shall provide national
treatment with respect to investment and to trade in
goods and services.

The concept of national treatment is a basic
liberalizing principle of international trade law.   It
is the foundation on which many of the obligations of
the GATT and the Canada-U.S. Trade Agreement are built.
The particular applications of national treatment and
exceptions to it are specified in individual chapters.

Chapter 2: General Definitions

PART TWO: TRADE IN GOODS
Chapter 3:   Rules of Origin for Goods

Annex 301.2:   Interpretations
The general rule of origin for goods to receive duty
free treatment for shipments between the Parties is a
change of tariff classification.   For a number of
industries (e.g. chemicals, footwear, machinery,
electronic, autos) this rule is supplemented by a 50%
cost of production test to ensure that the benefits of
the FTA tariff treatment will accrue to Canadian or US
producers.   The methodology agreed to for this test
provides that duty and taxes on materials originating
outside Canada or the United States and inland freight,
although incurred in Canada or the United States, will
be treated as foreign content whereas the total value
of offshore components that meet the rules of origin
will count towards the 50%.

Apparel made from offshore fabrics will qualify for
preferential FTA treatment into the U.S., up to the
following levels: 50 million square yards for non-
woollen apparel and 6 million square yards for woollen
apparel.   Above these levels, apparel made from
offshore fabrics will face MFN rates into the U.S., but
can benefit from duty drawbacks.   Apparel made from
Canadian or U.S. fabrics will qualify for preferential
FTA treatment into the U.S.   The corresponding levels
for apparel exported to Canada from the United States
are 10.5 million square yards for non-woollen apparel
and 1.1 million square yards for woollen apparel.

Fabrics made in Canada from offshore yarns and exported
to the United States will qualify for preferential
entry under the FTA, up to an annual level of 30
million square yards. This quota arrangement will
continue until December 31, 1992 and will be reviewed
within two years of implementation of the Agreement in
order to work out a solution satisfactory to both
Parties countries. There will be no corresponding
level for fabric exports from the United States to
Canada.

The FTA rules of origin have been specifically designed
to prevent goods processed offshore and returned to the
USA at reduced rates under the US tariff 807 provision
from qualifying for preferential FTA treatment. This
provision is used by US companies operating in Mexico.

Chapter 4: Border Measures

Article 401: Tariff Removal
Tariffs on certain telecommunications products such as
telephone sets and switching apparatus will be removed
immediately on January 1, 1989 or to three annual
steps.

Article 407: Import and Export Restrictions

407.2 specifies the parties' understanding that their
existing GATT obligations prohibit minimum import or
export price requirements.

407.3 makes it clear that when one country imposes an
import control on a product of a specified third
country, the other Party will not serve as a conduit to
the first Party; it also allows for the adding as a
condition to any exoneration from export controls for
bilateral trade that the product involved be consumed
in the other Party.

407.4 provides for consultations about actions to be
taken in circumstances where either Party might create
a distortion in bilateral trade by implementing a
restriction on imports of a good from third countries.

Article 408: Export Taxes
This article makes it clear that neither Party will
impose export taxes (i.e. taxes over and above those
levied on domestic sales) on exports to each other.

Article 409: Other Export Measures

409.1 (a) specifies the GATT circumstances
(conservation, short supply, domestic price
stabilization schemes) in which the use of an export
control by either country will be accompanied by
proportionate allocation of the reduced supply. It
specifies that in these circumstances, the export
control cannot reduce the amount available for export
below the amount exported relative to the total supply
which prevailed in the most recent 36-month period.
Total supply is defined as being all shipments from
domestic production, domestic inventories and other
imports as appropriate.

409.1 (b) requires that the export control not require
the disruption of normal channels of distribution or of
the normal product mix of the goods subject to the
control.

Chapter 5: National Treatment

Article 501, 502: Incorporation of GATT Rule, Provincial and State Measures

Article 501 incorporates the United States' and
Canada's existing national treatment obligations under
the General Agreement on Tariffs and Trade for Part
Two: Trade in Goods. Similarly, Article 502 provides
for the states and provinces to give treatment no less
favourable than the most favourable treatment provided
by the province or state to goods from the other Party.

Chapter 6: Technical Standards

Article 605: Accreditation

Provides for accreditation of each other's
certification bodies.

Chapter 7: Agriculture

Article 702: Special Provisions for Fresh Fruits and Vegetables

The conditions under which the existing tariffs on
fresh fruits and vegetables can be reapplied are
spelled out.

The text states that where the import price is below
90% of the previous five-year average monthly import
price and the planted acreage of the importing Party is
not higher than the previous five-year average (taking
out the high and low year), the MFN tariff rate can be
re-applied on a temporary basis. The text ensures that
planted acreage increases, as a result of possible
shifts from wine grape production to other fruits and
vegetables are excluded from acreage calculation. This
is a new element which will be of assistance to grape
growers who may be facing adjustment over the next few
years and wish to shift from grape to such crops as
tender tree fruits.

In the absence of this provision recourse to the 20-
year tariff "snap-back" provision for some fruits and
vegetables could have been prevented because of acreage
increases arising from wine grape adjustments.

In addition, the text notes that the tariff can only be
applied once a year nationally or once per year per
region, and that its duration will be for a maximum of
180 days.

Two days' notice and consultations are required before
application of the tariff.

The text then lists the products covered by this
article (all fresh fruits and vegetables, except those
that are already duty free).

Article 704: Market Access for Meat.
Article 704.1 provides that both countries will exclude
each other from the provisions of their respective Meat
Import Laws.

Article 704.2 spells out that when a Party takes action
against third party imports and the other Party does
not take similar action, the Agreement contains a
provision aimed at avoiding displacement which could
frustrate the effect of the quantitative restrictions
on third country imports.

Article 705: Market Access for Grain and Grain Products
The elements text indicates that import permits will be
removed when "support levels" are equalized. The legal
text spells out the details of the "technical
calculation". In addition, the text indicates that if
import restrictions are lifted, Canada reserves the
right to require end-use certificates or denaturing to
ensure that the integrity of the Canadian grain quality
control system is maintained.

The use of end-use certificates will ensure that U.S. grain does not enter Canada's grain handling system and thereby ensures that no U.S. grain is mixed with Canadian grain destined for export to third countries.

Article 706: Market Access for Poultry and Eggs

The elements text indicated that Canada would increase its global import quotas for poultry, eggs and products. The legal text spells out the actual size of the new quotas. The increases in the poultry import quotas are to agreed specified levels based on the 1982-86 actual import levels. There will be no subsequent re-calculation.

- The chicken import quota will increase from 6.3% to 7.5% of domestic production.
- The turkey import quota will increase from 2% to 3.5% of domestic production.
- The shell egg import quota will increase from 0.675% to 1.647% of domestic shell egg production.
- The liquid, frozen and further processed egg import quota will increase from 0.415% to 0.714% of domestic shell egg production.
- The powdered egg import quota will increase from 0.615% to 0.627% of domestic shell egg production.

Article 707: Market Access for Products Containing 10 Percent or Less Sugar

The elements text referred to "sweeteners". The legal text refers to "sugar". This change ensures that in determining the eligibility of a product for this exemption, sweeteners other than sugar will not be included in the 10 per cent calculation.

Article 708: Technical Regulations and Standards for Agricultural, Food, Beverage and Certain Related Goods

This article sets out in detailed form the principles to govern technical regulations and standards and establishes eight working groups to further the implementation of this section. Canada and the United States have agreed to work towards greater compatibility of technical regulations for these goods. This compatibility will not result in the lowering of any Canadian standards. In addition, the text guarantees that an open border policy for meat inspection will be maintained and limited to occasional spot checks to ensure compliance with inspection requirements. In addition, the text contains twelve schedules in an annex that sets out, for each specific area, guidelines for implementation.

Article 710:   International Obligations
This article specifically provides that both Canada and
the United States maintain their rights and obligations
under Article XI of the GATT.   This ensures that
Canada may maintain import quotas necessary to protect
existing or new national supply management programs.

Chapter 8   Wine and Distilled Spirits

Chapter 8 provides a detailed elaboration of the
obligations which were agreed to in the Elements of the
Agreement.

Article 803: Pricing
The wording sets out with specific dates, the timetable
agreed to in the elements.

Article 804.3:   Distribution
This article makes clear that the provision to
grandfather Quebec grocery story sales of wine applies
to the province of Quebec.   In addition, the text
clarifies that outlets (i.e. SAQ) must be available to
distribute imported U.S. wine.

Article 808:   Definitions
The definitions section clarifies that for Article 804,
wine store outlets that are grandfathered are those in
operation, in the process of being built, or where an
application had been approved.

This will ensure that those companies who had received
provincial approval and had made commercial plans and
commitments will be able to carry through with their
approved stores.

Chapter 9:   Energy

The Energy Chapter has given rise to a number of
misunderstandings as to its scope and content since the
publication of the Elements of Agreement.   The text in
a very detailed and clear way translates faithfully the
Elements in a way which Canadians will see safeguards
our energy interests.

It makes very clear that Canada has no obligation to
supply energy to the U.S.   However, in cases of short
supply, cutbacks in exports to the U.S. and the
administration of the cutbacks would be done in a fair
way.   The proportionality test for energy is identical
to that provided for all other goods.

The text acknowledges and indeed allows for higher
prices for export sales arising from the application of
a quantitative restriction but specifies that it should
not be imposed by government action.

In the Elements of the Agreement, Canada undertook to
eliminate only one of the three price tests the
National Energy Board applies to exports. The least
cost alternative test is being eliminated. In addition
the text makes clear that surplus tests can continue to
be operated by either party.

Article 902: Import and Export Restrictions
902.1 and 902.2 make clear that the trade agreement's
rights and obligations with respect to energy trade
restrictions are the GATT reasons for which such
measures can be taken. The obligations apply to
imports and exports, and apply equally to both Parties.

902.4 provides for consultations about actions to be
taken in circumstances where either Party might create
a distortion in bilateral trade by implementing a
restriction (e.g. an oil import fee) against third
country products.

Article 904: Other Export Measures
904(a) clarifies the way in which proportionality and
export price disciplines will apply in any situation in
which either Party implements export controls for such
GATT reasons as short supply, conservation, or domestic
price stabilization schemes. The proportionality test
for energy is identical to that provided in Article 409
for other goods.

904(b) acknowledges that higher prices for export sales
might arise from the application of a quantitative
restriction but, otherwise, should not be imposed by
government action.

904(c) provides that if energy export restrictions are
put in place for reasons relating to conservation,
short supply or domestic price stabilization schemes,
then governments may not require disruption of normal
channels of supply or normal product mixes.

Article 908: International Obligations
This article refers to the International Energy
Agency's Agreement on an International Energy Program
(IEP) relative to oil, to which both Canada and the
U.S. are already signatories; it makes clear that, in
the event of any unavoidable inconsistency between the
FTA and that 1974 Agreement, the provisions of the IEP
will apply.

Annex 905.2: Regulatory and Other Measures
Paragraph 1 makes clear that it is the third National
Energy Board (NEB) price test which is to be
eliminated. This test compares the prices in export
contracts to those for the least cost alternative for
the export customer. The NEB can continue to operate
its other price tests relative to the recovery of costs
and the price available to Canadians for comparable
service.

Paragraph 4 makes clear that, consistent with the
Agreement, surplus tests can continue to be operated by
either Party (e.g. by the NEB in Canada).

Chapter 10: Trade in Automotive Goods

There has been no substantive change from the Elements
of Agreement. The provisions in the Elements of the
Agreement on automotive tariffs, duty drawbacks, and
foreign trade zones are not part of Chapter 10 since
the general treatment provided for these subjects in
Chapters 3 and 4 cover trade in automotive goods.

Article 1003: Import Restrictions
This article specifies the schedule for phasing out the
embargo on used vehicles, such that after five years,
there are no restrictions on the import of used
automobiles and other motor vehicles.

Article 1005: Relationship to Other Chapters
This article contains a provision which would allow
manufacturers to average their calculations for
purposes of meeting the rule of origin.

Article 1006: Definitions
This article contains definitions of terms used in the
automobile chapter.

Annex 1002.1
This three-part annex lists the companies eligible for
various forms of waivers of customs duties.

Chapter 11: Emergency Action

Article 1101: Bilateral Actions

1101.2(d) provides that on termination of a bilateral safeguard action, the rate of duty shall be the rate which would have been in effect but for the emergency action.

1101.2 (b) and 1101.3 provide that actions may be taken after the transition period or may extend beyond the transition period only with the consent of the other Party.

Chapter 12: Exceptions for Trade In Goods

Article 1203 (c): Miscellaneous Exceptions (Fish)

The Elements of the Agreement provided for initiatives (elimination, phase-out, grandfathering) for an illustrative list of quantitative restrictions. Article 1203 (c) elaborates on the list by grandfathering existing east coast provincial acts, some of which have been used to control the movement of unprocessed fish. They include the relevant provincial legislation in Quebec, Nova Scotia, New Brunswick, Prince Edward Island and Newfoundland. With respect to restrictions on British Columbian exports of unprocessed fish, the two governments are pursuing at this time their rights and obligations under GATT in light of the recent panel finding.

Article 1204: Beer and Malt Containing Beverages

Beer was not dealt with in the Elements of the Agreement in a separate fashion. In the Wine and Distilled Spirits chapter, it was specifically stated that it did not apply to beer.

The treatment of beer is now explicitly laid out in the text under chapter 12 exceptions. Article 1204 applying to beer and malt-containing beverages makes it explicit that national treatment as spelled out in Chapter 5 does not apply to existing measures for beer and malt-containing beverages (beer, coolers).

Article 1204 grandfathers all existing practices concerning beer. The effect of this article is that existing practices cannot be challenged under the FTA. For future practices, beer will have access to the full range of dispute settlement protection of the FTA. (The U.S. has not, however, relinquished its GATT rights with respect to existing practices respecting beer).

PART THREE: GOVERNMENT PROCUREMENT
Chapter 13: Government Procurement

Articles 1301 to 1309: Government Procurement
Chapter 13 on government procurement of goods specifies
the federal government entities covered by the
agreement, sets out the transparency provisions or
procedures that will govern how procurements are
conducted, and outlines a joint commitment to work
towards further multilateral improvements in the GATT
Government Procurement Code. It sets out in detail
expanded procedural obligations for the purchases
covered, including national treatment for all potential
goods suppliers of both countries at all stages of the
procurement process (pre-notification, tendering and
bidding, evaluation of bids and awarding of contracts).
A common rule of origin is defined for eligible goods.

Annex 1304.3: Entities Covered
The annex incorporates the GATT procurement Code and
lists in all the federal departments and agencies
covered for Canada and the U.S.

Annex 1305.3: Principles Guiding Bid Challenge Procedures
The annex outlines bid challenge principles, which will
ensure that a reviewing authority shall accord timely
and impartial consideration to any complaint or bid
challenge by any supplier.

PART FOUR: SERVICES, INVESTMENT AND TEMPORARY ENTRY
Chapter 14: Services

The chapter establishes rules regarding the provision
of commercially-traded services, listed in the coverage
annex, across the border and within each country.
These rules will apply for all <u>future</u> laws and
regulations adopted by governments in regulating the
service sectors covered by the Agreement.

Article 1401: Scope and Coverage
This article clarifies that the services chapter
provides no additional rights or obligations regarding
investment in the services industries. It states that
establishment and acquisition of services industries
are covered in the Investment chapter.

Article 1402: Rights and Obligations
1402.2 states that a province or state shall accord to
persons of the other country treatment no less
favourable than the most favourable treatment accorded
to persons in the country of which it is a part.

1402.9 states that, with respect to trade in services, there are no obligations arising under this agreement regarding subsidies or government procurement practices.

Annex 1408: Services covered by the agreement
This annex lists a wide range of commercially-traded services covered by the agreement. Services provided by government and social services such as child care are excluded, as are cultural industries, legal services, all transportation modes and basic telecommunications. Financial services other than insurance are dealt with in a separate chapter.

Annex 1404.1.B: Tourism
Both parties have agreed not to use departure taxes or fees or currency restrictions to impede trade in tourism. Tourism-related services of a financial nature are included in the definition of tourism services.

Annex 1404.1.C: Computer Services and Telecommunications Network-Based Enhanced Services
The definition of basic and enhanced services will be as defined and classified by the respective regulators. No further benchmarks for these definitions have been included in the trade agreement.

The annex explicitly excludes any obligations regarding the establishment of facilities and offering of basic telecommunications transport services.

When a monopoly provider of basic telecommunications services competes in the provision of enhanced services, it may not engage in anticompetitive practices in the enhanced market. Separate accounting and other requirements shall ensure the separation of monopoly and competitive activities.

Annex: Transportation
The Elements of the Agreement stated that, subject to review by both parties, an annex would be included that clarifies the application of the agreement to future laws and regulations in the transportation section.

There is no transportation Annex because the U.S. was unable to bring the shipping industry under the discipline of the Services Code. No modes of transportation services are covered by the Services Code.

Chapter 15: Temporary Entry for Business Persons

Chapter 15 provides for temporary entry for a variety
of business persons. Schedule 1 lists the general
service providers who are covered. Schedule 2 lists
the professions covered by the new provisions for
professionals.

Chapter 16: Investment

The investment text has been clarified to make specific
Canada's right to retain Canadian ownership of existing
Crown corporations that are privatized and to preserve
existing Investment Canada threshold levels and
performance requirements for review of energy
acquisitions.

Article 1601: Scope and Coverage
1601.2 provides for the exclusion of transportation and
financial services (except insurance) and investments
relating to government procurement.

Article 1602: National Treatment
1602.4 provides that for a province or state national
treatment means treatment by a province or state to
investors of a Party no less favourable than the most
favourable treatment accorded investors of the country
to which it belongs.

1602.5 provides that any existing business operated by
a Canadian federal or provincial government is exempted
from the national treatment provisions of 1602.1 and
1602.2. Consequently, measures can be imposed on the
sale of these businesses such that they can be sold
only to Canadians, and conditions can be imposed
requiring control in the future by Canadians.

1602.6 provides that once a measure is introduced under
1602.5, it cannot be amended to make it more
restrictive.

1602.7 provides that if subsequent to the entry into
force of the agreement, a Canadian federal or
provincial government acquires or creates a new
business, this business is exempt from the national
treatment provisions of 1602.1 and 1602.2 for the
initial resale of the business to private investors.
While these businesses can be sold only to Canadians,
there would be no restriction beyond existing
grandfathered legislation on the subsequent sale of the
businesses.

Article 1603:   Performance Requirements
1603 proscribes the imposition of significantly trade
distorting performance requirements. It does not limit
Canada's ability to negotiate local employment, product
mandate, technology transfer, or research and
development undertakings with investors. Moreover,
there are no restrictions on the use of performance
requirements related to subsidies or government
procurement.

Article 1604:   Monitoring
This provision permits requirements to be placed on an
investor from the other country to provide information
for monitoring purposes.

Article 1609:   Taxation and Subsidies
This article provides that the provisions of the
Investment Chapter shall not apply to any subsidy or
any new taxation measures unless such subsidy or
taxation measures unjustifiably discriminate between
investors of the Parties or constitute a disguised
restriction on the benefits accorded to investors under
the Investment Chapter.

1602.8 allows for different treatment of investors from
the other Party to the extent required for prudential,
fiduciary, health and safety or consumer protection
reasons, and the where different treatment is
equivalent in effect to the treatment accorded to the
investors of the Party for such reasons.

Annex 1607.3
Paragraph 4, stipulates that in amending the Investment
Canada Act, the oil, gas, and uranium industries will
be exempted from the changes. This means that
threshold levels for investment review will not be
raised and the FTA's performance requirement
restrictions will not apply to these industries.

PART FIVE: FINANCIAL SERVICES
Chapter 17:   Financial Services

Articles 1701:   Scope and Coverage
Article 1701 sets out the relationship of this Chapter
to the rest of the FTA. Among other things, it
specifies which Articles of the Agreement apply.
Accordingly, the dispute settlement process, the
investment chapter (other than insurance services) and
the services code do not apply. It also specifies that
the commitments of this chapter do not apply to
provincial or state laws governing financial
institutions.

PART SIX: INSTITUTIONAL PROVISIONS

Chapter 18: Institutional Provisions

Chapter 19:   Binational Panel Dispute Settlement in Antidumping and Countervailing Cases

Article 1904:   Final Antidumping and Countervailing Duty Determinations

The Elements of the Agreement refer to "final orders" arising from determinations issued by the Department of Commerce and the International Trade Commission. The text defines "final orders" as including both positive and negative final determinations.

To maintain the integrity of the panel process, 1904.13 creates an "extraordinary challenge procedure" to allow a Party to challenge a decision where a member of the panel may be biased or where the panel has departed from a fundamental rule of procedure, or has manifestly exceeded its powers. This procedure is an extraordinary one and is not intended to allow for a review of the merits of the panel decision. By establishing such a procedure, there will be no need for domestic review where there are allegations of bias or excess of jurisdiction.

1904.5 provides for maintaining the rights of individuals to judicial review in anti-dumping and countervailing duty cases. Canada, upon the request of an individual, will request the establishment of a Panel if that individual would otherwise have had such rights under the domestic laws of Canada. The situation will be similar in the United States.

Article 1911:   Definitions: Final Determinations

To permit importers and exporters of both Canada and the United States a balanced opportunity in antidumping and countervailing duty cases, the Special Import Measures Act and the Federal Court Act will be amended to permit review by the panel of certain final determinations of the Deputy Minister of National Revenue. This ensures that these final determinations will be subject to review in both countries.

Annex 1901.2:   Membership of Panels

A majority of the five-member panel including the chairman will be lawyers, given that the panel replaces judicial review. However, in light of the breadth of the Trade Agreement, non-lawyers with familiarity with international trade law are also eligible to serve as panelists.

Chapter 20: Other Provisions

Article 2001: Tax Convention
This provision affirms that the existing tax convention between Canada and the United States continues to be fully operational. Nothing in the Free Trade Agreement affects the rights and obligations resulting from the tax convention.

Article 2002: Balance of Payments
2002 acknowledges each country's rights, now existing under international agreements, to take necessary restrictive actions for balance of payments reasons.

Article 2006: Retransmission Rights
2006 clarifies the understanding that each Party may determine the condition under which the right to equitable remuneration for any retransmission will be exercised. It also provides by 1990 for the establishment of a joint committee to review retransmission issues in both countries.

Article 2007: Advertising in Canadian Periodicals and "Print in Canada"
The final text amplifies upon Canada's agreement to remove the "print and typeset in Canada" requirement in Section 19 of the Income Tax Act. This will enable Canadian publishers to source their printing requirements for Canadian magazines and periodicals with the most efficient and effective printers in Canada or the U.S. and thereby ensure a competitive manufacturing environment for Canadian publishers.

Article 2010: Monopolies
The article provides that either Party may maintain or designate a monopoly. There are obligations to contain the impact of a monopoly on: discrimination in the provision of monopoly goods or services, and anticompetitive practices by the monopolist in any other market.

These provisions protect Canada's current federally and provincially regulated monopolies, and our rights to maintain and create new monopolies. The obligations to provide monopoly services on a non-discriminatory basis, and to prevent the monopolist from using its power to undertake anticompetitive practices in other markets are standard and well-established practices in Canada that will not affect the operation of current or future initiatives.

Postal Rates for Magazines
Canada has no obligation to phase out discriminatory
postal rates for magazines of significant circulation.
The U.S. tried to go beyond the October 4 Elements of
the Agreement to phase out the difference (1.5 cents)
between Code 3 and Code 6 periodicals and Canada
refused.

Chapter 21: Final Provisions

Article 2106: Duration and Termination
This article specifies that the agreement shall remain
in force unless terminated on six month's notice. Six
month's termination is a requirement of the U.S. Trade
Act for agreements negotiated under fast track
authority.

Index

411